THE DOLLAR DECADE

THE DOLLAR DECADE

Mammon and the Machine in 1920s America

Gary Dean Best

PRAEGER PUBLISHERS
Westport, Connecticut · London

Library of Congress Cataloging-in-Publication Data

Best, Gary Dean.
The dollar decade : mammon and the machine in 1920s America / Gary Dean Best.
p. cm.
Includes bibliographical references and index.
ISBN 0–275–97795–1 (alk. paper)
1. United States—Economic conditions—1918–1945. 2. Dollar, American—History—20th century. 3. United States—Social life and customs—1918–1945. I. Title.

HC106.3 .B483 2003
973.91'5—dc21 2002028761

British Library Cataloguing in Publication Data is available.

Library of Congress Catalog Card Number: 2002028761
ISBN: 0–275–97795–1

First published in 2003

Praeger Publishers, 88 Post Road West, Westport, CT 06881
An imprint of Greenwood Publishing Group, Inc.
www.praeger.com

Printed in the United States of America

The paper used in this book complies with the Permanent Paper Standard issued by the National Information Standards Organization (Z39.48-1984).

10 9 8 7 6 5 4 3 2 1

For my brother and sister:
Linda Sue Beattie
and
Thomas Lee Ullensvang

Contents

Preface

The 1920s was an introspective decade. Change was so pervasive and so rapid that the sources, nature, and future of the changes absorbed the attention of the masses and of scholars. As Charles Merz put it:

> whatever we say of the new America in which we live, at least we start with this: it is a brand-new America, and there is no section of the broad highway that leads from the New Jersey hills to San Francisco Bay over which a whole new layer of culture has not been spread within the memory of a generation of Americans still living.
>
> The triumph of the urban culture that has swept remorselessly across the countryside is the triumph of modern transportation. The prowess of the giant mills that have changed the habit of the nation with an avalanche of low-priced goods is built upon new methods of production which have been perfected only to be thrown aside for methods newer still. The standards of American life, the criteria by which each change is judged, the rules of thumb that once seemed everlasting principles, have been wrenched loose from their accustomed mooring by the progress of experimental science.[1]

It is unlikely that any generation before that of the 1920s had experienced such widespread change and been so acutely conscious of its effect on their daily lives.

Magazines and newspapers in the 1920s were awash with articles describing and analyzing one or another of the changes taking place. Authors wrote books on the subject. The incisive and sometimes lively writings of essayists like H.L. Mencken, Gilbert Seldes, Stuart Chase, Charles Merz, and Agnes Repplier are as readable now as they were for the generation of the 1920s. Editors compiled anthologies of essays by learned authorities on the impact of the changes for various aspects of American life, such as education, religion, or philosophy. One of the most noted of these was Harold Stearns, editor, *Civilization in the United*

States: An Inquiry by Thirty Americans (New York, 1922). Another, closer to the end of the decade, was Charles Beard, editor, *Whither Mankind: A Panorama of Modern Civilization* (New York, 1928). The trend culminated in the most exhaustive self-study of America ever undertaken by the federal government when President Herbert Hoover established the Research Committee on Social Trends to study the nation's society and to publish its findings, which were released in 1932.[2]

Not surprisingly, given the wealth of material available, some of the best books published on the 1920s since then have been anthologies of magazine and newspaper articles from the decade, such as George Mowry, editor, *Fords, Flappers, and Fanatics*, and Barbara H. Solomon, *Ain't We Got Fun?* (New York, 1980). And the best secondary work on the decade is still the one written from immersion in those sources, Frederick Lewis Allen, *Only Yesterday* (New York, 1931).

For that reason, this book, although it is not an anthology, relies heavily on quotations that convey a sense of the decade far better than any later writer can. It does, though, offer a slightly different perspective on the decade that I do not think is adequately conveyed by recent books—either anthologies or secondary sources. It was a complex and stressful decade for most Americans, and it has too often been portrayed as a frivolous era of flappers and flasks, à la F. Scott Fitzgerald. It is time for a more sober appraisal of the decade.

Acknowledgments

The research and writing of this book began while I was a Resident Scholar in the Social Philosophy and Policy Center at Bowling Green State University (Ohio), whose assistance is hereby gratefully acknowledged, particularly that of Fred Miller, director; Jeffrey Paul, assistant director; and Carrie-Ann Biondi, executive assistant. Mahesh Ananth did yeoman work as my research assistant, and Mary Dilsaver made the center seem like a second home during my weeks there.

Introduction

> The metaphysics of prosperity is a religion of the machine, with Ford and Mellon and Edison as its triune messiah, with Captains of Industry as its hierarchy.
>
> Silas Bent, *Machine Made Man* (1930)

In *Nickel and Dime Decade* I drew a contrast between the grim desperation of the 1930s and the carefree 1920s, based on what I had read of the 1920s in books that highlighted the frivolity of that decade with titles like *Ain't We Got Fun,* and *Fords, Flappers, and Fanatics*. When I began researching *The Dollar Decade* I expected that view of the 1920s to be borne out by my own research. Alas, it was not.

Instead, I discovered that much of the frivolity of that decade was the product of a sense of desperation not far removed from that of the 1930s. Unrevealed by most works on the decade is the extent of the stress and uncertainty that prevailed as a result of a variety of factors that combined to produce a profound sense of change and to cast many Americans adrift in a sea of normlessness. At the root of many of the changes was the sudden onrush of the machine in the 1920s, or perhaps one should say the money-driven machine, the impact of which cannot be overstated. One benchmark of the rise of the machine in American life was that 1929 was the first year in which cotton exports were exceeded in value by exports of automobiles and machinery, products of the machine.[1]

Sherwood Anderson found that "the machine dominates American life," both on the farms and in the towns. He was captivated by it, writing:

> I have felt the poetry of all this. I have felt the terror of it. After having written no verse for several years and after visiting the factories of the towns I have again the hunger.

> In some moods I want to be the poet of industry, of the machine. For the machine, as the American has developed it, I feel only admiration and love.[2]

R. Austin Freeman stated the case against the machine in 1921, writing that before the invention of the steam engine by Watt, production had been geared to demand, but after Watt the machine had continued to develop in accord with its own laws and disregarding the needs of man until it not only had met the original demand and ousted the craftsmen, but had continued to increase production past demand. As Stuart Chase pointed out: "The relations of supply and demand have become inverted. Under the regime of hand production the problem was to supply consumers with commodities. The problem now is to supply commodities with consumers." The result was that man "loses independence and self-reliance; he is readily subjected to regimentation and discipline. His sense of personal liberty is aborted; his sensibilities blunted and debased. . . . He becomes a watcher and listener, rather than a creator—a second-hand man."[3] Silas Bent wondered if

> because we read the same kind of magazines and newspapers, hear the same kind of music, are subjected to the same kind of political, educational, and social propaganda, wear the same kind of clothes and eat the same kind of food, [we] become as alike as the ants in a hill or the bees in a hive?[4]

Even the noise of the machines was tending "to standardize all of our nervous systems."[5] Clarence Britten added the standardizing influences of the movies, the Ford, the railroad, telephone and telegraph, and advertising. Even regional distinctions had been erased, leaving only distinctions based on money.[6]

An analyst of labor conditions in Detroit concluded that: "monotony may not be psychologically harmful; but it stifles initiative, and may operate as an industrial boomerang. Men with alert minds report that after eight hours of it, they cannot settle down to read or to think. They must find some emotionally violent form of escape in jazz, gin, the movies, tabloid murders, cross country motoring." The same rule applied to secretaries, clerks, and other office workers as a result of being tied to adding machines, typewriters, and other business machines.[7]

Ironically, as Freeman also pointed out, one impact of the machines was to create a sedentary society. As machines grew smaller they tended to take over more and more of the work previously done by hand or foot. In the domain of transportation, for example, "the motor has descended from the train to the car, from the car to the bicycle, and now we hear of a motor-driven 'scooter' by which the incurably sedentary man may save himself the labor of walking up the street."[8] Moreover, while the automobile freed individuals from their dependence on trains and other forms of mass transport, giving them greater mobility, it also had the effect of restricting their lives as compared to the freedom the bicycle had provided. Automobiles were confined to roads and streets, subject to speed limits, traffic jams, and stoplights, and required access to stops for oil, fuel, water, and air. Thus, at the same time that they increased human mobility they introduced new restraints into life, adding to those the machine was imposing elsewhere.

John Dewey observed late in the decade that:

Instead of extension of human control over purposes and their realization, machine-made and machine-bound civilization has deprived men of leisure and led to use of such leisure as they possess in mad search for amusement and foolish display. It has brought not freedom but enslavement to the machine. Work has been deprived of joy; artistic feeling has been eliminated from its performance and its products. The masses have been condemned to become appendages to the machines they tend; and those released from this fate manifest their boasted freedom for the most part only holding the activities of others in thrall. It is only heartless indifference which can behold in such a state of affairs a gain in human freedom.... Only a blind man would deny that characteristic traits of present life are a mad scramble for material commodities, a devotion to attainment of external power, and an insensate love of foolish luxuries and idle display.[9]

Freeman observed early in the decade that the machine had caused the "pleasurable states of consciousness in the worker" of premachine production, to be replaced now by "relatively unpleasurable" states.[10]

Everett Dean Martin, looking at education in the 1920s, found that:

Western civilization, because of its industrial and mechanical basis, is like an artifact, a construct, and assemblage of parts, rather than like a process of organic growth. Its unity is not given like that of a living thing or like that of early societies. Its unity must be consciously thought out by someone and all consciously utilized and controlled. Successful adaptation to it by the individual requires something more than the assent which was sufficient in earlier civilizations—it requires understanding. It must, to a degree that earlier civilizations did not find necessary, depend for its survival and advancement upon deliberately constructed programmes of education.

The reliance on tradition and custom as in a static society was no longer enough. Martin wrote:

Modern civilization is naturalistic, mechanistic, its rhythm the tempo of machines, each one of which is a creature of problem-solving intelligence. It is an unstable equilibrium of forces, the shifting patterns of which require of mankind ever more insight and calculation.... With rapidly moving machinery at their disposal men may not behave in one world and think as if they were living in another. In the face of every popular resistance—and resistance here is almost insurmountable—the educator must lead beneficiaries of the machine age to face the realities of the world [in which] they are living.[11]

The machine had also contributed to the attraction of the cities that was luring more and more Americans from rural and small-town America. The process of adaptation to urbanization has, however, been shown by sociologists to cause major behavioral changes, introducing, as it does, the change from a relatively static society to a dynamic one. Moreover, as historian Kevin Reilly has pointed out, urban life tends to be much more impersonal, shorn of the "surveillance and conformity" that are characteristics of rural and small-town life, so that in the city the migrant "was freer than his village cousin to choose friends, lovers, associates, occupation, housing and lifestyle." The city, in short, offered many new choices without the constricting standards and observation of rural and small-town America, but offered few new norms to replace them. As Martin put it: "The emergence of every urban civilization has brought with it, among other things, often of lasting gain for human progress, a period of cultural turmoil, intellectual ferment, and moral laxity. Our own promises to outdistance them all in these respect."[12]

Lewis Mumford wrote of the Machine Age city:

> The urban worker escapes the mechanical routine of his daily job only to find an equally mechanical substitute for life and growth and experience in amusements.... The movies, the White Ways, and the Coney Islands ... are means of giving jaded and throttled people the sensations of living without the direct experience of life—a sort of spiritual masturbation.[13]

Criticizing education in the 1920s, Martin wrote:

> The educator is like a manufacturer who, finding that his staple commodity is out of fashion, must turn his plant to the making of novelties of all sorts.... Hence the catalogue of a progressive institution of "higher learning" resembles nothing so much as a similar catalogue annually issued by Sears, Roebuck & Co.... Modern life is chiefly concerned with results. Thinking is subordinated. Much present-day educational psychology proceeds on the theory that we learn only by doing, and that learning is habit formation not essentially different from that habit formation which can be organized in animals by means of the conditioned reflex.[14]

In Eugene O'Neill's 1929 play *Dynamo*, the impressionable young son of a fundamentalist minister falls under the spell of the 16-year-old flapper daughter of an atheistic power plant superintendent. Betrayed by both the girl and his mother, he leaves home, wanders the country working at various power-related jobs, immerses himself in the study of science, becomes an evolutionist, and substitutes worship of electricity for Christianity. He returns home cold and cynical, takes a job in the power plant, but after succumbing to the temptations of the erstwhile flapper in a weak moment, he kills her and then sacrifices himself on the "altar" of the dynamo much as many American workers were "sacrificing" themselves to the machine in their daily work.[15] Few works of literature in the 1920s better illustrate the conflict between religion and science, and the impact of the machine on American life during that decade. The best and the worst of American culture during the 1920s was somehow traceable to American exploitation of the machine in the pursuit of profit.

In his book, *America Comes of Age* (1928), Andre Siegfried of the School of Political Science, Paris, wrote that the United States and Europe had drawn apart in the past thirty years. The United States had become more autonomous and independent as a result of its creation of a new civilization based upon a new conception of production and business. Absent the West any longer to conquer, Americans had turned to the conquest of organization. Europe was very much behind the United States in machinery. The French, for example, still valued the exercise of creative genius, the production of things of high quality and price, while Americans had embraced mass production.[16]

In an article for *Harper's Magazine* in the August 1927 issue, "The Outlook for American Culture," the Englishman Aldous Huxley, grandson of "Darwin's Bulldog," Thomas Henry Huxley, likewise described machinery as the principal driving force that was changing the world, and nowhere had the process advanced as far as in the United States. Conceding that labor-saving machines had produced a variety of blessings, including offering some degree of leisure and prosperity to almost everybody, making possible "a rich universal culture," he saw few signs that this fuller life had put in an appearance.

Wrote Huxley:

> A great many men and women—let us frankly admit it, in spite of all our humanitarian and democratic prejudices—do not want to be cultured, are not interested in the higher life. For these people existence on the lower, animal levels is perfectly satisfactory. Given food, drink, the company of their fellows, sexual enjoyment, and plenty of noisy distractions from without, they are happy. They enjoy bodily, but hate mental, exercise. They can not bear to be alone or to think. Contemporary urban life, with its jazz bands, its negroid dancing, its movies, theaters, football matches, newspapers, and the like, is for them ideal. They can live out their lives without once being solitary, without once making serious mental effort (for the work which most of these people do is mainly mechanical and requires little or no thought), without once being out of sight or sound of some ready-made distraction. The notion that one can derive pleasure from arduous intellectual occupations is to such people merely absurd. More leisure and more prosperity mean for them more dancing, more parties, more movies, more distractions in general. Most of the inhabitants of ancient Rome belonged to this type; so probably do most of the inhabitants of modern New York and London. And unless some system of eugenics is practised in the interval, there is no reason to suppose that the inhabitants of the great cities in the year 3000 A.D. will be radically different.[17]

The flap of the dust jacket of a book of essays edited by Charles Beard, *Whither Mankind* (New York, 1928), began:

> Science and the million machines born of science have profoundly altered the ways of men and women.
>
> The world of 1929 A.D. would seem an incredible dream—perhaps a nightmare—to the world of 29 A.D. or even of 1829 A.D. What kind of world is it? What are the gains and losses of the life it offers as compared with those of other civilizations the earth has known? Are the aeroplane, the modern news service, the intricate web of business based on tractors, rails and factory wheels, the central heating system, the magic control of disease—are these making robots of men and women—or demi-gods?

In the essay by Bertrand Russell on "Science," contained in that volume he wrote:

> The philosophy inspired by industrialism is seeping away the static conception of knowledge which dominated both medieval and modern philosophy, and has substituted what it calls the Instrumental Theory, the very name of which is suggested by machinery. In the Instrumental Theory, there is not a single state of mind which consists of knowing a truth—there is a way of acting, a manner of handling the environment, which is appropriate, and whose appropriateness constitute what alone can be called knowledge as these philosophers under it. One might sum up this theory by a definition: *To know something is to be able to change it as we wish.* There is no place in this outlook for the beatific vision, nor for any notion of final excellence.[18]

Nor, it appeared, was there a place for men much past the age of forty. In the premachine age the older a craftsman became the greater the skill and art he brought to his craft. Machines required speed and agility rather than experience, and once past forty, as the workers of Middletown learned, they were expendable. As the head of a machine shop put it: "I think there's less opportunity for older men in industry now than there used to be. The principal change I've seen in the plant here has been the speeding up of machines and the eliminating of the human factor by machinery. The company has no definite policy of firing men when they reach a certain age nor of hiring men under a certain age, but in general we find that when a man reaches fifty he is slipping down in production." The personnel manager of another company told the Lynds: "In production work forty to forty-five is the age limit because of the speed needed in the work. Men over forty are hired as sweepers and for similar jobs." And a superintendent of yet another told them: "The age dead line is creeping down on those men—I'd say that by forty-five they are through."[19]

Middletown workers and their families were very conscious of the uncertain future they faced. A former resident observed, upon moving back to Middletown, that the things he most noticed were its prejudice and superficiality. "These people are all afraid of something," he said. "What is it?"[20]

But the editor of *The Iron Trade Review* responded to concerns about technological unemployment by writing that industry needed more machines, not fewer. Leaders of industry, he said knew that "progress is relentless," that the world would no more stand still "now than when James Watt was experimenting with his mother's teakettle." As for technological unemployment, those leaders knew, too, that "in a country developing as rapidly as the United States a certain amount of maladjustment is inevitable," but those displaced could find employment in purely service occupations," like the thousands who were "operating gasoline-filling stations."[21]

From the preceding it will be seen that insightful contemporary observers viewed the decade in very different terms from historians weaned on F. Scott Fitzgerald and other portrayers of an equally shallow and frivolous decade. The influence of the Mammon-driven machine was everywhere in American life in the 1920s, to be viewed in everything from art to stock speculation. It was a decade filled with insecurity and apprehension, of normlessness and reaction both to and against the new influences. It has been customary to say of Americans in the 1930s that they experienced the inevitable hangover after their binge of the 1920s. It would be more accurate to say that in the 1930s the worst insecurities of people in the 1920s came to fruition, but that it was, in a sense, a relief for many to see the machine apparently discredited, and that hostility exhibited toward business and finance in the 1930s was at least in part because of the machine culture they represented.

1
The Revolution in Moral Standards

At the end of the decade, Joseph Wood Krutch wrote that morality and emotional lives reflected a world that no longer existed, that insofar as people adhered to a code of conduct they did so from habit, not because they could give any logical reason for it. "It is," Krutch wrote,

> not a changed world but a new one in which man must henceforth live if he lives at all, for all his premises have been destroyed and he must proceed to new conclusions. The values which he thought established have been swept away along with the rules by which he thought they might be attained.[1]

Changes in values, Krutch added, were, perhaps "the most momentous events in the life of the human race," far more profound than changes of government, for they were, "in effect, changes of God, and they involve a change both in his whole conception of the meaning of the universe and in the thing for which he lives. Every time a value is born, existence takes on a new meaning; every time one dies, some part of that meaning passes away."[2] One such value that seemed dead in the 1920s was love, which seemed to many novelists to be "a sort of obscene joke." In their books the characters were so absorbed "in the pursuit of sexual satisfaction, they never find love and they were scarcely aware that they are seeking it, but they are far from content with themselves." Love had become "gradually so accessible, so unmysterious, and so free that its value is trivial." What this signaled, however, was the "complete surrender of something which we have been accustomed to regard as one of the chief values in human life, and ... it leaves a mighty blank in existence."[3] It resulted in man being dehumanized and "life ... made to sink back to a level nearer that of the animal, for whom life is a phenomenon in which there is no meaning except the biological urge."

Man was carried "one step nearer to that state in which existence is seen as a vast emptiness which the imagination can no longer people with fascinating illusions."[4]

FREUD

It was commonplace in the 1920s to decry the "revolution" that seemed to be taking place in the morals of post–World War I America. Sin, however, was probably no more rampant in that decade than in those that preceded it. The revolutionary aspects lay more in the changed definitions and acceptance of heretofore "sinful" behavior, whether that behavior actually involved sin or not. For these changes, a great deal of the credit, or blame, was ascribed to the influence of Sigmund Freud.

A horned-and-tailed Freud was denounced from thousands of pulpits and in scores of Christian periodicals, but the direct influence of his ideas can easily be exaggerated. "Freudianism," as it was popularized by a multitude of writers and speakers, placed undue emphasis on certain of his concepts, to the exclusion of others, and in this way pandered to trends in sexual behavior that were already in motion by giving them a seemingly scientific basis. Freud, himself, was appalled by such misuse of his ideas, but was powerless to stop it. A writer observed in 1920 that Freud's theories were everywhere, and that one could "hardly pick up a newspaper or a magazine without finding psychoanalytic terms." They had, Edmund Wilson wrote, begun profoundly to color "the thought of the twentieth century, from psychiatry and mythology to the paintings of the Independents' Exhibition and Mr. Van Wyck Brook's extraordinary study of Mark Twain."[5]

Psychology was a relatively demure and noncontroversial discipline in the United States until 1909, when Clark University invited three of the leading European figures in the field to talk at the school's decennium. The three were Sigmund Freud, of Vienna, H. Ferenczi, of Prague, and Carl Jung of Zurich. Freud, especially, threw psychology into an uproar, both inside and outside the profession. His controversial views created dissent within the profession, which was not resolved through the 1920s, and the popular perception of his theories influenced the behavior of Americans all through the decade. By the end of the 1920s, however, Freud was ranked by some as one of the great minds of the twentieth century, the century's equivalent of Charles Darwin, the equal in stature of Albert Einstein. Freud, it was held, had taken Darwin's discoveries an important further step, by applying them to the psyche.

In popular culture, however, Freud spawned a host of what one psychologist referred to as pseudoanalysts who gave their own spins to his theories for popular consumption. The result was that much of Freud's terminology began to infiltrate common thought and speech, but without a real understanding of the background to that terminology. The science of psychonalysis, one psychologist wrote, was suffering "most of all from the hundreds and hundreds of psychoanalytic chatterers, from those eager folk who long so passionately to impart their smattering of knowledge." The result, he added, was "a specious science which has intrigued a tremendous public with its false and facile formulations" that was "so far from Freudian theory and so popular" that it deserved its own name—which he christened pseudoanalysis. Freudian designations, he wrote, had begun to replace such allegorical imperatives of an earlier generation, such as love, honor, and beauty, and had become "inflated far beyond their dictionary proportions" to the point of becoming dangerous, "apt to become emotional and ethical dynamite." Another critic wrote that Freud's followers had become so "engrossed with the cruder side of sexual life that their works might often be taken for contributions to pornography rather than to medicine."[6]

Another writer of the 1920s observed, "A magazine of terms—repression, libido, transference, compensation, and the like—was added to the quack's vocabulary," all of which only validated Freud's own concerns over the uses to which his theories would be put. Part of their popularity was no doubt due to their "scientific" respectability, but "their most constant users have never read Freud, or only superficially understood him, and are applying his language and ideas in amazingly inaccurate ways." What professionals most objected to about "pseudoanalysis" was what they called its "glorification of uninhibited self-indulgence." It was only "the abysmally ignorant," Dr. Karl Menninger wrote, "who accuse psychoanalysts of believing that self-control is the genesis of the neuroses and therefore a kind of modern Mephistopholeses," when in fact, "the Freudian thesis defines the neurotic patient ... as one who is failing to maintain his inhibitions, and needs help in mastering his escaping desires."[7]

Freud, wrote one observer, "rapidly became epidemic in America." As early as 1916, an informal survey found approximately 500 would-be psychoanalysts in New York City alone, although it was estimated that there were not more than six properly qualified to do so in the entire state. One could become a psychoanalyst through mail order instruction, or it was possible to learn it in schools of chiropractic.[8]

One area where Freudianism exerted an obvious influence was on the literature of the 1920s. As one literary critic wrote in 1924:

> Already a new literature has sprung up to welcome the new learning. Sherwood Anderson here, and Lawrence and Miss West and Miss Sinclair.... Their exhibit is of something deeper and richer than we find in their old-style contemporaries, precisely as one of Doctor Freud's technical studies seems to be desiccated and to hold a better converse with fundamental realities than the formulas of the eclectics. And yet in this literature generally, it must be admitted, there is an accent which is repulsive to the reading public; it deals too frankly with aberrations of sex, in the specific sense of the term.
>
> In this sense sex is still taboo in literature; it is obscene just as in the Greek tragedy certain parts of the fable were obscene and must take place off the stage. The literary adaptors of psycho-analysis have very boldly and with a rather crude art translated the most sensational feature of the science bodily into literature, where they are calculated to become accessible to the general public.

The effect on literature was that it was "bound to make an enormous accession of evidence for Freudism when it is studied for that purpose."

And for that matter, the Freudian psychology, if it keeps that name, will be far more than one man's work before it is completed. It will be like a medieval Gothic cathedral, for whole generations of scholars will have helped to put it together.... And when the grand edifice is completed, the result will be a complexity and yet a unification of doctrine, perhaps as imposing a structure as the world has seen.[9]

A writer in 1925 wrote that "mental furniture" went through fashions just as did interior decoration:

A few years ago, when the shadow of Freud came West to America and the Parlor Analyst eclipsed the Parlor Socialist, it might have been expected to pass on presently or be blotted out by a newer darker disc.... But no. Even to-day let some *ingenue* venture "I had the queerest dream—" and all at once we see a crowd, a host of parlor analysts. The obliging interpreters listen,—though this is hardly necessary,—look wise, and at the end exclaim in an "I know something about you" tone, "*Aha!* That means sex! You have a sex-complex!"

Now there may be something in it. But the answer is so simple, so easy, so monotonous, that it stirs suspicion. Our amateur seers seem to have fallen on a time of famine. The old-fashioned fortune-tellers and dream-readers gave more lavishly of color and variety,—a journey, a letter, a tall blond lady, a dark lean man, or at least a lean or fat year. Any passing gypsy would do better by you than that meagre rubber-stamp, "sex complex."[10]

George Sylvester Viereck wrote in that same year that Freud had "played an important part in the intellectual life of the world so long that, like Bernard Shaw, he has almost ceased to be a person." In the future, Viereck wrote, Freud would be referred to "as the Columbus of the Unconscious." Columbus, in seeking a route to the Indies, had discovered a continent; "Freud, attempting to find a new method of mental therapeutics, discovered the submerged continent of man's mind." Viereck wrote:

No educator can seriously pursue his profession without a study of psycho-analysis. No parent can assume parental responsibility intelligently without a lesson in Freud. No husband can understand himself or his wife without turning for guidance to the truths unearthed by Freud.... The lawyer and the judge, the teacher and the merchant, the lover and the creative artist, can no longer successfully conduct the difficult business of living without acquiring at least the rudements of psycho-analysis.... Freud, in other words, has modified the world's mental outlook. Having glimpsed the depths in our souls, Life can never again be the same.

Viereck added:

In America, more than anywhere else, not only scientists but poets, novelists, and playwrights are mastering the laws of psycho-analysis. Harvey O'Higgins, Rupert Hughes, among our older novelists, freely admit their indebtedness to Freud in their most recent novels. Sherwood Anderson, [Eugene] O'Neill, Ben Hecht, James Branch Cabell are unthinkable without Freud. Surely Jurgen is a traveler through the realm of the unconscious. Edgar Lee Masters, in his *Spoon River Anthology*, indulges spasmodically in psycho-analysis.[11]

Another writer in that same year wrote that Freud was "the God of psychoanalysis" and that seldom had "the personality of one man so dominated an intellectual movement as has Freud's."[12]

Aldous Huxley concluded, on the contrary, that psychoanalysis was only the latest in a long history of pseudosciences that included phrenology and astrology. It was, he wrote, immensely popular "among all classes except the scientific."[13] However, Professor William McDougall, perhaps the leading name in psychology in America in the 1920s, wrote that Freud had "done more for the advancement of psychology than any student since Aristotle," and devoted his book, *Outline of Abnormal Psychology* to mediating between Freud and his critics.[14]

"Psychology," a writer observed in 1929, "seems to have polarized all the cranks, quacks, and faddists who in the past gathered together under the banners of hypnotism, mesmerism, animal magnetism, Yoga mysticism, New Thought, Higher Thought, phrenology, occultism, and the rest." "Doctors of Psychonalysis" had begun to proliferate, their "degrees" having been bestowed by correspondence institutions of dubious standing.[15]

It follows from these misinterpretations of Freud and the popularity of pseudoanalysis that he was profoundly hated by those who were opposed to what they regarded as the licentiousness of the 1920s—in both behavior and dress—blaming him rather than the conditions that were producing that behavior. Men of the cloth railed at him from their pulpits and the Christian press admonished believers to ignore Freudianism's apparent invitation to sinful behavior. But by the end of the decade Freudianism was still alive and well when he observed his seventy-fifth birthday in 1931, having failed to fulfill the 1920 prophesy of one critic that his theories were "to psychology what cubism is to art—new sensation and rather interesting," but destined before many years to "take their place in our historical medical museum along with all the other curiosities which the centuries have accumulated."[16]

For some, though, the influence of Freud on American life in the 1920s symbolized the protest against the machine's influence, conditioning the literature of protest and revolt against it. As one wrote:

> Its predominant dogma, that individualism and the pleasure principle are in constant conflict with convention and the reality principle of the bustling world around us, seems quite in harmony with the complaint that the machine is coercing, depersonalizing and standardizing the globe.... [A] Viennese psychiatrist now colors a large part of our fiction, poetry, and drama. Following paths almost parallel, some of our essayists, historians, biographers, poets, and playwrights have attributed to the machine the repressions, complexes, neuroses and escape mechanisms of our febrile modern life. The forge, the factory, and the mill have supplanted *libido* in their symbolism.[17]

An editorial in *Catholic World* in 1930 summed up the views of that church on Freud's influence on the 1920s:

> Sigmund Freud has been called "the most influential thinker of our time, next to Einstein." Note the adjective "influential." No discriminating admirer of Freud would call him a *clear* thinker or a *profound* thinker. *Influential* is the safe word. Philosophers—of a sort—have appropriated Freudian ideas, but Freud himself is no philosopher. Nevertheless, he is the vogue, and hence he has influence. Novelists and dramatists, with even greater impetuosity than philosophers or moralists, have seized upon Freudianism and have made it popular. . . . [T]he poetic or dramatic quality of the Freudian ideas has much to do with their popularity. Freud's idea of "complexes" and of the "subliminal self," caught the popular imagination. His phrase "release the inhibitions" promptly entered into the speech of the man in the street. Indeed great portions of the Freudian vocabulary have become so familiar as to constitute a kind of argot, a pseudo-scientific jargon. That is to say . . . Freud "dramatized" himself and his psychological notions just as Babe Ruth dramatized himself and his home runs, or Rudy Vallee himself and his crooning melodies. There is no knowing just what will capture the fancy of the people, but when you've got them you've got them. . . . Hence Freud is "the most influential mind."

America in the twentieth century had become morally emancipated, the writer continued. Before the emancipation

> Puritanism was the dominant moral force, a hard, grim theology, based on the dogma of hell-fire and brimstone. Men were enslaved with a curious superstition called "conscience," or "the moral sense." Conscience made cowards of them all—cowards and miserable wretches. They groaned over their sins, and scourged themselves for their moral delinquencies. But came the deliverance! Darwin taught us that we are cousins to the beasts and hence essentially animals. Haeckel hammered home the corollary that there is no soul and hence no conscience, that religion is a superstition and morality is a matter of artificial restraint. Freud gave the *coup de grace* to all morality, old or new, by demonstrating that we are merely beasts—and uncommonly nasty beasts at that.[18]

EFFECTS OF THE WAR

In fact, of course, much of the revolution in moral standards owed its origins to the influence of World War I, rather than to Freud. Millions of American men who might otherwise never have left their counties or boroughs were transported to Europe and exposed to experiences only the more wealthy had heretofore absorbed. That experience, summed up by the popular song lyrics "How ya gonna keep 'em down on the farm, after they've seen Paree?" meant profound changes in the attitudes of a large percentage of a whole generation of American males. To this must be added equally momentous changes in the lives of women during the war years, when many were called upon to take the jobs in industry vacated by men in uniform, and to work in new jobs created by the war. Many of them were part of a great internal migration from rural and small-town America to the cities, which included many Southerners, both black and white. This migration, in itself, was portentous of major changes in their lives, since cities provide an anonymity lacking in small towns, providing for greater freedom in individual behavior. For women, in particular, the new employment opportunities brought financial independence and the opportunity to indulge in forms of behavior—like drinking and smoking—that had previously been lacking in the lives of many of them. As the president of the New York State branch of WCTU said: "The war has in no small measure been responsible for the spread of smoking in this country. Some of our young women as well as some of our young men have developed the habit. The cigarette was found to act as a sedative when no other kind could be found.... But the war is over.... There is no reason why we should carry over into the peace period a habit that was taken up as a war measure."[19]

Yet another contribution to the freer sexuality of the 1920s was the growing use of birth control devices, especially among the middle class.

Add to that the fact that political action by women had culminated in their enfranchisement in 1920. This evidence of their political muscle ennervated women and their organizations in the 1920s, encouraging them to believe that they could make further gains—such as passage of an equal rights amendment. Clearly, the contribution to self-esteem was enormous, and the rejection of older female stereotypes was a casualty, especially among women, themselves. Understandably, it opened an era when many women, at least, seemed to have good reason for believing that all things were possible of attainment, and for rejecting a postwar return to "normalcy" where their own status and behavior were concerned.

The "revolt" of the 1920s was particularly associated with the younger generation, and it was in the schools and colleges where much of its effect was felt, and where it was the subject of considerable analysis. Dr. Charles J. Smith, president of Roanoke College (VA) at National Lutheran Educational Conference in New York, was quoted by *Literary Digest* as having

> asserted that social wrongdoing is not now confined to any class or place, and that he has personal knowledge of its existence in theological seminaries. He gives particularly attention to a certain type of young woman. As he is quoted in press reports, he declares that "in every age women drank liquor; a few even enjoyed a smoke; many of them threw away their honor; but the world has never known the turning loose of such an army of hard-drinking, cigaret-puffing, licentious Amazons as walk our streets and invade our campuses to-day."

He asked what could be done "when the daughters of the so-called 'best people' come out attired scantily in clothing, but abundantly in paint, with a bottle of liquor not on the hip but in the hand-bag, dancing as voluptuously as possible in order to be attractive and appear popular, calling for frequent intermissions to give them opportunity to quench their thirst from the bottle; and then interspersing this with violent 'petting parties' in the luxurious retreat of a big limousine."[20]

The dean of Princeton University examined the "faults" of 1920s youth and pointed out that the older generation had not known the radio, movies, telephones, or automobiles, all of which he said were contributing to the disturbed state of youth. World War I, rather than raising up public heroes who were swept into office, as previous wars had, instead disillusioned youth and kindled a spirit of revolt against the generation responsible for the war. Prohibition, meanwhile, had engendered disrespect for authority and encouraged in youth a belief that nothing compulsory deserved respect. Movies had exposed 18-year-olds to more of life "than a person of that age would have dreamed of being familiar with a generation ago. 'They are thoroughly conversant with matter that we, perhaps fortunately, were ignorant of.'" Also at fault, he said, was the shrinking size of American homes, which drove the young to seek equivalence of the old home life elsewhere.[21]

Cambridge Associates reported a revolution in eating habits, with 75 million meals daily being served in restaurants, cafeterias, industrial lunch-rooms, hotels, schools, clubs, and other places." This meant 21 percent of meals daily were being eaten out, partly because of the servant problem, but more due to the automobile.[22]

Yet another academician traced the excesses of the "Jazz Age" to the automobile, which had made Sunday outings preferable to church attendance and thus shifted the moral and social background of the community. The telephone and typewriter also came in for blame due to their effect in speeding up American life, both in business and socially.[23] A prominent eastern clubwoman blamed the "alien" influences of communism, free love, and birth control, particularly the books of Bertrand Russell in advocating the teaching of birth control to boys and girls.[24] Economist Irving Fisher blamed the revolt of youth on the "drunkenness and disrespect of law of their parents."[25] A noted Baptist clergyman faulted "commercialized amusements, sensuous dances, best sellers, and the ever present downward drag of stage and screen" for the debauching of American youth. The popularity of evolution had brought "monkey morals," as America's youth sank "deeper and deeper in rank paganism."[26] A University of Georgia professor found a distinct correlation between crime and the use of coffee and tobacco, as well as one between automobile ownership and divorce.[27]

An important contribution to the obsession with sex was the publication of Havelock Ellis's multivolume *Studies in the Psychology of Sex,* which, as one observer noted in the 1920s, had succeeded "in freeing love . . . by lifting from mankind the burden of that sense of guilt which had oppressed so many and not infrequently poisoned what would have been otherwise a mighty and perfect experience." However, love had now become "so accessible, so unmysterious, and so free that its value is trivial.[28] Looking back from the perspective of 1928, a writer in *The New Republic* observed that the old taboos had "lost their compulsion," had lost them as part of the "same process of social evolution that has undermined the authoritarian principle in religion, politics and law." One cause was "backwash" of World War I, "the temper of cynical realism engendered by the war itself in many still youthful survivors, and by its sequel of folly and chaos in many still younger observers." It had caused youth to seek pleasure in the moment and at first hand, not vicariously. Another cause was the "degradation of the authoritarian principle." Instead of conservativism offering an inviting alternative, it presented in the 1920s "the disgusting spectacle of rank selfishness, downright fear of clean, hard thinking, passionate stupidity, barricading themselves behind age-worn dogmas that do not, on examination, support the constructions put upon them, and retreating in disorder from positions that are not sound enough even to earn respect." An example was fundamentalism among Christians, which tried to offer answers to questions that it was clearly not qualified to deal with.

"Another and less reassuring influence," he wrote, "arises from the popularization of what is (incorrectly) called the new psychology." This one had brought with it some "not altogether fortunate byproducts." He explained:

> One of them is the disparagement of the will (or, if you prefer, of the integrating power of active as opposed to passive cognative attitudes). The semi-educated have fastened avidly upon the idea of repression as the source of mental malady, and proceeded to infer that all will be set right by simply lifting the lid off one's particular private hades.

To this he added confusion over the terminology of psychoanalysis in the lay mind that resulted in

> a popular fixation upon certain recognizable impulses, that positively adds to the difficulty of controlling or educating them. Add to this fact the decay of restrictive taboos already noted, and the natural result is a situation to which even the cheapest journalism and the most popular movies bear witness.[29]

Another writer, also looking back on the 1920s, traced the "crisis in morals" to several causes: World War I,

> with its shattering effect on custom and character, and its severing of actions from their natural consequences ... the rapid and widespread emancipation of women, and their entry into all fields of economic and intellectual work. This revolution must necessarily affect sexual morals, as the independent woman, earning her living by her own exertions, cannot possibly keep up the same extreme sensibilities as the protected woman nor indulge in the same helplessness or narrowmindedness ... [and] a certain breakdown of religious orthodoxy....

Other important contributions had been made by psychology, which had taught "that much of our traditional moral language is based on false premises ... and has at the same time familiarized us with information about the spring of human conduct which ... often produces a paralyzing effect on the character and sometimes provides an excuse for depravity," and "the wide dissemination of knowledge about methods of birth control." Of the latter, he explained:

> The greatest non-moral deterrent to promiscuous intercourse throughout history has been the fear of pregnancy; that deterrent has now, to a great extent, been removed, and

those people—whether few or many—who were deterred from promiscuity only by fear of social punishment are now almost free from that fear.

As for psychology, "especially the theories of Freud, so much and so incompetently disseminated," their first effects had been bad in throwing people "into familiar contact with things which ordinary social instinct, from primitive times down to the present, treats with extreme reserve," and causing people to discover that "much, and perhaps all of our emotional and spiritual nature has a physical and often a grossly physical basis."[30]

The ever-declining price of automobiles, largely thanks to Henry Ford, made them accessible to more and more people in the 1920s and contributed greatly to the revolution in morals. As one observer noted at the end of the decade:

> The auto proved to be truly, as Ford said, the Great Liberator. It liberated the young people from the surveillance of their elders. They no longer had to spoon in the front parlor, or on the family veranda, or under the eyes of the neighborhood, walking where they might be recognized. They could climb into their flivver and disappear as completely as if they had eloped by railroad train in the old days. So they were free to carry on that moral revolt of modern youth . . . and the thunders of preachers and authors and moralists of all sorts are roaring around this new storm center of social unrest with terrifying fury.

The World War, he added, had "quickened the pace of the revolt" that began even before the war.

> The tribal ban on cigarettes was not the only one that was lifted for the benefit of the boys in the trenches. Any pleasure which they could snatch at was permitted to the youths who were about to die. A girl could not deny herself to the lad who was going to face death in her defense. Puritanism among the young came to a sudden and violent end, assisted by the automobile, by the general knowledge of birth control, and by the efforts of the Freudians to preach a more intelligent conscious ideal for the control of the sexual instinct.[31]

The revolution was not confined to the large cities, as many writers pointed out, because "the machine age has abolished most of the barriers which impede the exchange of mental and moral patterns."

> While it has been transferring the bodies of men to the cities, it has, with even greater rapidity, been spreading the ideas of the city to the country. By means of the cinema the styles of dress are universalized, and the styles of conduct as well. The "releases" from Hollywood induce emotional "releases" in Middletown the same night as in Chicago or New York. By means of the radio the same sermons and songs are brought to the frontier home as to the city apartment; and if the former are no longer accredited as creators of moral sentiments, at least the latter are. The machine has united the morals of the city and country in marriage—"for better, for worse, for richer, for poorer." But in this union the word "obey" has been retained, and it is the city which has assumed the masterful function of the old-fashioned husband in our nation's household of morals.

The traditional moral codes were based on "pre-machine-country conditions," and it was doubtful if a moral code developed for "a rural people living on the edge of a desert" had much relevance for people wandering in the "wilderness of our cities" amid "the allurements and advertisements of our machine age." The very release from tiring and time-consuming toil in the home, for example, that was a product of the machine was causing stresses in married life, releasing discontents that had formerly been drained off by "a woman's work." "The divorce rate has risen with the sale of vacuum cleaners and electric washers."[32]

No one, however, could speak with such authority on the revolution in morals and manners that had taken place in the '20s as Emily Post. "In the smaller towns," she wrote,

> customs may still be jogging gently along (I doubt it!), but in the great cities like New York, youth is out of hand. Set free from the restraining influences of the chaperon, girls and boys alike have been attacked with speedomania and excitementia. Thousands of them are looking out upon the road of life as though it were a roller coaster.... The ... typical young girl of America goes out alone with another girl or more likely with a man friend who stops for her and again sees her home. But what she does, how she behaves, even where she goes, her mother and father have no idea beyond what she happens to choose to tell them, or what they hear accidentally from others.[33]

The 1920s also developed its own slang, which originated mainly with the young of college and high-school age. One authority on slang explained its popularity in the 1920s on the fact that "classes mingle so much more. There are no hard-and-fast lines between classes any more. We are learning to speak each other's language. And when one set takes up certain slang expressions, the other set is soon apt to be trading it around."[34]

MUSIC AND DANCE

Jazz music and the dances of the 1920s came in for their share of the blame in contributing to the looser behavior of American youth. Jazz, according to one of those who helped popularize it, drifted out of New Orleans to Chicago in 1915, from whence it spread quickly to New York and the East by 1919.[35] The Jazz Age, according to a writer in the *Saturday Evening Post*, "began with Paul Whiteman's arrival at the Palais Royal cabaret in Longacre Square in 1920, and ended with Rudy Vallee. It was a fat period for jazz musicians, with Whiteman's earnings reaching as high as $648,000 per year, and a half dozen others not far behind. Whiteman's musicians earned from $350 to $650 per week." Whiteman's music was a revelation to the East Coast, replacing the "blatant and raucous" music heretofore associated with jazz with whispers, by comparison. "His brasses were muted, his banjo purely a rhythm marker, his saxophones and clarinettes confidential, his drums distant tom-toms rather than abused and protesting sheepskins." A recording contract was quickly offered and Whiteman's version of jazz was soon heard wherever there was a phonograph. And the popularity of Whiteman and similar bands began the night-club era. The writer continued:

> The jazz-boom was on.... The youth of America grabbed saxophones and left home and law school, never to see daylight again for many years. Dinner Jacket common [stock] crossed 1000. Musical-instrument factories installed assembly lines and worked three shifts. Instruments on twenty easy payments. How to play the avocado in six easy lessons. Gold-plated, silver-lined, diamond-studded instruments. High-school orchestras had to be locked up at night.[36]

Henrietta Straus in *Nation* described a 1924 concert in Aeolian Hall, New York City, by Paul Whiteman and George Gershwin, as "a new chapter to our musical history." Jazz was the "music of the melting pot." "Many of those who write, orchestrate, and play jazz," she pointed out, "are of Russian-Jewish extraction, and the elements of the Russian, negro and the native American are the components that are now simmering." It was an educational experience for those who jammed the hall, from the devotees of jazz to those of classical music.[37]

After hearing Gershwin's "An American in Paris," a prominent music patron referred to him as the "Lindbergh of American music." Otto Kahn said: "He is a leader of young America in music in the same sense in which Lindbergh is the leader of young America in aviation, and in more than one respect has qualities similar to those of the young and attractive Colonel—qualities which we like to consider characteristic of the best type of young America.... In the rhythm, the melody, the humor, the grace, the rush, and sweep and dynamics of his compositions he expresses the genius of young America."[38] The difference between classical music and the mellow jazz of Whiteman and Gershwin was described by some as the difference between high hat and brown derby.[39] Another described jazz as "a brazen little hussy, with jewels on her heels and a cigarette between berouged lips."[40]

For some, jazz seemed the perfect music for the Machine Age. As one author wrote: "The moan of the saxophone, the wails and shrieks of the other instruments, the broken rhythms, are indeed as reminiscent of the factory as baseball is indigenous to the United States." And in an age of the noise of the machines, what could be more appropriate than the noise of jazz?[41] Yet another saw it as an escape therefrom. James Weldon Johnson wrote:

> When white America is not straining under the spur of the money-making urge it yields for relaxation to the spell of Negro song and dance. A great deal of white America's leisure is spent in playing a black-face part; in a desperate effort for realization, in an effort to get back to the primeval joys of life, it strives to "pass" for colored, to be really Negro.[42]

Jazz quickly spread overseas, conquering much of Europe, and with the music went exports of its instruments. A former trade commissioner reported that in 1924 there were more American-made musical instruments in foreign countries than from any other country, $12 million having been sold in that year alone, more than the total of England, Germany, and France combined. And instruments had been exported to 107 different countries, with the American player piano one of the most popular.[43]

By 1920 lamentations were being heard that jazz was robbing classical music of some of its most talented musicians of the future. The *New York Herald Tribune* wrote that some musicians had "abandoned high-class music to play in the 'jazz' bands at hotel and restaurants where there is dancing, the reason being that they command wages as high as $125 a week for such work." But when the dancing mania had died out, as must inevitably happen, "these musicians will be unfit for the higher reaches of their art. Not only their ability but their taste also will be vitiated. One need not be a moralist to see how the dance music of to-day (the "Blues" type especially) has kept pace in degeneracy with the dance itself."[44]

Another writer blamed the popularity of jazz on World War I, saying "that the total releasing of individuality is where such a disturbance as the late war reacts for the bad on music and poetry. Normal bonds are broken. Artistic restraint is weakened." Therefore, "an after-the-war period becomes a time when extreme personal idiosyncrasy has scope to exercise itself, with all its associated extravagance, subversive independence, and eccentricity. It is also a time of impatience. The clever youth is free to try to find short cuts. He has opportunity to flout that compulsion to measured movement which is necessary in the production of permanent music and poetry."[45]

The music and dances, and the conditions under which males and females associated at these affairs, were subjects of considerable criticism in the early 1920s. When the *Literary Digest* surveyed the opinions of the editors of religious and student papers, college deans and presidents it found about an equal division of opinion between those who believed conditions to be bad and those who disagreed. A majority of religious editors believed the country was experiencing "something like an immorality wave." One college newspaper wrote that modern dance was "not based on the natural and harmless instinct for rhythm, but on a craving for abnormal excitement" that had "passed from slight impropriety to indecency, and now threatens to become brazenly shameless. From graceful coordination of movement it has become a syncopated embrace," and "American morals have undoubtedly degenerated with the dance."

Another student newspaper wrote that the clothing worn by women contributed to the indecency of modern dance: "When every dancing step discloses the entire contour of the dancer, it is small wonder that moralists are becoming alarmed. The materials, also, from which women's evening dress are made are generally of transparent cobweb. There is a minimum of clothes and a maximum of cosmetics, head-decorations, fans, and jewelry. It is, indeed, an alarming situation when our twentieth-century debutante comes out arrayed like a South Sea Island savage." Another wrote that some of the dances were "mere animal exhibitions of agility and feelings. There is nothing of grace in them, and such dances serve as an excuse for actions that would be severely censored anywhere but on the modern dance floor." A western college editor wrote:

To glide gracefully over a floor, keeping time to the rhythm and harmony of music, is a pleasant recreation and is pleasing to witness, but to jig and hop around like a chicken on a red-hot stove, at the same time shaking the body until it quivers like a disturbed glass of jell-o, is not only tremendously suggestive but is an offense against common decency that would not be permitted in a semirespectable road-house.[46]

The mid-'20s saw the inauguration of the dance most generally associated with the decade—the Charleston. It was introduced to the public by an Afro-American review called *Runnin' Wild*. A writer for *The New Republic* wrote:

The first impression made by the Charleston was extraordinary. You felt a new rhythm, you saw new postures, you heard a new frenzy in the shout of the chorus. You were aware that in all this novelty there persisted elements as old as the cakewalk and probably as native, as traditional, as the levee dances.... The Charleston as an exhibition dance employed to advantage what the extravagant shimmy had brought in—the quiver of the body otherwise motionless, the use of the torso in the dance; it added the movements of the hips, thighs, buttocks, made familiar since Shuffle Along—the characteristic negro freedom of movement, frank and engaging; the patting which accompanies the blues was varied to slapping, and the hand fell on any portion of the body, in a frenzy.... And then, the visual high point of the dance, these seemingly grotesque elements were actually woven, in the rhythm of the dance, into a pattern which was full of grace and significance, which was gay and orgiastic and wild.

He went on to say that "schools are teaching it, the movie houses hold Charleston contests, little children imitate its steps on the sidewalks and along country roads—I have seen them."[47]

With the end of the 1920s came what one writer called "a soothing antidote to the hyperthyroid accents and rhythms of commercial jazz" in the form of "Rudy Vallee's crooning. Sober, soft-toned, relaxed, crooning was almost like the music warning that the inebriation of the twenties was dissipating and that the hangover of the thirties was just around the corner."[48]

Vallee was besieged by "stage door Johannas" who waited outside for a glimpse of the man "whose specialty of crooning songs in a soft, romantic voice while his orchestra plays in muted tones, has brought him a tremendous vogue." It had all begun when Vallee had, as an experiment, begun "crooning" with his band, and had resulted in his crooning "his way into the hearts of a million women." Critics found his voice less than wonderful, but admitted that it was "so full of yearning and tenderness that it made the hearts of many feminine listeners beat faster. Here was a voice that brought romance and love, a voice that stirred the imagination and lifted one out of the humdrum of every day life." It made him almost overnight the "the ideal of a million women," leading him to become the replacement in many hearts for the late Valentino," of whom it was said by H.L. Mencken: "He was catnip to women." One evening while leading his seven-man band Vallee had begun "to sing the chorus of a song, and he was greeted with so much applause that he continued to make it a practice to sing with the band. It was when the orchestra went on the air that the radio audience heard his voice for the first time, and feminine hearts fell for its romantic appeal."[49]

Predictions of the demise of the "Jazz Age" began early in the 1920s, clearly cases of wishful thinking. In 1931 the *Literary Digest* found more agreement on the subject, writing:

> The Jazz Age will soon be one with the "gray eighties" and the "gay nineties." Lengthened skirts may be the outward and visible sign of a reformed and chastened spirit.
>
> At least so it seems to one who has become "period conscious," who sees cycles in human behavior as in the material affairs of man....
>
> The discarding of manners and morals began about fifteen years ago, when the saxophone assaulted diners, fantastic dances symbolized something more than mere leg freedom, and the night club was substituted for the home.
>
> As people grew interested in "liberation" they turned to sex, bolstered with the backing of Freud and Ellis, Huxley and Fairbank. Literature on sex, from being innocuous, reached the depths of noxiousness.
>
> Indeed half of the serious literature and fiction combined had a definite sex-appeal, at least for the sex-minded.
>
> Then came the radio. It put the popularization of "modernism"—of high-powered salesmanship, of stampeded personalities, of tooth-pastes, cigars, wristwatches, and other articles of domestic efficiency and smartness—in the same class as the selling of thousands of copies of books.
>
> Thus while we became sex-minded we also became money-minded. We had our prosperity, our big fling at self-indulgence.
>
> Now those who are exhausted as a result want to say good-by to all that.[50]

Reviewing the course that jazz had taken in the 1920s, Isaac Goldberg wrote in *Forum*:

> It was in the evolution of ragtime into jazz that the business of the arranger in Tin Pan Alley took on a new and a revolutionary significance. The jazz band, once Whiteman had reduced its fantastic improvisations to paper, became strangely enough an agency of musical subtlety. It created a new field for clever—and sometimes more than clever—musicians who dressed up the popular tunes for the particular band that employed them. Jazz, so largely an orchestral function, made the Tin Pan Alley public for the first time instrumentation-conscious. And not that public alone. It introduced new color, new combinations. Contrasted rhythms, blue notes, interwoven melodies, impudent improvisations—these blended into a new spirit that gave music a new pertinency to living.
>
> One man, George Gershwin, in himself has provided a quasi-symphonic repertory developed out of this so easily despised product of the musical slums. In 1924 the "Rhapsody in Blue," which has continued in unabated popularity and conquered Europe; in 1925 the too-little heard "Concerto in F"; in 1928, "An American in Paris" ... That jazz should have insinuated its way into the symphonic and operatic scores of a devitalized Europe provides, if nothing more, a highly interesting footnote in the history of modern music. For the first time in the history of the arts, Europe, through jazz, became a debtor continent to us.[51]

An English music critic wrote: "For millions of Europeans, America means jazz, and jazz means America." This was unfortunate, he wrote, because jazz was "the most dreary, the most brainless, the most offensive form of music that the earth has ever known." Accompanying the popularity of jazz in Europe, and only slightly less offensive to this critic, was American black spirituals, which had at least "a certain native charm." He concluded: "If the peace of the world is to be assured, let America, for heaven's sake, send us no more jazz and no more spirituals, but especially no more jazz."[52] Roland Hayes, a black singer of mainly spirituals, found no interest in his talents in the United States, but in Europe after World War I he "found recognition wherever he went, was recognized by the aristocracy of Paris and London, and was 'commanded' to sing before royalty." His European success led him to be accepted enthusiastically by audiences in both North and South once he returned to America.[53]

One of the most popular dramatic productions in the 1920s was a play called *Porgy*, which was a story of colored life, and which caused, according to the *Literary Digest*, "the deepest impression so far this season on New York's theatergoing public." The cast was almost entirely black, and the play was described by one critic as "the first fine performance I have seen given by a negro troupe." It was set in Charleston. Some critics found the play more moving than the book on which it was based, the spirituals sung in the play having much to do with making it come alive. One critic wrote: "To hear the 'spirituals' sung as they were sung last night is worth twice the price of a seat. . . . "[54]

THE VERDICT

The publication of Walter Lippmann's *A Preface to Morals* in 1929, made him a widely reviewed and quoted authority on the changing morality of the post–World War I years. Fundamentally, it was Lippmann's view that there was no divine sanction for human morality once one had concluded that all conduct had "purely, human, local, and temporal origins," and with the loss of divine sanction went any stigma of sin.[55]

A reader of Lippmann's book wrote:

> I have much sympathy with this young generation. It has seen so many myths exploded around it; not merely the Christian myth, but such things as self-denial, altruism, public spirit, that it believes in no myths at all. And you need to be very tough indeed to be able to do without *any* myths.[56]

2

Manners, Modes, and Fads

CIVILITY

Closely related to, and sometimes indistinguishable from, the revolt in morals, was one in American manners. In 1921, Benjamin De Casseres wrote in the *New York Times Book Review and Magazine*:

For the last two years every one who goes round this town a good deal has noted an increase in grouch. Everybody you meet bristles like a military brush, Answers are short; faces are long; curses are deep. Taxes and prohibition, maybe, People are silent, morose, suspicious, and their voices in public places are like unto a rusty saw cutting ice,

For De Casseres, the situation was in part a result of the departure of bartenders, as a result of prohibition, "the most courteous public servants I ever met." They had "set the manners of an age that has gone," and when historians in future studied "the decline of public civility in New York after the war, I believe they will lay it to the fall of the bar and the cafe table."[1]

One writer in the '20s observed that if it was a sign of good breeding now to disdain any show of appreciation, then America was "the best bred of all nations." The time was coming, he predicted, when Americans would no longer give or accept a tip, since "all classes are reluctant to betray appreciation or as much as consciousness of a kindness." "Good morning" and "Good evening," he also opined, were "doomed, mere refuse to be flung into the garbage can of decayed manners." He wrote:

Nobody believes any longer that to be civil with ease is to make one's self beloved; that good breeding goes hand in hand with common-sense and good nature. To be uncivil with ease is now the way to get on, and to get on the one thing to bother about.

"Be rude to one another" had become the golden rule, and bad manners had spread to infect all of "the fundamental things of life as well." He explained: "The contagion" had spread to art and to literature, "emancipating verse and prose alike from form and restraint," also to the theater, where it was "exalting cheap humor and vulgar display at the expense of a noble dramatic tradition." In government, it had reduced "the people's chosen representatives" to "wrangling and snarling like dogs over a bone," while in religion men of God were "shrieking hell and damnation to each other like angry fishwives."[2]

A hundred years ago," another writer observed, "the young girl who wished to ensnare the heart of a man would blush, and tremble, give a side glance and look down, and carelessly drop a rose from her bosom in the path of her pursuer," but now she was more likely to throw a dinner roll at him across the table, shouting, "Hi there! Catch it, you boob!"[3]

HOME AND FAMILY

One much-commented-upon apparent casualty of the loss of manners was marriage. Reno, Nevada had become the divorce capital of America, passing out decrees of doubtful legality but accepted so long as they were not challenged by the other party. As one writer observed, "A man would be expelled from his Rotary Club and a woman from her Garden Club if either should start to contest one of these divorces in court."[4]

Some blamed the "death to propriety" on advertising. Starting with the invention of halitosis, the prying eyes of ad men had penetrated into every corner of the home. "From basement to attic they crawl and dash.... they pry into the clothing, the weight, the digestion and every other intimate detail of mankind. They leave no room in America for reticence or reserve."[5]

Traditional domesticity was also supposedly suffering at the hands of another recent development—ready-to-eat foods. As the *Literary Digest* observed late in the decade, the home had become for many "merely a place to sleep and to wield a can-opener." A University of Chicago scholar, it noted, had told the American Sociological Society in early 1929 that between 1900 and 1920 "the number of restaurants in this country increased almost four times as fast as the number of families; between 1914 and 1925, bakery production increased 60 per cent, while population increased only 15 per cent, and from 1910 to 1920 the number of delicatessen shops grew 43 per cent, or about three times as fast as the population." For some, these statistics boded ill for traditional family life and its influence on values and manners. One newspaper opined that only radio might "save the family home from extinction." For others, however, the figures were only proof that household menus had become "far more varied and appetizing than formerly," and if a housewife was patronizing the bakeries and delis, it was evidence that she was seeking better meals for her family and making the home a greater attraction. The greater freedom from household work did not mean the decadence of family life; it could as easily mean just the opposite, giving the wife and mother more time for her husband and children.[6]

A Middletown butcher told the Lynds that the modern housewife had "lost the art of cooking. She buys cuts of meat that are easily and quickly cooked.... Folks today want to eat in a hurry and get out in the car." The Lynds observed further that the housewife's time was also saved by the increased use of bakery bread and canned goods, which had eliminated much of the need for home baking and canning. And thanks to refrigeration and cold storage and improvements in transportation, families now had access to fresh fruit and vegetables all year round.[7]

The New Republic agreed that family life was undergoing alterations, but denied that it was in danger. Surveying the contents of papers delivered at a conference "On Family Life in America Today," it found:

> The customary factors were cited as reasons for the declining importance of the home as an institution. It no longer has economic significance, since the manufacturing processes which once went on within its walls are now conducted elsewhere. Children in their late 'teens who still live at home, and even wives, tend increasingly to engage in outside remunerative work, and thus the dominance of the father, once backed by the club of grim necessity, has been much weakened. It has also been diminished by the general decline of authoritarianism, political and religious. The rising costs of land and residential construction make houses and apartments ever smaller, until there is hardly enough room for family life, in the old sense, and hospitality consists to an increasing extent in taking one's guests out to hotel, restaurant or theater. New sources of extra-mural activity are furnished by the automobile, the motion-picture theater, the enormously increased popularity of dancing.[8]

World War I had brought a temporary halt to all dispensable construction, thus creating a shortage of housing that drove rentals skyward until they occasionally absorbed as much as one-half of the family income. Families were driven to find ever-shrinking quarters, and little by little the qualities of traditional home life were lost—first the library, then the dining room, and then the parlor, while even the kitchen "shrank to a mere hole in the wall." The irony, one writer observed, was that the smaller living quarters often had no room for milady's laborsaving machines. Apartment living was blamed by some "authorities" for "the cocktail hour, the short skirt, shingled hair, and the public use of lipstick." It had also contributed to making of Americans a race of "nomads" who seldom stayed long in one home, by contrast with the rural tradition of living a lifetime on the same site.[9]

In their study of Middletown, the Lynds found not only houses but house lots shrinking—down to about 5,000 square feet. This naturally had implications for such things as children's play space, room for leisure-time activities, and privacy. "Houses," they wrote, "are crowding closer to the front paving-line and flowers and shrubbery must give way as the lawn shrinks to allow a driveway to the garage." Less time was being devoted to care of the lawn because of competition from the automobile and the movies for spare time, and "the make of one's car is rivaling the looks of one's place as an evidence of one's 'belonging.'"[10] The Lynds also found that, while the interior plan of houses had undergone little change, there had been some trend toward fewer and larger rooms, the "parlor" and the "spare bedroom" being the casualties.[11] In 1925 90 percent of the homes were wired and presumably lit with electricity. One of the great products of the machine age for housewives was linoleum, which eliminated the need for the carpets that had consumed so much time for housecleaning. This, combined with the smaller size of the home, the many laborsaving devices, canned, bakery, and delicatessen foods, and store-bought clothing, made life much easier for the 1920s Middletown housewife.[12]

The Lynds found that in the first half of the 1920s electric use had burgeoned in Middletown to the accompaniment of the purchase of a variety of electrical appliances, including irons, toasters, curlers, refrigerators, vacuum cleaners, toasters, washers, refrigerators, and ranges. Moreover, they found that "in April, 1924, 4,348 Middletown homes had a telephone, leaving about 5,000 without this tool. . . . Around the telephone have grown up such time-savers for the housewife as the general delivery system for everything from groceries to a spool of thread."[13]

The weekly washing and ironing of family clothes, too, tended to make markedly different inroads upon the time of housewives, with commercial laundries playing a larger role than in the past, although the tendency to send laundry out had been slowed by the increased used of electric washing machines and irons in the homes.[14]

During the 1920s Americans purchased 5 million electric washing machines, along with 8 million electric vacuums, 1.5 million electric refrigerators, and 13 million radios. Yet the use of such devices was still largely confined to urban America as electrification only slowly penetrated into rural areas. Less than a quarter million farm families enjoyed electricity in 1926, out of a total of approximately 6 million.[15]

Professor George Walter Fiske, of Oberlin College, accounted for the decline of the family by writing:

> In countless American homes every member is busy expressing himself with selfish abandon, obeying instinct and impulse without restraint, each running off on his own pet tangent, till the old home-centered life is no more. This subtle selfishness is killing out the old home loyalty which has been the cement of American society. The individualistic mother centers her interest in bridge and social climbing. The individualistic father is absorbed in fighting his competitors and "the plaguey unions." No wonder the individualistic sons and daughters pursue their own favorite sense pleasures, crushes, crazes, and intoxications, quite independently, each going his own separate way, and making the home chiefly a point of departure and reluctant return.
>
> Such centrifugal homes are seldom found in the country. They are usually urban or suburban, symptoms of overprosperity, social satiety, demoralizing luxury, and the sudden growth of commercialized sensational amusements. Rural life, in general, plods along in the same safe grooves; but city life finds a new thrill every week for every member of

the family, and thrill chasing absorbs the time and energy of the multitude who lose their ideals in the easy glamour of the city. In fact, the thrill is the chief pull to the city, for rural youth whom it entices are really more fun-hungry than dollar-hungry.

"Even our moral ideals are threatened," he wrote, "by the reckless speeding up of this automotive age, with its resulting nervous tension, overstrain, and restless, hectic city living."[16]

The Lynds found in Middletown that the people were learning how to adapt to new material things more rapidly than they were acquiring new habits addressed to persons and "non-material institutions." They wrote:

New tools and inventions have been the most prolific breeders of change.... Bathrooms and electricity have pervaded the homes of the city more rapidly than innovations in the personal adjustments between husband and wife or between parents and children.... At the same time that secularization is lessening emotional resistance at some points, the very swiftness of the penetration of impersonal institutions like automatic machinery, electrical devices, and automobiles, has, however, multiplied occasions for emotional exploding in Middletown through the discrepancies between these shouldering new ways and other habits upon which they force themselves. One need only mention the new friction spots between parents and children incidental to the incorporation of automobiles and movies into their world.... [17]

The Department of Labor reported that 1928 was the third year in which more families in cities were living in apartments than in single-family dwellings, and it was the first year in which new apartment houses exceeded in number both one-family and two-family houses. Homes in new buildings in 257 cities were provided for 388,678 families, of which 53.7 percent were in apartment houses. In 1921 only 24.4 percent of the families provided for were housed in apartments and 58.3 percent in one-dwelling homes. The percentage of apartments was even greater in the fourteen largest cities—67.2 percent. In Chicago and New York City it was over 80 percent.[18]

Standards were in flux. Stuart Chase wrote:

The psychoanalysts have lifted the curtain on a variety of matters long held suitable for discussion only in a brothel—if at all—and made them current coin at every "modern" dinner table. In brief the only dependable standard in sexual affairs seems to be that any sort of reticence connotes a serious, not to say perilous, internal conflict.

It was a time of a mobile population, constantly on the march in search of better things that rarely came, following chasing fads in occupations and in speculations, migrating relentlessly from farm to city. Chase concluded that "the indirect effects of mechanization have shaken us loose from ancient mental certainties. We are never adequately prepared for change, and resist it when it comes, but we are beginning to realize with some bewilderment that almost anything may happen."[19]

Walter Pitkin found Europeans most struck and bewildered by the brief time that Americans spent at home. Urban Americans, he wrote, were "never at home except when they have to be; they seem to feel out of place there. They eat and sleep within its walls, then rush off to work, to school, to the movies."[20] Much of this was the result of the automobile, which seemed even for a brief period to be making some Americans "seasonally nomadic," with winters spent in Florida homes, until the onset of the depression made it impracticable.[21]

DIVORCE

One aspect of changing family life was the increasing liberalization of views concerning divorces, and a related increase in their numbers. Many states followed the example of Nevada in making divorces easier to obtain, and at least some Protestant churches relaxed their attitudes toward them. In 1928 the Methodist Episcopal Church dropped its insistence that a valid divorce required evidence of adultery, and left the question of remarriage to the judgments of individual clergymen.[22] The rising numbers, however, fueled further concern that, in the words of a sociologist, "there is something radically wrong about our home and family life." He explained:

> The chief thing wrong with American family life is the unsocialized individualism of our standards with reference to marriage and the family. We have made these things matters of individual convenience, instead of matters concerning the welfare of our highest ideals and values. We have tried to build the family life upon selfishness, and we have failed.... We need to replace our pagan standards, pure individualism, with reference to the family and to the home life, with a more socialized Christian standard.[23]

Some went so far as to draw parallels between the United States and the fall of the Roman Empire in their common "laxity and rottenness of the laws of divorce."[24]

While men were filing for more divorces than were women, by about a 2–1 margin, it was women who were more likely to be charged with desertion (in half of the filings) or adultery (one-fifth). Female adultery outranked male adultery as a cause of divorce by 20.3 percent to 7.5 percent, figures that suggested the growing emancipation of women was at least partly responsible for marital ills. Some critics charged that one or both members of many couples were entering marriage with the thought of divorce already in mind and, with the growing laxity of divorce laws and the declining stigma of divorce, were embarking on a succession of marriages that some of them described as "consecutive polygamy." For some critics the only solution seemed to be the elimination of state laws on marriage and divorce, many of which were viewed as too liberal, and the substitution of a strict federal law that would cover all Americans.[25] By the late 1920s nearly one marriage in five was likely to end in divorce, a fact that spurred the Presbyterian Church to recognize divorces obtained only for "biblical" grounds—adultery.[26] Only the onset of the depression, and the resultant economic securities of the 1930s, stemmed the onward tide of divorce.

BOOZE

Drunkenness, it should be pointed out, was seldom listed as a cause of divorce in the 1920s, which should not be surprising since this was the decade of prohibition. Nevertheless, it was still given as a cause in some cases, indicating that the consumption of alcohol in America had not ceased, despite the law that came into effect in January 1920. Thereafter the only alcohol legally manufactured and sold in America was industrial alcohol, to which one of forty denaturing substances approved by the government had been added to make it unfit for use as a beverage, and which were very difficult to extract. But prohibition did not put a finish to drinking. As a writer in the liberal *The Nation* observed midway through the decade,

> A social law, a law dealing with the personal habits of a people, should be an expression of social custom; when it anticipates custom it misses its function and does harm. Resistance in such cases is inevitable. The public is not given to thought, but it has an uncanny way of arriving at results. It has a subconscious but keen appreciation of speciousness and tyranny and injustice, and it acts accordingly.

Prohibition, one critic argued, had been approved in wartime, when the people wanted to "hurt themselves," as psychological compensation for the suffering at the front, but in peacetime it was "liberty that now appeals, not sacrifice." Thus, the passage of prohibition in wartime, and the widespread defiance of it in the postwar years, with 1,300 known saloons in Philadelphia alone in October 1923, and 43,155 arrests for drunkenness in that city in 1922—more than any year *before* prohibition.[27]

O.O. McIntyre wrote of New York City that it was filled with "thousands of speakeasies that have supplanted the old-time swing-door beer saloon since prohibition." He added:

> These are mostly in basements where you ring the bell and ask for Louie. Once they were old brick homes. They serve meals for $1 that could not be furnished elsewhere for $6. Any variety of booze is on tap from cocktails to cointreau. Now and then there are police raids but the courts are so clogged with cases that if the accused lived to be 100 years old they would not face trial.

Moreover, he pointed out, prohibition had cost New York all of its best restaurants, except for Lindy's, the others having been replaced by "a flood of Chinese chop-suey caravansaries with dim lights, shadowy booths and $1.25 table d'hote dinners and huge orchestras."[28]

Initially, the thirst for "booze" had been slaked by supplies remaining from before prohibition. Then, after a variety of experiments, bootleg breweries and distilleries had turned to corn sugar for their raw material. After first trying to stop the diversion of the existing stocks, government agents had turned to preventing the use of industrial alcohol. But by the second half of the decade it had become apparent that the manufacture of booze had assumed factory dimensions with its large-scale purchases of yeast, corn sugar, and other ingredients, and federal agents had begun to concentrate on the task of interrupting that flow. Between 1921 and 1927, for example, the production of corn sugar in America had grown from 152,000 pounds to 905,000 pounds.[29]

Charles Merz's definitive work on prohibition, *The Dry Decade*, made a convincing case for his assertion that Congress passed the Eighteenth Amendment and the Volstead Act only to put the contentious issue of prohibition to rest, but was so little committed to it that it never appropriated enough money to enforce the law. Instead, when faced with criticism of the obvious and widespread violations of the law, the response of Congress was to pass more laws without significantly increasing appropriations.

Clearly, Congress had intended that the states would carry much of the burden of enforcement, and the federal government continued to exhort the states and municipalities all through the 1920s to do so, but without significant success. The states were, in fact, showing no more inclination to spend money enforcing an unpopular law than was the federal government. In fact, says Merz: "They were spending for the enforcement of the Eighteenth Amendment approximately one-eighth of the sum they were spending for the enforcement of their own fish and game laws."

The federal government tried by a variety of tactics to stem the flow of alcohol, but with an inadequate force to deal with any of the means by which alcohol reached consumers—whether smuggling, illicit distilleries, or illegal tampering with legal alcohol. The force of federal agents was, in fact, inadequate to deal with any one of the various sources, and it was a travesty to expect them to cope with all of the them. Tens of thousands of arrests were made, and thousands of sources interdicted, but these only dented the tip of the iceberg. Still, they were more than the judicial system could handle. As with enforcement, Congress refused to appropriate the money for an adequate number of judges to deal with the cases. And arrests seldom led to convictions or appropriate punishments, anyway, since the law was unpopular with juries and judges.

The uneven nature of state enforcement led, by default, to a kind of system of "local option," in which some states and municipalities ignored the liquor traffic, while others tried fitfully to enforce the law. For the most part it was the larger industrial states and their urban centers that tended to ignore the law, and agrarian states and small towns that tried to enforce it.

One device tried by federal agents on a nationwide basis was the padlocking for one year of those buildings where illicit liquor activity was discovered. This resulted in the curious instance of a redwood tree in northern California being padlocked, because its base had been hollowed out to contain a still. But even padlocking was ineffective, since not enough agents were available to ensure that the padlocks remained in place for the entire year.

Perhaps because they were preoccupied with other matters, including the war in Europe and the possibility of American participation, organized opposition to passage of the Eighteenth Amendment and the Volstead Act was limited largely to the brewery and distillery industries, together with the American Federation of Labor. The obvious self-interest of the first two naturally reduced their effectiveness. As the 1920s went on, demonstrating not only the ineffectiveness of prohibition, but also its negative effects in promoting lawlessness and wholesale corruption of government officials, a broader-based opposition arose that by the late 1920s was able to compete on a more even footing with the prohibitionists. By the end of the decade it seemed clear that either the definition of "alcoholic liquors" would be liberalized to include beer and light wines, or the Eighteenth Amendment would be repealed.[30]

A writer reported of North Carolina in *American Mercury*:

> Any hotel porter or bellhop in the State can get you, on three minutes' notice, any required amount of liquor. Generally the management shuts its eyes to the fact that its help is selling it. Patrons demand service. Usually the hotel servant works on a commission basis for some established retailer, who in turn has dealings with a wholesaler. The small distiller who once peddled his own liquor has disappeared.... I know of at least three distilleries that are financed by respectable banks.
>
> Rarely are any of the larger operators or distributors caught. Some of them pay tribute regularly and others are not bothered by the local authorities. I have accompanied Prohibition agents when they went to collect their tribute. It is the small fellow, the man who totes it around on his hip, who gets hauled up, The courts are congested with his like. The formerly decorous and profoundly venerated Federal courts have become tribunals of obscene comedy, on a level with that which goes on in the police courts.[31]

While the Justice Department in Washington, D.C., where the enforcement of prohibition was under the zealous direction of Assistant Attorney General Mabel Walker Willebrandt, made every effort to marshal a nationwide war against alcoholic beverages, the commitment fell off rapidly at the state level, and even among many federal agents outside the capital. Indeed, a writer in *Collier's*, after much research and consultation with Mabel Walker Willebrandt, concluded that the United States was on average 38.5 percent "wet"—i.e., that much of it was free of enforcement. He claimed that "the thirty-one border or seaboard States and a few inland States are the wettest. On the Atlantic seaboard, for instance, the average dampness is 58¼ per cent." Wettest was New York City and its environs; the driest states were Kansas, Utah, and Idaho. The District of Columbia was not listed, but was estimated at 60 percent. Politics, he wrote, had caused enforcement to break down, with too many political appointees responsible for enforcing prohibition.[32]

New York City's reformist Committee of Fourteen warned that the speakeasies, night clubs and dance halls of the 1920s had "evolved an American counterpart of the Geisha girl." Prohibition was being indicted by the press as the cause of the problem. The report said:

> She is employed for the main purpose of increasing the sales of liquor, food, and other drinks; incidentally, she is to provide esthetic, social, and sexual entertainment for the men customers.

> Her sex appeal largely accounts for her success. She is the successor of the old-time rustler who worked in bars on a commission basis many years ago....
>
> The speak-easies and night clubs are now too numerous to succeed from the sale of liquor without the added attraction of "hostesses." Their use in these places did not become general until the last two or three years. The greatest demand appeared in the fall of 1927 when agencies and clubs became bold enough to advertise for recruits. So far as is known the only paper to accept these advertisements is one daily tabloid.
>
> These advertisements have had the result of drawing not only local girls into this occupation, but also girls from outside places in various parts of the United States.
>
> Other hostesses are recruited from "closed" dance halls which in turn advertise extensively for "young, attractive girls over eighteen, experience unnecessary." Still others are known to have been inmates of houses in Albany, Troy, Detroit, and other cities still tolerating such resorts.
>
> It is believed that the night club and speak-easy have been directly responsible for a marked increase in the volume of vice. This is especially true, because they provide a place for operations.... [33]

Charles Merz found that the drugstore soda fountain, too, had at least in part replaced the bar since prohibition, writing: "This is the new American bar, and it is in part the product of good advertising, in part the child of Prohibition, in part the natural sequence of a 'servant problem' which makes meals at home more troublesome, while men work farther from their homes and women work in offices." While the soda fountain antedated prohibition, he wrote, they had only recently burgeoned to about 30,000 in number and begun "to put on airs." "In an age of bustle, rush and ragged nerves," he wrote, "they are re-fuelling places for a jaded nation. Here, after a hard day, or a hard night, is a handy first aid station and a pick-me-up." An additional attraction was that they sometimes added alcohol to drinks for regulars. In addition, the drugstores purveyed a variety of alcohol-laced patent medicines. It was a sign of the times, he wrote, that nowadays federal judges were impounding barrels of dandruff remedies, hair tonic, and benzoin lotion on the suspicion that they had been "prepared and intended for other purposes than mere medication of the scalp." The soda fountain, he wrote, had "much about it that is characteristic of our background. It has our prompt adoption of whatever is most recent and most perfect in mechanical devices.... It has our national ability to make speed whether or not the occasion warrants: a drug store dinner can be ordered, served, and eaten in ten minutes."[34]

TOBACCO

The well-mannered lady of pre–World War I America did not smoke—at least not in public. The war years changed all that. Taking on men's work, women obviously felt they were entitled to some hitherto male perquisites, including cigarettes. The right to vote, beginning with the 1920 election, only further confirmed them in that conviction. As one female war worker observed: "If Congress admits that women have a right to vote, I'd like to see them stop us from smoking. If a woman wants to smoke, she'll smoke. You might as well try to stop a volcano from smoking."[35]

Others, however, saw in the trend the pernicious influence of advertising by the cigarette companies. Noting that $60 million was being spent in the early 1920s on selling cigarettes, including the use of testimonials of politicians, athletes, and movie stars, Senator Reed Smoot actually introduced a bill in Congress that would have censored cigarette advertising. Reed referred to the cigarette companies' advertising campaign as "unconscionable, heartless and destructive attempts to exploit the women and youth of our country."[36]

By 1924 smoking had become so pervasive that the editor of *Good Health* magazine, John Kellogg, was advocating that refuges be set aside where non-smokers might escape exposure to cigarette smoke. Noting that as recently as the previous century smoking was a practice of a small minority, with smokers confined to designated areas, Kellogg wrote that the situation had now been reversed. "Smoking," he wrote, "has become so nearly universal among men, the few non-smokers are practically ignored and their rights are trampled upon."[37] Walter Pitkin computed that Americans smoked 1,000–1,200 cigarettes per year, sometimes as many as 10,000, and that the typical family spent $70 per year on them.[38]

Kellogg was critical of colleges and universities for not doing more to discourage smoking among students, but the following year Bryn Mawr College actually lifted its ban against smoking by its female student body. The move came in response to a petition from the student government. The president of the college explained her decision by observing that "a regulation prohibiting smoking can no longer depend on the authority of conscience and convention which made up public opinion, and it is no longer effective in a self-governing commonwealth." Smoking rooms would be provided in each residence hall. Newspaper comment was generally favorable, with the *Indianapolis Star* viewing female smoking as just a "flapper movement" fad. It explained that the Midwest

> still looks askance at the one who indulges the habit in public, altho privately the cigaret has long since lost the element of novelty. Young girls think it smart; some women think it bohemian. Others enjoy smoking and see no reason why they should be criticized. Their argument does not readily admit an answer.

But the *Buffalo Evening Post* viewed female smoking as but a part of a general "coarsening" of young womanhood that included also "the exposure of nakedness in public appearance, of overpainting the face and lips, and of petting parties." It added: "It may be true that women have the same right as men to drink and smoke and indulge habits peculiar to masculinity, but that means the lowering of the standards of womanhood to the level of men."[39]

Good Housekeeping noted in 1929 that the production of cigarettes had doubled in the 1920s—from 53 million to 106 million—and found much of the increase attributable to the rise in female smoking, especially by young women. It wrote: "The number of girls under twenty-one who now smoke cigarettes is said to be greater than the number of boys who smoked twenty years ago. It is a common sight, at least in the business offices of New York, to see young girls sitting at their desks smoking." It found the increase spurred by greater and more skillful newspaper and magazine advertising, the influence of movies and radio, and of billboards. The fad among women to be slim had spurred the tobacco companies to emphasize the "slimming" effects of cigarettes. Marshaling testimony from doctors and coaches, the author of the article sought to discourage both boys and girls from taking up the smoking habit, but admitted that it was a difficult task, writing:

> Whoever knows girls knows that, if left to themselves, they will fall victims to the cigarette propaganda even more easily than the boys did. They have certain temperamental qualities that make them particularly susceptible to shrewd advertising appeal. Almost every girl would like, if she could, to be the Duchess of Sutherland, and if she can not be the duchess, she would like to do as the duchess does. If the duchess smokes, that seems, to many a girl, to be a reason why she should do the same. Girls, like boys, are influenced by the habits of those whom they suppose to be their superiors. Boys begin smoking to be "manly." Girls begin smoking to demonstrate that they are strictly modern and up-to-date in their views and habits of life.[40]

Catering to the aforementioned desire to be slim, the American Tobacco Company unleashed an advertising campaign for its Lucky Strike cigarettes that was built around the slogan "Reach for a Lucky instead of a sweet." Actress Helen Hayes was featured in advertising that linked smoking with a trim figure. Candy manufacturers responded with commercials and ads touting the ill effects on health that resulted from smoking. A chain of candy stores warned: "Do not let anyone tell you that a cigarette can take the place of a piece of candy. The cigarette will inflame your tonsils, poison with nicotine every organ of your body, and dry up your blood—nails in your coffin."[41]

The New Republic reported that the "war" soon expanded and was being carried on with deadly earnestness. Philip Wagner reported that American Tobacco had committed over $12 million to the fight, and the candy industry's side was equally well financed. One cigarette, however, had managed to bridge the gap between the two sides. Old Gold cigarettes told Americans: "Eat a Chocolate. Light an Old Gold. And enjoy both! Two fine and healthful treats!"[42]

The onset of the Great Depression caused reduced cigarette sales. *Business Week* reported in 1931 that cigarette sales were dropping nearly $1 billion per month. Thirteen states were taxing cigarettes from two to three cents per package, and the federal tax was six cents. To evade the high cost of cigarettes, many Americans had turned to rolling their own, a move that was anathema to both the cigarette companies and the states being deprived of tax revenue. Cigarette companies quickly began to offer their own brands of tobacco for hand rolling and to unleash advertising campaigns to promote their sale.[43]

Contrasting the success of the prohibitionists with the failure of those who sought to ban tobacco from America, Frances Warfield profiled the leading antitobacco crusader, Lucy Page Gaston, in an essay for *Outlook* magazine. Born in 1860, Gaston had begun her antitobacco crusade in 1899 through a variety of organizations she formed, such as the National Anti-Cigarette League, chartered in 1901. Yet, as Warfield pointed out: "The United States now produces more than fifty times as many cigarettes as in 1899, when Miss Gaston founded her first anticigarette organization."[44]

FADS

Late in the decade Stuart Chase wrote: "Look at the fads which follow one after another in crazy procession—bicycle riding, ping pong, golf, bridge, mah-jong, jazz, crossword puzzles, bobbed hair, antiques, prohibition cocktails. Look at the steady drift from the farm—where the *mores* have ever been powerful—to the cities—where they were always more tenuous."[45]

If female smoking can be classed as a fad of the 1920s, it shared in common with other fads of the decade that they all originated with, or were promoted by, those whom most Americans admired. Mah-jongg, one of the earliest fads of the 1920s, originated with society matrons on New York's Fifth Avenue. The bobbing of women's hair originated with movie actress Irene Castle, and golf was at first the sport of the wealthy. In short, these fads did not originate with the working classes, but rather spread to them from the top down. It was so, also, with the most popular fad of the 1920s—the crossword puzzle. According to *Literary Digest*, such puzzles had appeared in magazines and newspapers for at least a decade without attaining the dimension of a fad. Only when "a group of well-known writers of New York" popularized them, did publicity create a fad among the masses:

> The cross-word puzzle soon found its way into the news and editorial columns, into comic strips, vaudeville acts and the radio. From eye to eye and ear to ear the story of cross-words traveled. Not to know of them, not to have worked them, soon stamped one as being behind the times.

"Millions of people," it wrote, "seek no further happiness than that supplied by a cross-word puzzle and a dictionary."

The craze really took off when two young men, Richard Simon and Max Schuster, formed a publishing company and followed the suggestion of Simon's aunt by bringing out a book of the puzzles in 1924. Discouraged by the reaction of booksellers and others to the idea, they initially printed only 3,600 copies. A magazine article the next year described the reaction:

> Inside of a month the demand began to grow. New editions of the first book came out in rapid succession, A second followed and sold like hot cakes. When the third book was

published, it *started* with an edition of forty thousand copies! Approximately three quarters of a million of these books have been sold, and still the demand keeps up.

Other publishers have followed suit. There are all kinds of crossword puzzle books, including several for children. There is a Biblical one, containing only words which are found in the Scriptures. There is a "celebrity" book, made up of crossword puzzles which have been constructed by famous people. There are Yiddish puzzles for the Jews; and so on almost without end.

One interesting result of the mania has been reported by the publishers of dictionaries. They declare that their sales, since the crossword furor started, have been unprecedented.

One university was including crossword puzzles in its curriculum, a professor at another was offering a prize for a puzzle with two different solutions, and dictionaries were in such demand that some libraries were prohibiting their use by crossword solvers. Correlations had been found by psychologists between performances on crossword puzzles and intelligence tests. Clearly they were not a fad for morons and could only flourish in a society with a high level of education. Psychologists found another explanation for their popularity in the fact that they were a rare fad that "costs virtually nothing and requires the development of no special physical dexterity, the acquisition of no unusual equipment, the learning of no rules." It required only a pencil, and perhaps a dictionary. It also satisfied "a long list of the fundamental desires of human kind."

Social distinction, sex, imitation, group loyalty, cooperation, competition, pleasure, play, amusement, humor, curiosity, activity, and constructiveness—all of these ingrained, instinctive wants of man are satisfied merely by printing letters in the proper squares.[46]

The *North American Review* regarded crossword puzzling as "the only satisfactory form of solitaire yet devised by the fertile brain of man." Unlike the more common variety, this one did not rely heavily on one's luck in the draw of the cards, but on knowledge and ability. It was "an intelligence test whose outcome no one need know but yourself." The successful puzzler "swells up visibly and may even cackle a little, like a hen which has laid a triumphant egg which had never been laid before. He feels the thrill of creative genius, and of establishing order and good sense in the very midst of chaos."[47]

The *New York World* wrote, with tongue in cheek:

It is remarkable that organized opposition to the cross-word puzzle addiction has not yet reared its head. Of course it will. The dissipation until lately has interfered only with relatively unimportant matters, such as domestic economy, the keeping of business engagements, and the dispatch of affairs in general. So it has been condoned.

Difficult as it is to find anybody engaged in his accustomed employment, things contrive to get done, and until they go utterly to smash, an anti-puzzle league may find difficulty in forwarding prohibitory legislation.... But a really serious indictment of the craze is uttered by the president of an athletic union, who asserts that it interferes with the training of football players, sprinters, and other young men engaged in like activities of paramount importance. The country might waive the injury to law, to medicine, and all such minor avocations by the intemperate hunt for synonyms, but it is horrible to contemplate the outcome suggested by the sporting official, namely, that the athletic supremacy of the United States is threatened by the cross-word puzzle.

If the Bill of Rights permits, Congress may see its duty clear to bar the dictionary to all athletes. Should an anti-puzzle drive gain headway, devotees at large will do well to stave off absolute prohibition. They must hold out for a puzzle a day at the minimum.[48]

So popular did mah-jongg become early in the decade that two of the most important items in American trade with China consisted of exports of cattle bones to China, where they were bleached and carved into mah-jongg sets for export back to the United States. A mah-jongg set could be bought for anything from ten cents at a dime store to $5 at a department store, with more elaborate ivory sets selling for as much as $200.

American missionaries in China complained that the American fad for mah-jongg was undercutting their work in China, where mah-jongg was essentially a form of gambling that they were trying to discourage. The *Springfield Union* wrote:

For centuries the Chinese have been laboring with their hands in a slow way to make Mah Jong sets for the limited number of Chinese that could afford them. So long as the business was confined to a Chinese demand it was comparatively limited. It made severe requisitions on the supplies of bamboo and ivory.

But suddenly all this changed and the astonished Chinese found themselves overwhelmed with demands for more Mah Jong sets in a week than they could make in a dozen years. The supply of bamboo was plentiful, but the ivory ran out. Then the shin-bones of Chinese calves became insufficient, and the beef-packers of Chicago had to ship tons of shin-bones to China. Even then the problem of meeting the demand was impossible without a radical change in the Chinese methods of labor, and an American business went in and "standardized" material and labor. All of this, however, was to the considerable discomfiture of American missionaries who were teaching that gambling was a sin.[49]

The discovery of Tutankhamen's tomb in the mid-1920s unleashed one of the more transitory fads in 1924, when it seemed everybody was talking of King Tutankhamen, reading stories of King Tutankhamen in the magazines, seeing pictures of King Tutankhamen in the rotogravure sections, reading bulletins of King Tutankhamen in the five-star finals. Egyptian bracelets were the rage. Egyptian silhouettes were favored in the styles. Egyptian dining rooms were being built in all the best hotels. Sixty-five colleges introduced new courses in Egyptian history. Barnum & Bailey's circus had an Egyptian clown.[50]

A more important and enduring fad was unleashed by Henry Ford midway in the decade, when his own pursuit of American antiquities created an interest among the American public in the treasures of the past. Some found it ironic that the man most responsible for unleashing the modern machine culture on America should simultaneously rekindle an interest in the simpler past. The Metropolitan Museum in New York City set up an American Wing to recreate a picture of life as it had existed for earlier generations, and many cities set to work to try to restore bits of their past. In 1926 the *New York Times* reported: "The craze for early American antiques of all sorts is sweeping the country."[51]

Just as Americans were copying the risqué French magazines, so were the French, in turn, adopting American fads. A Parisian fashion designer wrote in early 1927 that "we in France are slaves to the American influence; to what else can one attribute the passion for wealth, the worship of money which has been so evident with us in recent years and which has certainly not been a characteristic of French life in past ages?" He went on:

> American, too, is the tendency which our young ladies manifest when they affect a masculine appearance and a martial swagger—the vogue of cigarettes and pajamas! Along with that, the necessity of providing for the future has turned many of them into lawyers, doctors, manufacturers, chemists, mechanics, and these professions perceptibly modify their garb, their manners, and often their moral attitude.... Even more American are the implacable and hypertrophic rhythms of the new dances, the blues and the Charlestons, the din of unearthly instruments, and the musical idioms of exotic lands. I should estimate that for another fifteen years we shall have an ascending graph of jazz-bands and negro fanfares, which in their turn will give way to something newer, weirder, and more outlandish. The thrall of American music, which with Paul Whiteman seems to have reached its paroxysm and its zenith, will die away, just as that of the gypsy rhythms which now seem so naive and old-fashioned to us.
>
> The further this American spirit spreads, and the more we indulge the taste for these alien dances, the more masculine and the more severe will the fashions for women become. Already we have been treated to women in dinner jackets, and we shall soon witness a revival of trouser-skirts under various guises.... And the trousers for women will not be a mere short-lived fad; they will become as inevitable as bobbed hair, which is here to stay.[52]

THE IMPACT OF ADVERTISING

One phenomenon of the 1920s that intruded into every life was the remarkable growth of advertising, which, like so much about the 1920s, had its origins in World War I in the efforts of the government to promote sales of its Liberty Bonds and build support for the war effort. As Stuart Chase described it:

> The Committee on Public Information during the War provided us with the supreme example of the attempt to standardize opinion by propaganda; an example which not even the spirited drives of Old Gold cigarettes and Lux toilet soap can equal. Seventy-five million copies of thirty different booklets, printed in many languages, were circulated throughout the United States, and millions of additional copies abroad. Seventy-five thousand "four minute men" made 755,190 speeches in 5,200 communities, explaining the proper philosophical alignment of the words "democracy" and "war": and the principle of giving until it hurts.[53]

Foreign visitors, a *New Republic* writer observed in 1919, regarded the advertising they experienced as "saliently and essentially American." S.N. Behrman added:

The advertising man, the genius of America, is usually young, good-looking, sartorially perfect, with sleek hair and parti-colored shoes. Consciousness of the eminence of his position in American business has made him as complacent as Douglas Fairbanks. He does not conceal his awareness of the fact that he is the cornerstone of the most respectable American institutions; the newspapers and magazines depend on him; Literature and Journalism are his handmaidens. He is the Fifth Estate.[54]

An author of poetry for advertising defended his trade by writing:

Many a starving Chatterton to-day is making a comfortable living. Artists are no longer penniless, but grow opulent decorating the advertising pages of magazines. While this is not artistically ideal, it is humanly more comfortable for men of doubtful muses.[55]

In fact, many magazine writers of the 1920s were complimentary of the art and poetry that graced advertisements, one of them writing, after giving examples of noteworthy advertising art, that it was "time for dilettanti and scoffers to cease their scoffing, for fine work in advertising . . . is making a very real contribution to the sum total of aesthetic achievement in this country." Even the usually critical *New Republic* admitted that some of the poetry was of quality, printing:

Lightning on the hills
Clamor of wind
Whimper of rain
Storm dead ahead.
Hold to it
In spite of the gale
and the slippery hills
the sharp and slithery curves
Safe home.

which was from an advertisement for Socony gasoline. It concluded: "One begins to believe that all our young literary men are in the agencies; their books are often like ads and their ads like ads too."[56]

Further glossing advertising's image was its involvement in health campaigns. The National Tuberculosis Association in 1919 enlisted some of what *Literary Digest* called "the highest advertising brains of the country" in its Christmas Seal campaign, with the objective of wiping out tuberculosis in America. In Great Britain advertising was being used in a campaign against venereal diseases. There seemed no reason to doubt that a method so effective in selling toothpaste and tires could be equally effective in spreading the gospel of health.[57]

Nevertheless, advertising had its detractors. Stuart Chase attacked the "wastes of advertising" as part of a series on waste in America. Two quadrillion words, he pointed out, came off American printing presses in a year—11 billion linear miles of words, or enough to circle the solar system—and well over half were advertising copy. Advertising, he observed, was "the life blood of quackery, and the patent medicine industry." Over $1.25 billion was spent on advertising every year, and it made up 40–75 percent of the contents of newspapers, meaning that over half the nation's consumption of newsprint pulp went into advertising, with all the hewed timber that represented. An estimated 80 percent of the nation's mail consisted of advertisements, much of which ended up in the wastebasket unread. Advertising employed an estimated 600,000 workers, from copywriters to psychologists.

Chase complained that the purchasing power of the nation was not increased by advertising, that it created no new purchasing power, and in fact drew workers away from productive employment. Advertising only moved purchases from A to B, making B rich and bankrupting A, and in the meantime reducing purchasing power by the amount spent on salesmanship. While admitting that some advertising was essential in a functioning society, Chase estimated that only 10 percent of the 1925 level was necessary, since the remaining 90 percent consisted only of "largely competitive wrangling as to the relative merits of two undistinguished and often undistinguishable compounds—soaps, tooth powders, motor cars, tires, snappy suits, breakfast foods, patent medicines, cigarettes." Moreover, much of advertising was devoted to the packaging and not the product it contained—the "glitter of a shaving stick holder, the unique shape of tonic bottles, the gold foil about a cigar, monogrammed cigarette boxes, powder puff containers," all of which focused attention away from the product and on "the splendor and the glitter of the container."

Pointing out that one dollar was being spent in America on advertising for every 70 cents spent on all levels of education, Chase concluded:

> And yet when all is said and done, advertising does give a certain illusion, a certain sense of escape in a machine age. It creates a dream world; smiling faces, shining teeth, school girl complexions, cornless feet, perfect fitting union suits, distinguished collars, wrinkleless pants, odorless breaths, regularized bowels, happy homes in New Jersey (15 minutes from Hoboken), charging motors, punctureless tires, perfect busts, shimmering shanks, self-washing dishes, backs behind which the moon was meant to rise.[58]

Author Sinclair Lewis observed that individuality in America was now being exercised by buying the specific products that advertising had convinced all to use. "In these lucrative magnificences," Lewis wrote,

> the man whose life is completely bounded by the 7:49 and 5:16 trains and the Bonanza Movie House, and his wife whose life is even more determined by those same boundaries, vicariously find something like a decent and self-respecting and heroic life.[59]

J. Thorne Smith attacked advertising as "America's cruelest and most ruthless sport, religion, or profession, or whatever you choose to call it. With an accurate stroke, but with a perverted intent, it coddles and toys with all that is base and gross in our physical and spiritual compositions." It was "the graveyard of literary aspiration," in which those who had failed as writers turned their talents to blackjacking those who had rejected their talents into "buying the most amazing assortment of purely useless and cheaply manufactured commodities that has ever marked the decline of culture and common sense." These "fanatics" were "continually boring into the pocketbook of the public and extracting therefrom a goodly quantity of gold and silver," even while they stimulated the overproduction of goods that "created unnecessary unemployment and hardship" whenever there was an economic depression.[60]

Having attacked advertising, as earlier noted, Chase charged a few years later that the "Age of the Salesman" was creating flaws in the American character. He wrote:

> The final objective of the salesman is to put it across, to get away with it, to secure the order. The signature on the dotted line becomes the Supreme Good. It follows that any methods involved in this consummation, are, *ipso facto*, good methods. The new ethics is thus built on the ability to get away with it, by whatever means.

For most people, Chase wrote, "the doctrine of the main chance is part and parcel of the law of economic survival." It required becoming a "yes man," and "for a yes man to have a sense of honor is unthinkable." As for the consumer, caught in a "net of primitive stimulus and response," and "stripped of all standards of judgment, his native sense is overwhelmed with psychological reactions which reduce him almost to an automatic idiot, and he never knows whether the thing he buys is worth the money he pays for it, whether it is a good product ridiculously overpriced, or whether it is just so much junk."[61]

But the "most curious and the most significant item in the whole phenomenon of changing ethics," Chase wrote, was

> the ever growing number of barrels of holy water with which business is being sprinkled—nay drenched. Commerce is taking upon itself all the sanctions of the church, and so slowly but surely transforming its common street behavior into a semisacred cult whose rituals are not to be profaned. . . . To the older ethics this alliance between business and religion appears as cant and hypocrisy, but to the new it is accepted as sound and self-evident doctrine. The unbridgeable chasm between behavior animated by selfishness . . . and behavior animated by the true spirit of unselfish service—is utterly ignored.[62]

The impact of the depression on advertising was immediate and drastic, with advertising expenditures slashed by about one-fifth in 1930.[63]

3
The Quest for Beauty

DESIGN

In their initial quest for novelty after World War I, clothing and fabric manufacturers found inspiration in the museums, borrowing, as one writer described it, from the costumes of "Arab chieftains, Chinese mandarins, guildsmen of medieval Japan, the tribes of the frozen Siberian tundras, the graves of ancient Peru, the ceramics of Mexico, and the Indians of our own plains and woodlands," in the process searching "the art history of the universe in an effort to add distinction to the home furnishings and costumes of America." Symbolic of the new trend in design was a major exhibit in the American Museum of Natural History in late 1919. At the exhibition:

> A number of the leading representatives of decorative industries and artists combined ... to show what actually had been accomplished in America. The idea back of the exhibit was twofold: in the first place, to show the general advance in American decorative arts, and secondly the more important ... concern was to show how these arts had benefited through museum contacts.... All these materials were presented in such a manner as to show the correlation between modern production and ancient source of inspiration....[1]

By contrast with this preoccupation with past and distant cultures for inspiration, the machine was already exerting its influence on design, as some had begun to recognize. Among the many great debates of the 1920s was that over the aesthetic value of the machine and its products. The battle raged at all levels, from architecture to commonplace decorative household items. Detractors of the machine, and they were legion, deprecated its products as ugly and tasteless, as must invariably be the case, they said, when the emphasis was on quantity through mass production. As one critic put it, "The extinction of craftsmanship and its replacement by machine production" exerted a very appreciable influence on general culture," as the "habitual contemplation of ugliness produces, first tolerance and finally complete acceptance." It produced "a machine mind," which found "satisfaction in purely mechanical qualities, in geometrically regular form, in smooth finish, in perfective repetition." This "atrophy of the aesthetic faculty," he wrote, was not confined to the masses, but was also found "among the governing class and even among scholars and men of learning."[2]

New York City's Metropolitan Museum of Art, however, weighed in on the side of the machine's defenders with a 1924 exhibition devoted to industrial art. A defender of the machine's influence wrote:

> There have been those who have seen in the machine just another tool inviting mastery at the hands of the craftsman, the creative designer, the artist—a tool infinitely complex and recalcitrant, but yet only an extension of the human brain and hand not essentially different from the ax, the adze, the awl, the plane, the gage, the amazing variety of tools in the guildsman's kit as those are viewed in historical retrospect against the flints of paleolithic and neolithic man. For them, "cheap and nasty" has not been an inherent characteristic either of democracy or machine production, but an incident in the slow struggle of the soul of man to reassert the dominion of beauty and excellence over this strange new extension of the human brain.

The "vindication of this faith," he wrote, "is forecast in an exhibition of industrial art at the Metropolitan Museum, New York."[3]

By contrast with those who decried the impact of mass production on their surroundings, a few had begun to see in it the early stages of a modern style. Lewis Mumford was one of these, writing of the early 1920s lunchroom that:

> its excellence is due to the fact that it has been made by a machine, and that it exhibits the accuracy, the fine finish, and the unerring fidelity to design which makes machine work delightful to everyone who knows how to take pleasure in geometrical perfection.

Admittedly, the new style was in its infancy, but it showed a capacity for growth and change now that had been absent earlier in the Machine Age. Of the opportunities and challenges Mumford wrote:

> To create designs which will respect the logic of the machine and at the same time have regard for the vagaries of human psychology is the problem whose solution will give us a satisfactory, genuine modern style.[4]

Walter Pach agreed that the "steel bridges, the steel buildings, the newly designed machines and utensils of all kinds, show an adaptation to function that is recognized as one of the great elements of art," even though it had not yet been fully appreciated by the public.[5]

Easily one of the greatest and most observable of influences on design in the 1920s was advertising. From a relatively minor industry at the beginning of the decade, the corps of designers swelled by the end of the 1920s to the point where no American could avoid their influence in countless ways daily. It was largely under the impetus of advertising that the new style came on with such a rush in the 1920s. Late in the decade, Gilbert Seldes wrote:

> Six years ago some of the finest industrial designers were unable to find work to do; in 1928 a single central agency placed fifty-three designers of textiles in contact with manufacturers in one month; a year later the same agency had calls for 200 ... and was unable to fill the demand.... Within eighteen months of the first exploitation of radical departures in furniture, glassware, silver, and so on, all these things were being produced by large-scale factory methods. You cannot be sure you are touching wood when you rap on the table; it is just as likely to have legs of chromium-plated steel and a metal top, In ten months one designer worked on some thirty-five different objects, ranging from trucks to table glass, from refrigerators to fountain pens, for each of which he created a new design, a new form; at the least, a new color scheme.

Much of the stimulus for the new designs came from The Art Center in New York City, what Seldes described as "a central institution ... with the single object of creating a new level of taste and a new, entirely native style in the arts," to whom manufacturers came for advice on design.

The result was, Seldes wrote, "that everything we touch and see and use in our daily lives is being changed in shape and color, that the visual aspect of America is being transformed." One of the principal agents in the change was advertising, which insisted that it could not sell products unless they were pleasing to the eye of the consumer. The result was that the influence of advertising was involved from the inception of the designing process, rather than only being felt when it was time for the product to be marketed. As Seldes put it, the advertising artist "began to operate inside the factory instead of outside it in a studio." For the most part, such painters tended to be illustrators like Rockwell Kent, or the designers of theater sets, like Joseph Urban.

Seldes was particularly struck by "modernist" furniture, not only its angles and "efforts to be striking and smart," but also the use of "new woods, of cork and insulating material, of new kinds of glass, of steel and copper—all the things which come from the experts and engineers." It was not an age in which houses were being built for the display of works of art, but instead, as Assistant Secretary of Commerce Julius Klein put it:

> Art has come to the dish pan, to the washstand, to dust mops and to the garage.... Even for commodities such as electric washing machines, the manufacturers declare that artistic design is getting to be a more important factor every year.... Art is on our floors and art is on our roofs.[6]

Lewis Mumford observed in 1929 that, despite resistance, "attempts at modern design have been made in almost every department of furnishing and decoration," with much of the initiative coming from the nation's largest department stores. Noting that furniture manufacturers planned to sell "a new suite of furniture to every family in America *every six years*," Mumford pointed out that the goal could be attained only by producing shoddy goods or by continually changing styles. These new styles, like *art moderne*, were, Mumford sneered, only serving "the purposes of salesmanship."[7]

An exhibition at Macy's department store was showing how modern decorative art could be applied to the home. Lee Simonson, designer for Theater Guild Productions, was responsible for the exhibition, and said he had "attacked the problem just as I would the staging of a play." "The setting, as well as the 5,000 exhibits, is made to tell the story of modern industrial design." The exhibition consisted of fifteen furnished rooms, in which, he said:

> We have avoided the use of wood wherever possible.... I believe that wood is not a modern building material. It has outlived its usefulness. The important thing is to develop materials that will eliminate the great labor that has gone into the finishing of woods. This is essential if beautiful objects are to become inexpensive and prevalent enough for general use. The high finishes traditional in furniture are a relic of the old days when craft labor was abundant and cheap. Why continue this practise in a day when all the emphasis is placed on labor-saving devices for the home? I predict that metal will be increasingly used in modern ornament and furniture. Its beauty is in itself. Its finish is inherent in the nature of the material. What remains to be done is to work into it color and texture, and this some chemical process will eventually solve. I believe the exposition will demonstrate the effectiveness of this theory: it is illustrated by the metal, asbestos and cork which are used in its construction.... In other words, the art of to-day is capturing the discoveries of the scientist in his laboratory for the purpose of combining utility, beauty, and economy to meet the needs of present-day life.

President Coolidge agreed:

> We need to put more effort into translating art into the daily life of the people. If we could surround ourselves with forms of beauty, the evil things of life would tend to disappear and our moral standards would be raised.... Our country has reached a position where this is no longer a visionary desire, but is becoming an actual reality. With general prosperity, with high wages, with reasonable hours of labor, has come both the means and the time to cultivate the artistic spirit.[8]

With similar ebullience, the head of a New York advertising agency declared that "open plumbing has become one of the fine arts in America."[9]

John Cotton Dana, creator and director of the Newark Museum, said: "Study the beautiful lines of American bathtubs, plumbing fixtures, and modern electrical refrigerators if you want to see beauty wedded to utility." His museum was devoted "primarily to the bringing of beauty into the machine-made things that we use in our every-day life, especially in the home." A pioneer in this kind of enterprise for over a decade, he now saw decorative art being exhibited all over the country, and he regarded department stores as "the museums of today."

Dana wrote:

> We hear a good deal about this "new spirit" in the arts these days. What is this new spirit? Briefly, it is the spirit of the machine. We are a machine civilization. Our things are made by machines, and because of that, some years ago, we had settled down to believe that we

must either have ugly things or do away with machine production. We see now how wrong that idea was, and that the machine is leading us to new vistas of design in the objectives of every-day life. The machine is freeing us from the cast-off art clothing of the past.

The modern movement in the decorative arts is really a movement toward machine art. The severe simplicity which is characteristic of modern design is a search for technical form, which is fundamentally a form of simple lines with a minimum of surface decoration. This technical form to meet the demands of machine production must be of a geometric simplicity, and the beauty of that kind of form depends upon mathematics and upon the fact that we can apprehend and appreciate it clearly. The art is industry which produced the modern American bathroom and kitchen is an art of to-day. It derives from the life we are living, a life in which machine production, highly organized industry and commerce, science and invention play the dominant roles. Ours is not a period of revery and reminiscence. It is pointed toward the future. And so we do not want art in industry which is reminiscent of the art of the past. A new epoch is here.[10]

Late in the decade Lewis Mumford wrote:

By transforming technology, the physical sciences have created new forms and patterns, in instruments of precision, in machines and grain elevators and warehouses and bridges; and the artist has seized upon these forms as fresh materials for his art. A subway station, for instance, with its regular piers, its monotonous surfaces, its sudden crystallization of color in red and green signal lights, presents an aesthetic experience. The hardness, the abstraction, the absence of surface variations, which characterize machine work, the intricate relation of parts, the lack of subtle modulations in color, the uniform illumination of electricity—all these things belong particularly to the modern world and have not, in the precise form, existed before. To these new products of exact technology the modern artist has become sensitive. Dismissed as mere utilitarian ugliness in one generation, they come back to use through the purer experience of the artist, as things of beauty....

Mumford added:

During the last thirty years we have become more conscious of the aesthetic possibilities of the exact arts; and it is no accident that our new instruments, the automobile and the aeroplane, are not the weakest but the best of our machined products, a distinction which they share with American kitchen equipment and bathroom fixtures. Under our very eyes, an improvement of design has taken place, transforming the awkward mass and the broken lines of the primitive auto into the unified mass and the slick streamlines of the modern car; or, by an even greater revolution in design, turning the imperfectly related planes of the push-power aeroplane into the more buoying, gull-like tract plane of today, with body and wing both gaining in beauty as they were adapted more carefully to the mechanical requirements of flight.[11]

It was a decade of fads, in large part cultivated and spread by advertising. As Charles Merz described it:

The stage was set in this America for a rapid flux in fads and interests, and a rapid flux in fads and interests was the inevitable goal of the great machine of modern industry itself. For with competition keen, with overproduction a constant menace, with a relentless demand for reducing costs and with cost-reduction usually dependent upon quantity output, the great machine had to cultivate new fashions in order to unload its goods.

This it did to the tune of a billion dollars' worth of advertising launched at the American public every year in an effort to create new styles, shorten the period between them as they came along, make people who were behind-times feel uncomfortable and out of date, train the public to want new things before it had used up old ones and develop the average man's desires until they far outreached his needs.... So rapidly were fashions changing, so regularly were new fads arriving, and so distracted was the modern merchant, trying to keep pace with his supply on one end and his market on the other, that trade conventions spent hours deliberating what was now in style.... Radio sets went Florentine one year, only to go Louis Quinze the next and Jacobean twelve months later. Styles in furniture, styles in diets, styles in wall paper and styles in floor coverings varied with the seasons. New cigarettes, new shaving creams, and new laundry soaps appeared from nowhere, covered the billboards with their claims, and wrote their virtues in airplane smoke against the heavens. Zipper galoshes, lizard-skin shoes, Russian boots, and Helen Wills eyeshades scored new triumphs in the market. Colour made its appearance as the handmaid of industry. Linoleum dropped its prim triangles for the rich lustre of a Turkish rug. Bed linens went all colours of the rainbow. Scorning the colour-blind conservative who had been satisfied all these years with what it described as "hospital white," the Lady Pepperell Company began advertising sheets in orchid, maize and nile.[12]

ARCHITECTURE

A writer on American architecture in the early 1920s wrote that it was growing constantly more complex, but, "fortunately and perhaps necessarily, it is also growing more reasoned. There is very little experimentation or exploitation of egotistic originality in the more important buildings of this country to-day. It is a period of architectural sanity, combined with architectural ingenuity and a remarkable degree of consistency." The sole exception he could find of a truly original trend in architecture was among the so-called "American Secessionists," which included Louis H. Sullivan and Frank Lloyd Wright, but whose work the author seemed to have difficulty understanding or appreciating.[13]

Such a stodgy approach to architecture was as dated in the 1920s as that in industrial design. It seemed to Lewis Mumford to represent an attempt by Americans to retreat into a past of Gothic and Renaissance buildings, or, as he put it: "The critical weakness of the romantic architect is that he is employed in creating an environment into which people may escape from a sordid workaday world, whereas the real problem is to remake the workaday world so that people will not wish to escape from it."[14] By the late 1920s the Machine Age was clearly exerting an impact on architecture, notably on such a project as the Telephone Building in New York City, where the designers "approached their problem from the point of view of designing something with respect for this present Machine Age," thinking in terms of what could be done with the labor of to-day, with the construction of to-day, and with the machinery of to-day, to give to each material the form, decoration, and color distinctly its own.... In the Middle Ages, the men who designed the things that we admire worked with respect for the means available for carrying out their conceptions. The modern architect must do the same; he must learn to use the machine as a basis of design if his work is to be indigenous to this period.

After World War I, America had been "ripe for architectural innovations," as a result of its prosperity, the need for new buildings, the plentitude of steel, her freedom from traditions, and her adaptability, and all of these were contributing to "the new architecture that she is producing"—an architecture that was "characteristically American in that it is useful first, then beautiful."[15]

It was the influence of Louis Sullivan that came closest to fulfilling this criterion in the 1920s. Mumford said of Sullivan that he "was perhaps the first mind in American architecture that had come to know itself with any fullness in relation to its soil, its period, its civilization, and had been able to absorb fully all the many lessons of the century. One might call him the Whitman of American architecture." Of Sullivan's contribution, Mumford wrote that he abandoned "the tedious and unmeaning symbolism of older cultural forms; a modern building could no more wear the dress of the classic than the architect could wear a peruke and sword." And not the least of Sullivan's contributions was his role as teacher of Frank Lloyd Wright. "In Wright," Mumford wrote, "Sullivan's best ideas found actual expression more convincing than in his own work."[16]

"Necessity, Mumford wrote, "became the handmaid of art in modifying the sky-scraper. As it has come to reach higher and higher into the blue it shuts out the sun from the street, and the people below walk in a perpetual twilight. A zoning law was inevitable, but the soaring spirit prevailed, and towers began to rise on towers as straight walls gave way to set-backs and the sky-scraper takes on a new beauty." One architect, Alfred Bossom, found his inspiration in the great pyramids of the Maya, who were, he said, the first Americans to construct tall buildings.[17]

The skyscraper, one observer noted, was "essentially a machine itself," and it had produced a myriad of problems for the cities—"the problems of relating tall buildings to their communities, and the communities to the whole city of which they form the parts." The skyscraper was creating these problems faster than it was providing solutions. It was driving city fathers to create urban plans and even regional plans in order to accommodate the density of workers being concentrated in downtown skyscrapers. The alternative was "a hodgepodge of miscellaneous buildings and unrelated, overcrowded streets."[18]

The American City surveyed skyscrapers in 173 cities of 50,000 or more, and found 36 had one or more buildings over 20 stories, 4,778 buildings over 10 stories in height, 377 more than 20. New York City had 188 over 20 stories, Chicago 65.[19] But Stuart Chase pointed out that while the latest skyscrapers were undoubtedly beautiful, they stretched so high into the clouds that their beauty could only be appreciated from a plane or by seagulls. But Chase agreed "that the case of art is not hopeless in the Power Age."[20]

Many new arts have come to birth; skyscrapers, lordly engineering structures in cement and steel, the curve and sweep of motor highways, photography, the moving picture, stage setting and lighting, the design of automobiles, airplanes, ocean liners, and a great variety of mechanical products, fabricated with their technological limits, and as perfect and lovely in their own way as a Sheraton chair in its.... Architecture, painting, sculpture, music, the theatre, literature, structural engineering, design—not one is languishing in Western civilization. You may not like the output either in whole or in part, but you cannot deny the vitality....

It was too bad, however, that so many promising artists were being seduced by advertising.[21]

A common target of architectural critics was the American home, which grew smaller in the 1920s, as a result of high building costs, but which showed little adaptation to the Machine Age. One sacrifice to higher costs was the parlor, typically the entertainment center of the home. But the architecture of homes continued past ideals—Cape Cod cottages, columned colonials, and other models little changed from the nineteenth century. The iconoclastic Henry L. Mencken, usually a critic of everything the "booboisie" held dear, uncharacteristically identified himself with them in taking up the defense of their architectural taste against its critics, writing:

We live in a Machine Age, but there are still plenty of us who have but little to do with machines, and find in that little no answer to our aspirations. Why should a man who hates automobiles build a house upon the principles which went into the Ford Model T? He may prefer, and quite honestly, the principles which went into the English dwelling-house of the Eighteenth Century, and so borrow them with a clear conscience.

I can sympathize with that man, for in many ways he is I and I am he. If I were building a house tomorrow it would certainly not follow the lines of a dynamo or a steam shovel; it would be, with a few obvious changes, a replica of the houses that were built in the days when human existence, according to my notion, was pleasanter and more spacious than ever before or since.

When humans began to "live in houses as coldly structural as step-ladders they . . . cease to be men, and become mere rats in cages."[22]

Florida, with its emphasis on exotic architecture had set the standard for similar real estate booms elsewhere in the country along Italian, Spanish, and other foreign themes. As Charles Merz described it:

A new world arose in Florida—a world of fronds and palms and palaces, of Moorish shops, Italian streets, Castilian clubs and Neapolitan ice cream.

The sensational development of Florida's most famous boom is sometimes supposed to constitute a unique chapter in the history of America, but we are unobserving if we do not recognize that this same transformation of the plain into the spectacular is now in progress in many sections of the country.[23]

Linking it to developments elsewhere, Stuart Chase wrote that it had led to the "most chromatic, not to say fantastic, experimentation ... in house decoration. New composition materials, new designs for skyscraper bookcases, bathroom fittings, playroom appurtenances—appear upon the market every day." Even in stodgy New England one could now find in any suburb "the century-old house with a Moorish palace on one side and a Spanish villa on the other." American conformity had been much commented upon, and Chase agreed that "Main Street towns may all look alike," but he added the caveat that one could not "be sure from one year to the next in what the likeness is to consist." Standardization ruled, "but it is the standardization of infinite variety and perpetual change, and thus uncomfortably close to a contradiction in terms."[24]

ART

In the fine arts as in other aspects of the 1920s, American tastes were torn between the traditional and the new directions. Many American art lovers of the decade doubtless agreed with William Lyon Phelps' description of painter John Singer Sargent as the greatest living American artist. A more critical appraisal in the *New York Herald* refused to rank him with greats like Manet and Renoir, but did say that in "his sense of values and in his brush-work" he ranked with them. Another critic agreed that no living artist, not even Monet, could compare with Sargent in his "command over his instruments." Sargent, he said, had "that ability in a measure recalling the miraculous days of the old master."[25]

Many young American artists studied in France in the early twentieth century, where they were in at the birth of Fauvism and Cubism. Labeled the American "modernists," these painters continued to reveal the influence of French modernism through the 1920s, liberating American art from the stodgy academicism that derided it in alliance with much of the American public. Gradually their works discovered an America that had been ignored by the academicists and began to strike a resonant chord with art lovers. Gradually, there developed two groups of painters who were inspired by the American scene. One of these was less concerned with realism than the other, and included abstractionists. Among these were a variety of artists who were clearly influenced by the machine.

The influence of the machine on painting in America in the 1920s was everywhere apparent, among both American and foreign-born artists. In the latter category was Francis Picabia, who, in the words of one art historian, "saw machinery as the prime metaphor of modern society and, particularly, of love." Machines took the place of humans, for example, in his depictions of sex. For Giuseppe Stella the prime attraction was the American city, its buildings and its bridges, such as *The Voice of the City of New York Interpreted: The Bridge*, which shows the Brooklyn Bridge against a backdrop of skyscrapers. Even Georgia O'Keeffe, who would later abandon the theme for New Mexico, did some extraordinary depictions of New York's skyscrapers, including *The Radiator Building—Night*. Charles Demuth concentrated in the 1920s on industrial America, with paintings of such things as grain elevators, water towers, and factories. Charles Sheeler moved from photography to painting and specialized in machines of the 1920s like elevated railways. Other painters, like Stuart Davis and Gerald Murphy, painted the products of the machine age, bottles and jars, safety razors, and fountain pens in their still lifes, even if sometimes in abstract.

The principal characteristic of the paintings of these machine painters was their absence of nature, with virtually everything in them man-made. Many of those who rejected this conception of art, including Georgia O'Keeffe, were drawn to Santa Fe, New Mexico, which acted as a place of exile for those artists seeking a return to the primitive. Here O'Keeffe painted for a quarter of a century, becoming in the process America's most famous female artist.[26]

The realists included John Sloan, Glenn O. Coleman, Charles Burchfield, Thomas Benton, and Rockwell Kent. But perhaps the greatest realist of the period and of the twentieth century was Edward Hopper, whose paintings included a touch of satire.[27]

One of the curious phenomena of 1920s art in America was the dominance of women in art matters on a scale unknown elsewhere in the world. Walter Pach wrote that American men were "engrossed in the drive of work, their leisure goes to sport and to the forms of entertainment that call for the smallest amount of mental effort," so that it was women who were the principal buyers of paintings and sculpture, and they, therefore, who influenced painters and sculptors.[28]

FEMININE BEAUTY

A year after the end of World War I an American magazine wrote:

> Important and interesting work has been done for the sake of making the scarred and mutilated veteran of the war a handsome man. The veteran is provided with a new nose or a new upper lip as required. Special pains are taken to make this new nose shapely and to take the graft for his upper lift from the top of his head so that he may not be deprived of the ornament of a mustache.

Such experiences had revolutionized the field of cosmetic surgery, which before the war had been regarded as "a shady business."

> Physicians were then decidedly chary of doing operative work for purely esthetic reasons. Altho besieged by men and women who felt that their happiness in life depended on the alteration of some offending feature, they discouraged them or even refused pointblank to operate, with the result that quack institutions throve on the treatment of facial defects.

Now, however, the cosmetic surgery associated with the war had brought such advances in technique that it was likely to "give the civilian population in peace times the same benefits enjoyed by the soldier in times of war," and should be taken out of the hands of quacks "and given a legitimate status in the profession."[29]

A dozen years later, when cosmetic surgery had become fairly common at the end of the decade, its "legitimate status" had still not spread very broadly in the profession. *The New Republic* found that "Conservative surgeons are still holding aloof from all connections with the beauty racket." Skilled surgeons were able to command $500 fees for face-lifts, while those women who were willing to take their chances could get them from quacks for $50.[30] A writer in *Good Housekeeping* estimated in 1930 that there were only a half-dozen surgeons in the United States whose experience from the war made them fully qualified to do plastic surgery. These six concentrated mainly on reconstructive surgery for accident victims and "would rather turn coal-heavers than be thought of as 'beauty doctors.'"[31]

For women not willing to undergo the risk and expense of plastic surgery, there was a wide array of cosmetics available in the 1920s with which they could attempt to achieve a similar result. *Harper's* wrote:

> A quarter of a century ago perfume, rice powder, and "anti-chap" for the hands constituted the entire paraphernalia of a woman's boudoir table. Now that table looks like a miniature chemist shop. . . . Rouge, lipstick, tints for hair and nails, dark paste for lashes and brows are established aids to superior grooming. Regardless of age, background, and social status, women have accepted the new standards borne in by incessant waves of propaganda, As a result feminine beauty, once the Creator's business, is now Big Business's.

American women, it reported, were spending nearly $2 billion annually in over 40,000 beauty shops, and American manufacturers were producing $178 million worth of beauty products per year, to which were added $10,500,000 worth of imports. This amount of spending on beauty, it wrote, rivaled that "devoted to education, to good roads, to armaments in peacetime." The beauty business was "a clear reflection of the morale of American womanhood."[32]

The alleged impetus given to the quest for feminine beauty by prohibition was described in the *New York Times* by the owner of two beauty salons:

> It is very easy to trace the growth of the beauty parlor business to prohibition. When men drank, they were not so critical. Their wives and sweethearts looked attractive to them without the assistance of beauty parlors. Now, however, men remain clear-eyed all evening and notice wrinkles, pallor, straight hair and unsparkling eyes. As a result, the women are flocking to beauty parlors and we have to turn many away every day.[33]

An equally convincing case was made by others, however, that it was feminine drinking that was driving women to the beauty parlors and to the use of cosmetics in order to "cover-up" the consequences of their "growing recklessness of behavior," worrying not at all about the effects of late nights out and excessive drinking because of confidence that "next morning a facial treatment can smooth away the puffs and creases, that rouge will hide the pallor, that lavender powder will cover the redness of eyelids, and that little drops will brighten the dulled pupils." Indeed, some were blaming the beauty parlors and cosmetics manufacturers for these excesses, but the author cautioned that "repairing the damage is a different thing from causing it." The causes lay

> deep in war and post-war psychology, in the pace of our machine age, in feminine independence and the enfranchisement of youth. Likewise, the results of the Volstead Act and the failure of authority represented by church, state, and the family are consequences of this same individual determination to live one's own life and to live it hard. Women cannot enjoy themselves unless they look young. But rather than heed the cautious counsel of prevention ... many women prefer to undergo radical treatment. It offers the only means to waste one's youthfulness and have it, too.

Thus the 500 percent increase in the value of beauty preparations since 1914, and the popularity of cosmetic surgery. Women, she found, were having face-lifts, even as far away as Paris, "with all the nonchalance with which they order a permanent wave."[34]

The cosmetics industry reported at the end of the 1920s that American women were using annually 4,000 tons of powder and enough lipsticks to reach "from Chicago to Los Angeles by way of San Francisco," plus "52,500 tons of cleansing cream, 26,250 tons of skin lotion, 19,100 tons of complexion soap, 17,500 tons of nourishing cream, 8,750 tons of foundation cream, 6,562 tons of bath powder and 2,375 tons of rouge." American women were spending $10 billion per year on their appearance. The cosmetics industry, with expenditures of over $16 million, had become the third largest advertiser in magazines in 1928, some of which carried ads for as many as sixty beauty preparations. The influence of the admen was also felt in the exotic packaging and naming of the products.[35]

Faith Baldwin concluded that romance had "become a business; as standardized as anything else in modern life; as cut and dried as a political speech; as articulate as a vacuum cleaner salesman; as artificially stimulating as an ancient aphrodisiac; and a matter of mass production." Love and romance, she wrote, had "become trademarked goods, shoved over an enormous counter into the hands of the consumers who, content with the wrappings and descriptive booklets, are of no mind to inquire into the origin of their purchases, and still less inclined to take a trip through the factories."[36]

DRESS

Little need be said about men's dress in the 1920s, which changed little from the previous decade. Men were not clothes conscious and resisted any attempts by London to dictate new styles to them. Walter Pitkin estimated that the American male bought a new suit only about every fifteen months, and similarly got by with fewer and fewer shoes, the opposite of trends among women. Nevertheless, there was a trend already visible by the end of the 1920s toward more comfortable attire. In this sense, the change in the occupants of the White House in 1933 marked the transition from an "old order" in menswear to a "new." Out went Hoover's tall, stiff, detachable collar, and in came the soft shirt collar of FDR. Gone also from many wardrobes were hats, garters, undershirts, and vests. And the depression meant longer intervals between the purchase of new suits.[37]

Women in the 1920s began to copy the fashions of movie stars and other stylish women. Those fashions tended to be more daring than was usual. In mid-1921, the *Literary Digest* looked at the debate raging in the nation's press over morality and its relationship to women's fashions. The YWCA, it found, was conducting a nationwide campaign among high-school girls to promote modest dress and behavior, while the Women's Auxiliary of the Episcopal Church had begun holding meetings with girls throughout the country on the subject of "upholding standards." The Catholic Archbishop of Ohio had condemned such dances as the "toddle" and the "shimmy," and also "bare female shoulders." The *Literary Digest* added that the New York State Assembly and Senate had passed a law empowering the Commissioner of Licenses to censor dances, and that a number of state legislatures were considering bills aimed at regulating women's dress. In Utah, for example, such a bill provided fine and imprisonment for women who wore in public skirts higher than three inches above the ankle, and one in Virginia would prohibit the display of more than three inches of her throat, while gowns must not have skirts higher than four inches above the ground. A bill pending in Ohio would not allow more than two inches of decolleté, nor any "garment which unduly displays or accentuates the lines of the female figure." Moreover the bill decreed that "no female over fourteen years of age shall wear a skirt which does not reach to that part of the foot known as the instep." Similar legislation applying standards of various lengths had been introduced in the legislatures of New Jersey, South Carolina, Kansas, Iowa, Pennsylvania, and "a full dozen other states."[38]

An observer noted in mid-1920 that it was becoming increasingly difficult to distinguish between classes on the basis of clothing, so quickly did all adopt the same style. The same was as true of manners. Part of the reason was that many of the advantages "till lately the privileges of a few," are 'becoming common.'"

> Compulsory education has been but a dwarfed variety of the real thing. The way from the primary to the secondary school is now barred only by a turnstile ... given force and industry, the passage from one to the other can be made. Keen, alert, hard-working, and perhaps rather pushing, the representative of the many arrives among the few.... Till lately ambition might be roughly said to have been the prerogative of the abler boys in the secondary schools—we mean by ambition the intense desire to make a success of life.... Now able boys everywhere are ambitious. We are in the face of a huge ambitious crowd.[39]

A few years later another observer commented on the fact that "out of the mass of people of diverse and varying origins, we have developed a truly national spirit on an almost incredible scale." He explained:

It is picturesquely revealed among other things in the average attire of the average American, man or woman, boy or girl, down to the veriest tot in the kindergarten and in the cradle. This uniformity of characteristic attire in surprisingly good taste, and with a bewildering variety that allows individual choice an unparalleled range—the standardization of an unexampled high-class excellence in clothes for all and not only for the privileged few—is the real American miracle.

It was, he said, "difficult to overestimate the social, the economic, and even the political and spiritual value of this nation-wide distribution of ready-to-wear clothes of good cut and good quality."

This ready-to-wear clothing or, as its pioneering sponsors say, clothing in which "made-to-measure methods have been adapted to clothes you can put on in a shop and walk out with," is so extraordinary a contribution to human self-respect, freedom from all class distinction, that it is only the fact that we are so near to it and take it as a matter of course that the deeper meaning and value of the convenience escape us.

It was a purely American phenomenon since in Europe "caste and class are still the bane and burden of their civilization."

The annual output of ready-to-wear clothing was in 1925 running to $5.5 million, he wrote, with the crucial beginnings of the trend dating from the 1880s.[40] Nor were the styles much influenced by Europe, despite their attempts to do so. The colors of clothing began to become less subdued a few years after World War I. In the first few years of the decade, the influence of the war could still be noted in the popularity of somber shades, especially black, which was attributed by a French designer to the fact that many women were still in mourning. But by the middle of the decade pastel shades were in vogue.[41]

Bruce Bliven wrote of a representative flapper named Jane in 1925 that:

She is, for one thing, a very pretty girl. Beauty is the fashion in 1925. She is frankly, heavily made up, not to imitate nature, but for an altogether artificial effect—pallor mortis, poisonously scarlet lips, richly ringed eyes—the latter looking not so much debauched (which is the intention) as diabetic. Her walk duplicates the swagger supposed by innocent Americans to go with the female half of a Paris Apache dance. And there are, finally, her clothes.

These were estimated the other day by some statistician to weigh two pounds. Probably a libel; I doubt they come within half a pound of such bulk. Jane isn't wearing much, this summer. If you'd like to know exactly, it is: one dress, one step-in, two stockings, two shoes.... Her dress ... is cut low where it might be high, and vice versa. The skirt comes just an inch below her knees, overlapping by a faint fraction her rolled and twisted stockings. The idea is that when she walks in a bit of a breeze, you shall now and then observe the knee (which is not rouged—that's just newspaper talk) but always in an accidental, Venus-surprised-at-the-bath sort of way. This is a bit of coyness which hardly fits in with Jane's general character.

Jane's haircut is also abbreviated. She wears of course the very newest thing in bobs, even closer than last year's shingle. It leaves her just about no hair at all in the back, and 20 percent more than that in the front—about as much as is being worn this season by a cellist (male), less than a pianist; and much, much less than a violinist. Because of this new style, one can confirm a rumor heard last year: Jane has ears.

The corset is as dead as the dodo's grandfather.... The petticoat is even more defunct. ... The brassiere has been abandoned, since 1924. While stockings are usually worn, they are not a sine-qua-nothing-doing. In hot weather Jane reserves the right to discard them, just as all the chorus girls did in 1923. As stockings are only a frantic, successful attempt to duplicate the color and texture of Jane's own sunburned slim legs, few but expert boulevardiers can tell the difference.

This "uniform" was being worn not merely by all other women her age on the East Coast, but also

by all of Jane's sisters and her cousins and her aunts. They are being worn by ladies who are three times Jane's age, and look ten years older; by those twice her age who look a hundred years older. Their use is so universal that in our larger cities the baggage transfer companies one and all declare they are being forced into bankruptcy. Ladies who used to go away for the summer with six trunks can now pack twenty dainty costumes in a bag.[42]

Carrie Chapman Catt looked at the new vogue of trouser wearing by women and argued that they "were originally a a female garment and without apology were deliberately stolen by men." She added:

As late as 1914 there were more women in the world who wore trousers than skirts, and also more men who wore skirts than trousers. If, having exhausted other sources of variety, the French Fashion Trust now decides to put women back into their own trousers for a while, there is nothing shocking in it.... A more exciting question is: Will the London Trust put men back into their own skirts?

The French Fashion Trust had decreed that only silk was fashionable for women, she wrote, with the result that "the American cotton textile industry is in ruins, cotton growers are planting other crops, and factories are running short time." Inquiring at several fashionable New York shops she learned that none had stocked a cotton or linen dress for more than a year. The French Trust had, however, totally missed the spirit of the postwar years in emphasizing women's legs. "It was cruelly unkind," she charged, that, at the moment when mankind was painfully attempting to recover its stability of mind after the most upsetting of wars, there should have been laid upon it the additional mental shock occasioned by the sudden sight of millions of women's legs." She predicted a rebellion by women against the fashion dictates of Paris.[43]

When Paris designers dictated lower skirts and tighter waistlines, the rebellion that Catt had predicted seemed imminent. Fannie Hurst wrote in *The New Republic*, "Let's not wear them!" Women had previously allowed themselves to be led like sheep according to the dictates of Paris, and this submission had been "the most dependable and constant factor with which the international industry of dress has to deal." She wrote:

It is only natural that during the last ten years, in the ferment after the War, should have occurred what are perhaps the most radical changes in women's dress since fashions began.... The reasons, in the light of the world cataclysm and the resultant social changes, are significant.... The fashions of the last ten years not only establish the most radical departure in the history of woman's clothing since woman first donned clothing, but they eloquently represent her new psychological, sociological, economic, and political status.

In part this growing independence from the dictates of Paris no doubt stemmed from the fact that the French influence was much diminished during the war years. The war had cut Americans off from that influence and had given new stimulus and confidence to the American fashion industry, as well as greater acceptance of its products. The domestic industry had the opportunity to develop "a true American idiom in clothes" that "insists that a dress guarantee freedom of motion; and it seeks tact in adornment and imagination in draping of fabrics."[44]

By contrast with women's lives and dress in Queen Victoria's time, between 1920 and 1929:

Woman's new and varied activities came to create a demand for more utilitarian clothes. Short hair seemed to synchronize with the close-fitting hat, or vice versa, the hip-flask probably inspired some designing mind with the cute idea of the boyish form. Woman's emergency jobs, during the War, made the short skirt a prettified novelty. Corsets rode low on the Ferris wheel of fashion. The female limb became a leg and the silk stocking business an industry.[45]

A writer in the *Independent* in 1927, commenting on the "Whale of a Difference Just a Few Years Make!" wrote: "Nowadays, a woman wakes to put on one layer of silk and a two-yard, kneelength dress, runs a comb through her boyish bob, and steps out. Not so the girl of yesteryear, she drew a long breath—her last till bedtime—and then took her daily dozen pulls on the long strings that did her up for the day."[46] A woman wrote in *North American Review* that it was, in fact, the women who dictated fashion—it was the "sheep" who made the decisions of what to wear.

Irene Castle bobbed her hair. The sheep liked Irene Castle and they liked the idea of short hair as freedom added to more freedom. The idea spread like wildfire in dry stubble. Dear, snowy locked old sheep even hurried to come under the shears. In vain men shouted their annoyance and tried to drive the sheep out of their comfortable sunny barber chairs. Hairnet manufacturers passed away in their sleep. Plain basement barbers became Specialists in Coiffures overnight. Haircuts became trims and prices soared from fifteen cents to $1.50 plus the tip.

High fashion may start many things as, no doubt, it does, but the sheep finally decide the matter.... Ladies of fashion may amuse themselves by letting their hair grow. They may let down the length of their skirts and bring solace to the worried textile manufacturers. But the sheep have got it into their heads that short hair and short skirts are as comfortable as no corsets. They like being shorn of hair and cloth. High fashion doesn't have to patronize this salt lick unless it wishes. The sheep are satisfied and these things will stay. Wait and see![47]

But in the mid-1920s Paris began to decree a return to eleven yards to the gown, instead of four, long gloves and long hair, and the woman shopping had not much choice in the matter. Not only were the simpler styles no longer to be found, but it took more courage than most women had to be conspicuously out of fashion. And so "the ridiculous spectacle is seen of millions of women about to climb back into corsets, trains, long gloves, and coiffures." It was time for a revolt. "Down with the corset and up with the hemline!" should be the rallying cry of all women who did not "want to be bullied into doing something as undesirable as it is unwelcome."[48]

The New Republic reported in late 1929 that since midsummer a "furious war of fashions" had "been raging on both sides of the Atlantic." While the length of skirts, the location of waists, and other matters were part of the war, "the principal question," it wrote, "is the figure that women should present to the world—whether it is to be that of a long-stemmed Christmas tree, or that of a weeping willow with a broad crown and branches that sweep to the ground." The willow look was better for the textile industry since it involved more cloth and it was backed by those who would benefit by that look—not only textile mills, but corsetmakers, and merchants who profited from changes in style. The Christmas trees were led by women "who believe in liberty and comfort for their sex, and who are willing to fight for their beliefs," but they were "receiving little help from other women, the mass of whom, like the mass of men, are willing to follow fashions blindly," but they had the support of "manufacturers of silk stockings, whose present business is threatened by longer skirts." "Comparative freedom of action for women," it noted "has coincided during the last six years, with comparative freedom in clothing. Will the new styles—the tight waists, the long skirts, the weeping-willow profile—symbolize their return to bondage? The prospect is unlikely."[49]

Looking at a picture of a woman wearing the new style, *The Nation* wondered if it weren't looking at an 1892 picture. It wrote:

> Much white paper has been utilized of late years for remarks, mostly adulatory, on the emancipation of women. Women were free, we learned; they were no longer slaves. They could vote, swear, smoke, and stray out nights. They had legs; on the last point there could be no possible shadow of doubt whatever. We learned that the entire weight of a modern flapper's garments, including her shoes, totaled about 22 ounces, and we saw in the Sunday rotogravure sections the flapper pictured in stages of undress which made the statement perfectly credible. In the midst of all the cries of joy there were certain faint moanings of distress. If it took only three yards of material to make a dress, what was to become of the silk industry? If corsets were never going to be worn any more, what was to be the future of the American whale?

Despite the protests, however, and the occasional exception, *The Nation* found at the end of the decade that skirts were somewhat longer "than the knee-length scarves of only yestermonth."[50]

It meant, the *New York Times* reported, "the demise of the flapper and the new age of the siren."

She knows very well the ways of the world. She has character and background as well as long skirts and a deep-back decolletage.... She is as modern as the airplane and the backless bathing suit.... She handles men with the combined skill of both her parental continents [Europe and America] ... She no longer has to bother about smashing tradition or demonstrating her superiority to convention. In this she is the flapper's debtor, for that young person abolished surplus clothes and surplus manners with the same enthusiasm she devoted to acquiring gin and cigarettes. By sheer force of violence she established the feminine right to equal representation in such hitherto masculine fields of endeavor as smoking and drinking, swearing, petting, and disturbing the community peace. They need no longer to be the subject of crusade.[51]

4
The Impact of Radio and Movies

RADIO

Late in the decade Stuart Chase observed that on the very night he was writing there were 30 million Americans "in their homes listening to sounds coming out of a small polished box." Many of those 30 million were "listening to a song which one machine [the radio] has caught from another machine [a recording device], which was caught, lidless and blind by the first machine from a more or less bored singer vocalizing into its dead and impersonal face.... We are not playing ourselves; we are being played to—and at three removes from the original source."[1]

The Lynds studied Middletown on the very eve of the "radio revolution" in the 1920s, but already found the radio "rapidly crowding its way in among the necessities in the family standard of living." Working to its advantage was its "accessibility." As the Lynds explained it, even those of modest means could, with a little skill, assemble parts easily obtainable from the dime stores and gain access to the same programs as the wealthy. As a result, the radio was now cutting into the time previously spent on reading, moviegoing, even driving. It would, they wrote, doubtless function "as yet another means of standardizing many of Middletown's habits," along with the influence of such other factors as national advertising.[2]

A writer in *Forum* noted that people were opening "a valve and the music comes out, just as water or gas comes out of other valves." Describing the relation to the Machine Age, he wrote:

> Music is losing its aesthetic and emotional caste because we are coming increasingly to confuse it with the mechanical rhythms and noises of the world in which we work and

live. We turn on the music when we are at home because we are keyed up and tense—because it replaces and compensates for those rhythms and auditory stimuli which we have left behind in streets and office.

By "mechanical rhythms" I mean mechanical intervals as well as the mere noises of motor cars, subways, telephone bells, buzzers, and so on; these intervals are the period of time during which we wait alertly for a reaction—intervals which go to make up the sum of wear and tear and general nervous dissipation.

A few of these intervals which affect all of us are: the time between the red and green traffic lights; the interval between the picking up of the [telephone] receiver and the answering of central; the interval between the opening and closing of a subway door; the interval between the placing of a piece of toast in a machine and its jumping out to be buttered and eaten while hot; and, in general, the feeling that life is short and that not merely "success" but survival are attained only by constantly leaping this way and that.

When, on returning home, we switch on the radio to "see what's doing," we are actually continuing the auditory and consequent nervous stimuli of our offices, subways, or factories.... most of us, suddenly stranded in the quiet of our homes, tune up the radio to keep our nerves from quieting down. It is not so much *what* the radio or phonograph is playing, as that it *is* playing.

Music, he concluded, was "now more of a public utility than an art."[3]

Dr. Frank Conrad of Westinghouse began after World War I to experiment with voice and music transmission over his radio, instead of Morse code, twice a week. When Westinghouse saw that stores were advertising radios to listen to Conrad's broadcasts, they told him to shut down his little station and let Westinghouse back him in a real station that would go on the air election night 1920 and broadcast the returns.

Competition began in the fall of 1921. Three new stations took to the air in September, one in October, one in November, twenty-three in December. Most of them were small, but each added fuel to a flame that was sweeping the country. Radio shops sprang up in the cities; mail-order stores carried the business into the small towns. The radio craze was on. By the end of 1922 there were 508 stations broadcasting in the United States. By the fall of 1926 the number had risen to more than seven hundred, and there was pandemonium![4]

In 1920, but twenty-five people were able to listen to the results of the presidential election. Eight years later an estimated 9 million radios received the news of Hoover's victory for some 50 million listeners. Americans spent $850 million on radios and parts in 1929.[5]

After beginning the 1920s with cheap crystal sets and headphones, radio rapidly evolved both qualitatively and quantitatively. Between 1923 and 1925 production of crystal receivers declined, but there was an enormous increase in production of multitube sets and speakers. Ten times as many of the more sophisticated sets were produced in 1925 than in 1923, and four times as many speakers, all of which indicated, *Literary Digest* observed, that "the public has definitely adopted radio as a permanent investment, and is buying sets that will give efficient long-time service."[6] Yet it was estimated in 1926 that only 5 million of America's 28 million homes were yet equipped with radio sets. In that year there took place the first move toward permanent radio broadcasting on a national scale with formation of the National Broadcasting Corporation by the Radio Corporation of America. RCA was the largest distributor of radios in the world, and it was expected that sales of sets would be stimulated by improving quality of programming.[7]

The rapid growth of radio in the 1920s seemed to some to threaten existing institutions, particularly the press and theater. A newspaperman recalled after the 1924 presidential election that on previous election nights he had "looked out from newspaper office windows upon a sea of faces upturned toward bulletin boards" to follow election returns, but in 1924 the crowd was sparse, as the curious gathered at home in front of their radios for the results, instead. It was a fitting climax to "the first radio campaign"—one that had been aired over the "family hootodyne" from the convention speeches to the final results. What would the rise of radio do to newspapers? A war between the two forms of media was unlikely when in that year, alone, twenty-two newspapers also owned radio stations, including the influential *Chicago Tribune*. For this particular newsman, at least, it appeared that radio was destined to play an increasing role in the dissemination of news, but as an ally of the newspapers rather than an enemy.[8] But *Literary Digest* wondered if it were not likely that more people would listen to political speeches on radio who would never listen to them in a stuffy hall, and if that were true then *Radio* magazine might be correct in its prediction that radio would now supplant the press as the major force in influencing public opinion.[9]

Sports—whether boxing matches or games—rapidly became one of the most avidly sought broadcasts on the radio. A sportswriter recalled that one of his "greatest moments" in sports had been a "September evening back in 1923 when four of us sat hushed and hunched around two ear phones listening ... to the stalwart Mr. Firpo as he knocked Mr. Dempsey through the ropes." "Why is it," he asked,"

> that sport is so entrancing and so interesting over the radio? Well, mostly, I suppose, because it makes demands upon our imagination. Thus when we are told that "it is Yale's ball on Princeton's two yard line," we do not need to be told any more. We can picture the whole scene.... And we are stimulated thereby. Just as we are stimulated when with three men on base and the score tied in the ninth inning of a World's Series game we hear that fatal; "Ball three ... Strike two.... " This, our imagination tells us, is the mighty moment. For the truth is that we can see the whole scene much better than we could were we on the field.[10]

As for the theater, a spokesman described radio in 1925 as "the greatest menace the theater has ever faced." Another observer, however, argued:

> The present scare among the theaters can be likened to the introduction of the first moving-pictures, and will soon pass. We still have a commodity the public wants, and neither the moving pictures nor radio can replace the theater, where you can both see and hear the artist.

And some experience seemed to indicate that airing show tunes over the radio only increased the theater box office.[11]

One editor pointed out in 1925 that radio was producing a revolution—"the greatest, we imagine, since the coming of printing."

> It is a social revolution, not a political or economic one, for it changes how people learn, think, laugh, kill time, worship, and set their clocks. It depends upon the native potency of the spoken word or the sounding note repeated instantly to millions of listeners.... It goes with you—in an automobile, up in an airplane, down under the sea in submarines, into the Arctic with Macmillan, into the Tropics with Beebe, on the Twentieth Century Limited [railroad], in camp, in the library. The world is with you wherever you are (it never was before in human history!), but it is not "too much with you" for a click of a switch and you are alone again.

Experiments had already begun with offering university classes through the air, and churches, too, were feeling competition from radio sermons.[12]

The "extraordinary" thing about radio, Gilbert Seldes noted, was that it was "the one form of domestic entertainment which from the beginning has been inexpensive," cheaper by far than the early phonographs or home movie projectors. While the "fatuities which come over the air are unbelievable," there was nothing to prevent the listener from turning the dial to another station, and the variety available was almost limitless. But, Seldes complained, the greater part was "intellectually sub-tabloid," copying from the tabloid "advice on manners and morals, the witty sayings of little children, the prizes for last words in limericks, the optimistic uplift." One of the "stars" of radio, however, was jazz, which was "the most reliable thing on the air," with "always two or three good bands playing," and jazz music actually seemed to come over the radio better than classical symphonies, which required delicate adjustment. However, radio stations reported rarely getting requests for more jazz. Instead, the public seemed to want what they called "classical music," but which turned out to be "intermission pieces from the repertory of the vanished theatre orchestras."[13]

Charles Merz, however, was more complimentary, writing that radio had produced "an avalanche of bands.... whose fame the radio has broadcast into millions of homes reaching all the way from city flats to the loneliest farms in the wheat country.... It is the brass bands, the popular airs, the harmony boys and the ukuleles that have made the radio famous," and it was to them that radio devoted most of its time—about 60 percent, most of it during the peak listening hours of evening. Merz concluded:

> Into a nation that lives at top speed most of the day and comes home much too wide-awake to settle down, the radio brings a stimulus for tired nerves and something to distract us from the dull business of staying put at home.... We tune in—on a mighty rhythm to which millions of people are marking time, the pulse-beat of a nation.... If it is true that from twenty to thirty million Americans are listening in on the radio every evening, then for a large part of that evening they are listening in on the greatest single sweep of synchronized and syncopated rhythm that human ingenuity has yet conceived.[14]

Pitts Sanborn wrote that jazz was "mechanical and synthetic," and "merely a by-product of the Machine Age." He explained:

> We are witnessing the triumph of the great American machine; ingenuity to the fore. Machine, with its gramophone, its reproducing piano, its radio, and now its talkies, has become a Columbus breaking the seal of human repression. Suddenly the message of music is carried to millions. People who never heard a symphony orchestra are now partaking of the best.... The stevedore on Cherry Hill, with his two-tube set can sit and listen to the same concert as Mr. Astorbilt with his de-luxe superheterodyne. Perhaps the tired magnate will turn to jazz. And perhaps Mr. Stevedore, who five years ago had never heard of Schubert, will find "The Unfinished Symphony" on the program, and carefully tune in.[15]

A writer wrote in *Survey* magazine that while isolated on a mountaintop he had tried to tune in the news.

> But the air was full of jazz. The Florida Theater in Jacksonville was broadcasting vaudeville from the stage.... The Goldman Band was pouring very good Wagner into the air from the Million Dollar Pier at Atlantic City.... The radio was performing its nightly miracle, but King Jazz yielded no lot of his time to let the air carry word of what was happening.... Science had created this wonder, but jazz had seized the fruit to distract the people.

Clearly a better and more responsive news system was required.[16]

Legendary broadcaster Graham McNamee noted in 1926 that the industry was still relatively small—"1200 announcers scattered among the 540 radio stations scattered around the land"—and new—"started by the first pioneers only four years ago." He wrote:

> It seems perhaps much longer than that, now that so many millions are accustomed to tuning in each night; but if you think back you will remember that it was only in 1922 that you got your first radio set, something you put together yourself if you were handy, or purchased somewhere under a manufacturer's label that is now forgotten. Not long after that the first radio magazine came out. The game is younger, you see, than the motion-picture industry, which is still called an infant.... In those four short years fortunes have been made and lost, huge factories have sprung up all over the land, tens of thousands of radio stores have been opened, and the air is full of myriad voices spreading news and messages, music and song to a listening world....

When McNamee joined radio with WEAF there were only three stations, recently opened, and his station worked from only two rooms and with a few people, broadcasting only four hours per day. Four years later the station occupied an entire floor and employed 100 people, while broadcasting an average of nine hours per day. With no hookups the earlier audience had been limited to tens of thousands of nearby listeners. In 1926, thanks to hookups with other stations through the facilities of AT&T, his station could reach as far as the Pacific coast and be heard by many millions.[17]

Already by 1924 radio was being credited with an influence on politics. Many observers credited radio for Coolidge's overwhelming majority in the presidential election, the Republicans having largely dominated the airwaves that year. Part of the reason, some suggested, was the very different impressions the two parties had given when their conventions were broadcast—the Republicans well organized and carrying through smoothly to the end, the Democrats long, drawn-out, and rancorous, with speeches filled with strident religious bigotry and sectional prejudice. And when the Democrats did finally get around to nominating John W. Davis, he turned out to be a candidate without a "radio voice" or a "radio personality." *Literary Digest* wrote that Davis's

> voice sounded gray and colorless and lacked conviction.... But "Silent Cal" had the magic quality of voice and personality that got him across over the radio from the outset. His clear, natural, well-modulated voice was easily heard and every word understood. It carried a suggestion of restraint and rang with conviction and common sense; to the average citizen listening to him over the radio it mirrored accurately the man behind the voice.[18]

The GOP was estimated to have spent at least three times as much as the Democrats and eight or ten times as much as LaFollette's third-party bid. Looking to the 1928 campaign, observers expected radio to play an even more important role. As *The New Republic* observed, radio had grown enormously since 1924.

> The number of receiving sets in the United States is now estimated all the way from about six million up to eight or nine.... The potential audience is probably twenty millions, and perhaps more. The linking up of many stations for simultaneous broadcast of the same program, in 1924 still a rarity, is now a regular daily and hourly matter.

Reception on radio sets had also improved, and more were now powered by electricity rather than batteries.

As for the 1928 campaign:

> The conventions will doubtless be broadcast, because neither party would dare to admit that it feared to let the country overhear its deliberations. But such broadcasting will not constitute an important item on the campaign program, which will consist for the most part of speeches specially made before the microphone in the studio, by candidates and others. In their access to radio and film, the Republicans were likely to have the same advantage they historically enjoyed with the press. Even as most newspapers were owned by wealthy businessmen who leaned Republican, so it was with radio station and motion picture studio owners.

The New Republic wondered: "How can a true democracy exist when the channels of discussion are, in general, closed to one set of ideas and open to another?"[19] Others, though, expected a better showing from the Democrats in 1928, since Al Smith had "made more effective use of radio than any other man in public life."[20]

The *St. Louis Post-Dispatch* estimated that a total of $2 million was spent on radio in 1928, about evenly split between the two parties, with each side using about fifty hours in nationwide hookups. Radio was credited with increasing voter interest and turnout, particularly by women, with the vote in 1928 measuring 10 million more than in 1924. *Literary Digest* wrote:

> Eight years ago, reports David Lawrence in a Consolidated Press dispatch from Washington, there were about fifty people at the capital who had radio sets sufficiently accurate to capture the broadcasting by KDKA at Pittsburgh. In 1924 there was a small hookup of a few stations, through WEAF, reaching a few millions. But this year.... at least 40,000,000 people were able to listen in on the candidates' speeches.

Radio revealed personal qualities and defects and seemed certain to be of even greater influence in 1932 and subsequent elections.[21]

Radio seemed to offer a variety of potential uses as it increased in reliability and popularity during the 1920s. Station WOR in Newark, New Jersey began to offer an exercise class over the air to musical accompaniment every day at 7 A.M. With an estimated 50,000 listeners doing exercises with its leader, A.E. Bagley, the program was billed as the largest gymnasium in the world.[22] Some colleges utilized the new device to offer courses by radio to distant learners. Kansas State College was one of the first to offer a "College of the Air," as they called it, which carried courses and entertainment to listeners all over the state. By 1925 forty radio courses were being offered covering a wide spectrum of topics and interspersed with concerts and other features to give radio students a feel for campus life. Applications for enrollment in the "College of the Air" had come from virtually "all States of the Union."[23] Radio had also begun by the mid-1920s to experiment with broadcasting plays over the air.[24]

It was estimated that of 700 radio stations in the United States, 1 of 15 was owned by a religious organization, and if those owned by sectarian colleges, and so forth, were included, it would be more like 1 in 10. One-half of all stations included some kind of religious worship.[25]

The importance of the ear in an age when radio was emerging as the dominant source of news and entertainment obviously put those who were hard of hearing at a disadvantage. But the 1920s provided a solution for that handicap with the invention of what was described as "spectacles for the ears," the first effective hearing aids.

MOVIES

Early in 1919 a writer in *The New Republic* reported of a visit to a suburb shortly after sunset, and of the spectacle that entranced him. From all corners of the town came streams of people, all headed in the direction of the local movie theater and its screening of Mary Pickford in *The Little American*. He wrote:

> On that night, all over our continent, similar processions were streaming into the temples of the movies. You could see these worshippers, in the mind's eye, coming over a million hills, along the streets of a hundred thousand such little towns, eager to laugh,

to weep, to be horrified, to love, to envy, to desire, to hate, to suffer, to be revitalized with every sort of emotion, to escape from their smaller selves into the general life of sympathetic imagination, to learn dissatisfaction and be led to aspire, to have adventures and see Beauty and be played upon by all the eloquent appeals of imaginative art.

He concluded after the movie: "You had only to see the faces of the people coming out of the theatre to know that they had been to the altar of all the old gods of human nature."[26]

In the mid-1920s, the Lynds found nine motion picture theaters operating in Middletown from 1 to 11 P.M. daily the year around. Their fare was enjoyed by "about two and three-fourths times the city's entire population" during a typical month. It was an opportunity for vicarious living. But the Lynds also found some educators complaining that the movies were contributing to "the 'early sophistication' of the young and the relaxing of social taboos.... The judge of the juvenile court lists the movies as one of the 'big four' causes of local juvenile delinquency."[27]

Not surprisingly, the popularity of movies created problems for stage productions, particularly in the smaller cities away from Broadway. As one observer described the situation:

To these smaller cities a generation ago came most of the well-known "stars" and most of the successful plays, stopping for a night and passing on. Sometimes there would be one visitor a week, sometimes two, three, or even more if the city was large enough to support so many. Since the development of the motion pictures, however, there has been an astonishing change. Shown at first in small, cheap houses down a side street, the movies progressed rapidly into the main thoroughfares, and then took possession of the playhouses themselves. The managers for a while looked upon them as a gap-filler, something to keep the doors open and the pennies coming in after Sothern and Marlow left on Tuesday, until John Drew came on Friday. But it was not long before the managers discovered that the profits from the films were more than the profits from the plays; a film is rented for a comparatively small fee, and no part of the receipts has to be shared, nor paid out to stage hands.

By 1920, however, the movies had begun to challenge the theater even on Broadway itself. Motion picture companies were buying control of some of the most respectable theaters and backing plays in those and other theaters with an eye to locating dramas that might make suitable movies. The concern of critics was with the diminution of quality that they forecast resulting.[28]

A broader question grappled with already at the beginning of the decade was the value or danger of movies to society. A critic of movies wrote that "learning to think was a slow and laborious undertaking" for mankind, but "learning not to think is proving a swift and congenial task and the shortest cut to success has been supplied by the movies." The earliest movies had been "all for instruction and information and edification. Amusement did not enter into their programme." But, she added, that could not have paid well, for now the play had become the thing. The danger was that the movies were impressing their "unintelligent standard of happiness on to the crowd," which was particularly perilous in a democracy where the crowd ruled. The movies, she concluded, were "worse than a sedative—they are dope." Movies stupefied and hypnotized, inducing apathy in a world in which work needed to be done, they were "more demoralizing than Bolshevism to the proletariat and intellectuals like."[29]

Others charged movies in the 1920s with "setting up false, often meretricious, standards of behavior, of luxury, of feeling and of thought," and thus doing more than even radios in damaging American life. Yet both radio and movies, their critics acknowledged, had "served as a means of filling hours set free by the machine—hours which their devotees have not learned as yet to devote to the enriching possibilities of real leisure."[30]

Others, however, found the movies performing another useful function before the advent of sound. Deems Taylor believed that motion picture theaters in the early 1920s were performing a more useful force in educating the nation musically than either the phonograph or the player piano. He explained:

> Music has always been a necessary accompaniment to motion pictures, in order to compensate for the uncanny silence in which these photographic wraiths unfold their dramas. Starting with a modest ensemble of piano and glass crash, the motion picture orchestra has gradually increased in size and quality . . . so that the larger houses to-day can boast a musical equipment that is amazingly good.

The result was that orchestras had begun to play as prominent a role as movies. It meant, Taylor concluded: "At last the average man is going of his own accord into a public hall and hearing music—real music—and discovering that he likes it. The picture house allows him to pretend that he is going solely to see the films, and needn't listen unless he wants to."[31]

A 1921 article in *Saturday Evening Post* reported that the movie industry was already the fourth largest in the nation and still growing. Its total receipts of $750,000,000 per year was larger than the combined income of all the nation's public utilities. The 15,500 movie theaters were estimated to be capable of holding 8 million viewers, while an additional 1,200 were under construction at an approximate cost of $72 million. An estimated 250,000 people were involved either directly or indirectly in the movie business every day. More than three-fourths of the world's movies were being produced in Los Angeles, where 100 producing companies operating in 52 studios produced films valued at $100 million per year. Exports of films totaled $11 million in 1920 and were 47,000 miles long.[32] Americans were estimated to be paying $7.15 per year to view movies, most of which cost anywhere from 11 cents to 17 cents, 10 percent of which was a federal tax.[33]

Americans, one writer observed, were continually trying to find an outlet for their "creative energies. Some get it in prize-fighting, base-ball, the theater, lodges, politics, newspapers, but they find it most of all in the movies." Meeting this demand had transformed moviemaking into "a great industrial and business enterprise." Profit making required that the moviegoing public be given beautiful women, handsome, heroic-looking men, enchanting clothes of the latest style, massive, realistic settings. The producer must be able to command the genii to transport his audiences into all the strange corners of the earth. No fantasy may be beyond him. To make any drastic change in this accepted program of pleasure is to gamble at least a hundred thousand dollars; it is often from a quarter of a million dollars upward.

So long as this formula was successful with moviegoers there was little likelihood that it would be altered.

Critics of the movies, this observer noted, failed to appreciate that movies were a "social and economic phenomenon" of the masses, whereas the fine arts were "aristocratic in their environment; they are nourished by the few, and made for them." The broadening of popular education was not likely to change that, nor to induce producers to release movies of more artistic content. After all, a generation was fortunate if it produced "one fundamental work of art in its time."[34]

For those who in the twenty-first century happen to catch a black-and-white silent movie from the 1920s on a classic movie television channel, it is difficult to appreciate the excitement and controversy that this medium engendered, so alien is it from our conception of motion picture entertainment. Technological advances in the industry late in the 1920s, however, transformed movies almost overnight into a form of entertainment that can still be appreciated eight decades later. These advances were the advent of sound and of color.

Of sound, Gilbert Seldes wrote in *The New Republic* in August 1921:

The moving picture synchronized with sound has come upon us rather like the War [World War I]. It had been talked about; each step of preparation had been announced; its Balkan stage was reached a few years ago in the imperfect projection of jazz-bands and Metropolitan stars—and suddenly it has arrived and found us almost entirely unprepared for it.

Seldes's own reaction was negative. The introduction of the "talking device" would, he forecast, lead "to a great extent the filming of stage plays," leading to an intensification of the competition between theater and movies and the diversion of the movie industry "from the exploitation of its own capacities." Seldes could not recall a single "good picture" that would have been enhanced through the addition of speech. But directors, he concluded,

think that you can add tone without changing the delicate equilibrium of the picture. It shows how little they know or care about the movies, and for them the speech-mechanism is a godsend, for it offers a novelty and again postpones the day when their feeble intelligence and atrophied imagination will be driven out of the movies.[35]

R.E. Sherwood found it comical that those most concerned about the dire effects sound would have on cinematic art were the same ones who, a year earlier, had

noticed the screen only as one would notice a road-side sign-board, which shut off part of the landscape and added nothing of beauty to the rest. Those who once spoke of the movie as the back-house of the drama are now protesting loudly because the Vitaphone, the Movietone and the Photophone are degrading a noble art!

While admitting that the talkies released so far were of abominable quality, Sherwood nevertheless argued that they were "exercising a profoundly salutary influence upon the movie industry and that the revolution which they caused will come to be known, in time, as a memorable Renaissance" that had rid the industry "of the fat-headed incompetence and stupid conceit that has dominated the movie during the protracted period of its infancy." Their incompetence could not be tolerated by the new masters of the industry—those who held the patents on the new sound devices: General Electric, Western Electric, AT&T, and RCA. The talkies represented "the expected victory of a superior form of industrialism over an inferior one." The machine had intruded and hereafter would be dominant.

As for the theater:

Well-nigh ruined already by competition offered by the film parlors, the dance halls, lonely suburban roads (suitable for evening parking), the radio and countless other alibi-providing menaces, how will the theatre survive against this new invention which assails the eyes, ears, nose and throat at one and the same time?

Movies, Sherwood observed, could now cater to select audiences rather than catering to the masses as in the days of silent movies. Citing Warner Brothers' production of Al Jolson in *The Singing Fool,* he noted that it had been produced more cheaply than a Broadway review and had recovered its cost through showing in one theater in one city. "The Warners," Sherwood wrote, "don't have to worry whether or not the square-heads in Kokomo or the peons in Chihuahua consider 'The Singing Fool' good entertainment. They, and all the other film producers, are at last in a position to thumb their noses at the rabble." But every viewer attracted to higher-quality movies like this one was a customer lost to the theater.[36]

In 1928 there were many promising developments in photography, movies, and television. George Eastman developed Kodacolor film and processing, hailed by the head of RCA as "the greatest development in photography since the moving picture itself." Advances in television in both England and the United States made it possible to broadcast a scene without artificial light. As for talkies, 600 theaters had contracted for talking motion picture equipment.[37]

By June 1929, a year of talkies had led to the virtual disappearance of silent movies. First-run theaters on Broadway were showing fourteen talking movies and only three silent ones. "It looks," a writer in *The Nation* opined, "as if the silent picture as an entertainment for the masses were definitely facing extinction."[38] The most successful of the early talkies were, in fact, largely musicals, or "song pictures," like Al Jolson in *The Singing Fool* and Fannie Brice in *My Man*. Admittedly, the cinema versions of these two great talents were not the equal of seeing them in person, but they were more than most Americans could have dreamed of only two years earlier. Moreover, the sound quality of the singing voice was markedly better than that of the spoken one in 1929. One observer predicted the filming of "full-blown" musical comedy" once sound quality was improved and color added.[39] In 1929 Fox introduced a new wider screen, called Grandeur, that stretched across the full width of the stage, and all theaters began to scrap their old equipment and buy it. The result was an increased "genuineness," a "fluidity and a vividness which the present-day screen does not afford." For the times it was almost a stereo effect.[40]

In the late 1920s Charles Merz wrote:

> Twenty million Americans go to the movies every day.... One American in every six, in other words, now finds time to visit the movies not once a month or once a week, but once a day.
>
> The business of making celluloid dramas now ranks with steel and motor cars among the ten great industries in the United States. Its invested capital, says the Film Year Book of 1927, is a billion and a half. Another billion comes in annually from the sale of tickets at twenty thousand theatres. Two hundred and thirty-five thousand people are employed at the production studios. One hundred and fifty million dollars is spent each year upon new pictures. Eight hundred feature films were made last year, in addition to twenty thousand shorter pictures and several million feet of news reels.

The secret of the movies' success, he wrote, was their "attempt to state life in as simple terms as possible," reducing all "primary things" to "manageable units in the movies." And the movies never failed their viewers' expectations.[41]

The Nation observed in early 1930 that the talkies had clearly come to stay.

> Not only have the most important producers ceased to make anything else, but the "wiring" of even the village nickolodeons has gone on so rapidly that the silent movie house is already almost a thing of the past. The wave of public protest predicted by certain critics never showed the slightest sign of materializing, and audiences, instead of troubling themselves about the alleged threat to an independent art form, accepted dialogue as an obvious addition to their favorite entertainment. Probably only America could have released so rapidly the capital and energy necessary to revolutionize an industry overnight, but the revolution is already a *fait accompli.*

Moreover, the technological revolution was continuing, with constant improvements in sound quality.[42]

This was bad news for those who had made their living by furnishing live music in the theaters as background for silent films. As one writer observed:

> Almost every cinema emporium in the country, deciding that music was one thing it could not do without, hired instrumental groups, ranging from three players in the small houses, to 100 or so in the coruscant palaces of the cities. Just before the advent of sound film, the orchestra was virtually the most important part of the movie program, the main attraction.... An enormous and unprecedented demand for musicians was created by the movies, both directly and indirectly. As people began to hear more and better music, they demanded music with other things than film—with meals, in chop suey houses, in summer resorts, etc.

The success of Al Jolson in *The Jazz Singer* in October 1927 was the beginning of the end for silent movies and their musicians. That movie, which had cost less than $50,000 to produce, grossed $1.5 million—three times as much as most silent movies costing $200,000 to make. Musicians had survived the advent of the phonograph and radio, but once all movie theaters were wired for sound and accompanied by canned music from the best orchestras, "the fiddler will go the way of the colorful but economically outmoded telegrapher."[43]

By 1930 the movie industry had also been invaded by color. At first imperfect, it seemed to many critics to detract rather than add to the quality of movies. But Alexander Bakshy brushed such criticism aside after viewing *The Vagabond King,* which revealed "the enormous possibilities that are latent in the use of color." Bakshy wrote:

> The naive enthusiasts who have been denouncing color in favor of black and white as the only "art" form of the movies must be either color-blind or simply ignorant of the art quality that distinguishes one sensation from another. There can be no doubt that color is one of the most important means of cinematic expression.[44]

VAUDEVILLE

The branch of the entertainment industry that proved to be least able to resist the onslaught of radio and motion pictures in the 1920s was vaudeville. In an article headed "Vaudeville Must Be Saved," Alexander Bakshy pointed to the decline of vaudeville on Broadway. There was, he pointed out, only one vaudeville theater remaining, the others having been torn down or converted to movie palaces. A foreigner visiting Times Square "would hardly suspect the existence in this country of that unique and ancient art." Paradoxically, vaudeville seemed alive and well in the rest of the country. RKO, the principal vaudeville enterprise, operated 700 theaters served by 25,000 performers, with an average weekly attendance of some 12 million patrons. Only five of the theaters served up an all-vaudeville program, the others dividing their fare with movies. Bakshy found the problem in the declining quality of vaudeville that was less recognized in the "provinces" than in the cities. Like the movies, vaudeville was being mass-produced by its promoters to satisfy the tastes of the masses. Moreover, some of the best talents had abandoned vaudeville for the musical comedy stage—George Cohan, Al Jolson, Eddie Cantor, Fannie Brice, Will Rogers, W.C. Fields, and Fred and Adele Astaire, for example. If vaudeville were to survive it must be original and inventive, with real talent.[45]

A few months later Bakshy was even more pessimistic about vaudeville's future, writing:

> The vaudeville stage platform today is the survival of the early nineteenth-century theater. Even more than the stage of the modern legitimate theater it betrays no effort to provide a physical foundation, a pedestal, a rostrum, for a frank display of the performer's

talents. Vaudeville's attempts at pictorial effects are usually of the good old late-Victorian type, and, if modern, shriek with the vulgarity of the cheap magazine covers. In music it still clings to jazz and sentimental songs. The whole atmosphere of the American vaudeville today is compounded of routine effort and second-rate talent. It is time that vaudeville woke up.[46]

A 1930 article in the *Saturday Evening Post* reemphasized the point that vaudeville nationally had shrunk from eighty theaters to just five. Clearly this was not enough to support quality vaudeville, nor very many vaudevillians. First had come the competition of silent movies, and then

> Just about the time vaudeville, shorn of its glory and prestige, was getting nicely calloused from being kicked around, a new exterminator entered the scene and started prussic aciding the works. What is this ruthless destroyer that has kicked over and splintered the venerable [profession]? Yes, Oswald, talking motion pictures.

And talkies were here to stay. The worst was yet to come for vaudeville. Its days were numbered.[47]

THEATER

An analysis of the impact of the war on the theater, written in 1919, concluded that wartime had rendered both orthodox and iconoclastic dramatists "stranded." A.B. Walkley wrote:

> That was because the war had changed our "values" and shifted our points of view. Such changes, while they leave works of pure art inviolate, are fatal to works constructed on the Shavian principle of using art merely or mainly to gild the propagandist pill.

But Walkley took solace in the theory that wars produced great dramatic outbursts and wrote: "If this be a right reading of history, the greatest of all dramatic upheavals ought to be confidently expected after the greatest of all wars." But he admitted that to attempt "to forecast the theatrical future would be the last imbecility."[48]

Some thought they saw the beginnings of this "upheaval" in what was referred to as the "New Movement," or the "New Theater." Oliver Sayler found its guiding purpose that of making "the experience of attending the theatre more vivid, to restore the thrill, the terror, the exaltation, the ecstacy of sitting at a play." But as of 1921, Sayler found the new movement confined almost entirely to set designers, who had "progressed more rapidly than the writers and actors and producers of plays." For the movement to attain fulfillment would require that they "stimulate their co-workers with some of their own enthusiasm or they will have to learn the other crafts of the theatre and perform the whole task themselves." There was, in fact, evidence that both of these things were happening, but the greatest lack was an absence of playwrights for the new movement, with the exception of a few like Eugene O'Neill.[49]

Four years later, however, Montrose Moses made a similar point when he wrote of the "New Theater" that the "revolution" in the theater had until that point been waged largely by the scenic artist, who was "opening greater vistas to the American playwright; he is the one putting the theatre in its proper place as an art, and asking the writer for the theatre to so consider it." Alas, there had been but little response from American playwrights, who tended still to be imitative. There were none who could be counted upon to "maintain a level of high thinking, a level of brilliance, a level of whimsy," equal to that of European playwrights. Only Eugene O'Neill used "consistently what is out of the conventional order.... He is the one man of the American theater to-day whose quality of soul is to be detected in all he does."[50]

Well before the onset of the Great Depression, however, the theater was mired in its own depression. One of the first indications of trouble in the industry was the sharp decline in "road" bookings—the traveling performances of road companies of Broadway shows in other towns and cities. Another was the fact that many investors who had heretofore underwritten theatrical productions were now putting their money, instead, into the burgeoning movie industry. Fault-finders found numerous reasons for the decline of the theater and varied solutions. Arthur Hammerstein, producer and theater owner, predicted at year's end in 1928 that stage productions were "doomed and within five years the theaters can be turned to more useful purposes, such as garages." Talking pictures, he said, had "about finished playhouses which did not have the silver screen." But Hammerstein also blamed discord within the industry, as well as "continued use of antiquated playhouses, incompetent theatrical managers, inability of legitimate-theater managers to organize for their own protection, evils in ticket-selling, and high salaries of popular actors."

For some, the solution to many of the problems was to learn the business management techniques of the movie industry. As one producer put it, the theater pursued a "public be damned policy," by contrast with the "public-be-pleased" policy of the movies, which put great emphasis on consumer comfort, service, and satisfaction. One example of this was that many theaters were not well ventilated, while scarcely a movie house could be found that did not offer this comfort for its patrons. Movie theaters were among the first to adopt air conditioning, with the first installed in 1917 and over 300 by 1930. By 1929, in fact, there were complaints of theaters being overcooled.[51]

For optimists, the popularity of dramatic productions at the high school and college levels, as well as the success of hundreds of "little theater" groups across the country, showed that theater was not dead, and that an audience remained for Broadway productions if they were of high quality and well managed.[52]

Theater critic George Jean Nathan derided the notion that the talkies were a threat to the legitimate theater, writing:

> At the moment, they are a novelty and are attracting the crowds that a novelty habitually attracts. In these crowds there are naturally some theatregoers who, drawn by cu-

riosity, want to see what all the shoutin's for. But the announced notion that these theatregoers will abandon the theatre in favor of the talkies, simply because the talkies cost less to see, is cousin to the notion that the same theatregoers are in the habit of abandoning plays like "Strange Interlude" or "Holiday" in favor of "Potiphar's Wife" or "Back Seat Drivers" simply because one can get into them at cut rates. The talkies will in the long run appeal only to that more ignorant public which has taken the movies to its bosom.

Indeed, Nathan predicted that the talkies would eventually prove less popular than the silents, since censorship made it impossible for them to offer the lascivious productions that had for several years been the principal attraction of the silent movies.[53]

But Nathan also deplored the absence of an audience for quality theater outside New York City. Chicago, he pointed out, had spent $3,500 on a drama by Eugene O'Neill in the same week that it spent $45,000 on an Al Jolson musical, and the same was true of the other large cities. The message was clear: "Honourable drama spells ruin; legs, lewdness and sentimentality spell riches." Part of the problem, Nathan admitted, was the lack of competent playwrights, only two or three retaining "in their hearts a determined and uncorrupted purpose. Take away young O'Neill . . . and there is next to nothing left." Others had begun brilliantly, but had been corrupted by commercialization and had ended by being only "ticket salesmen."[54]

A *New Republic* writer was willing to concede that the talkies might make inroads into the legitimate theater, but asked if that were really something to be deplored if the result was better plays and better acting. What did it matter if seventy of the eighty-five old theaters in New York City should be converted to movie palaces, if the remainder were putting on first-rate productions? If that were the result, then it would indeed be "a golden age of the theater."[55]

The 1920s was a decade of business consolidation, fueled by Wall Street, and the entertainment industry was no exception, with theater ownership consolidating under a few large interests and those, in turn, being bought up by movie production companies. Such consolidations brought not only Wall Street money, but also the influence of financiers in the operations of the industry. One result was the intrusion of advertising into virtually every facet of the business. As one critic observed: "The song-writing business has 'gone advertising' almost completely. Every song you hear nowadays is a theme song for one motion-picture or another," and it was likely that the trend would spread to other branches of industry. Advertising was also beginning to appear in the theaters. Music publishing houses were being acquired by the large motion picture companies, and songwriting had begun to be prostituted to produce advertising ditties for products like Maxwell House coffee and Prophylactic toothbrushes.[56]

A long-time actor-producer wrote:

The real estate speculator has seized upon the theater, and far too many are being built. They are a drug on the market. The housing of plays within them has become a great commercial industry, necessitating all sorts of labor efficiency. Plays and their productions are assembled like so many Ford automobiles, and surrounding their creation and presentation are unions and protective associations, pacts and despotic rules. Managers, actors, dramatists, scene painters, electricians, carpenters, stage hands, wardrobe women, musicians, advance agents, business representatives of companies, treasurers, and even dressers, ushers, and stage doorkeepers are all herded in individual groups as unionized as are miners and bricklayers. Mergers of theatrical enterprises are popular and effective, and shares may be purchased on the New York Stock Exchange.[57]

A Broadway actress decried the proliferation of theaters in New York City, which was decreasing both quality and profits. She wrote:

Theater-building, you see, is not an artistic venture. It is merely a real-estate speculation. Theater-owners don't care a continental what happens to the drama. After this has ceased to exist they will still have their property, the buildings and the land on which they stand. The buildings can be converted into moving-picture houses, or even garages, at a trifling cost.[58]

Analyzing the decline of the Broadway road companies, *The Nation* found:

Whatever the artistic sins of the moving-picture industry may be, it has for a long time been conducted upon business principles far more enlightened than those adopted by the legitimate theater. For fifty or seventy-five cents one may have a comfortable seat in a cleaner theater than one is likely to get for four times the price in a regular playhouse, and one may be reasonably assured of politer treatment while one has been buying it. Much fun has been poked at the regimented ushers and the ornate lobbies of the movie palaces but they represent a shrewdly calculated reaction against the indifference of the theater manager to the comfort of his public.... "Hey, Rube!" was the battle-cry of the old-time circus, and it still expresses the spirit of many managers of traveling companies. They come into a town to get as much as they can as quickly as they can, and when they have worked the suckers they depart. No wonder they have lost out to the local movie. At bottom it is a matter of what the trade journals call "showmanship," and there is no doubt which of the contending forces best understands what that means.[59]

5
Business and Life

RETAIL BUSINESS

That there were revolutionary changes in American business in the 1920s is well known. Those changes were as pronounced in the retail sphere as elsewhere, with the impact of the machine felt even there. The Lynds found that in Middletown, specialization was growing in retail trade, with branches of chain stores pushing out established merchants. From April 1924 to January 1925 "three Middletown clothing stores and one shoe store were taken over by selling agencies having at least one store in another city, and four new chains entered the city with one or more branches." They found: "The whole business structure is dominated by the necessity for keeping costly machines busy." Businessmen were operating according to the "set of rituals prescribed by 'business,'" and they seemed "subject to almost as many restrictions as the machine dictates to the worker who manipulates its levers."[1]

Retail buyers were also often pulling levers, as more and more items began to be sold through vending machines in the 1920s. In 1928 an estimated $25 million of business was done by these "robot clerks." Silas Bent wrote that, in addition to the usual candies and chewing gum:

> Electric washing machines are now fitted with coin devices, so that for twenty-five cents the housewife can get laundry work done automatically for thirty-five minutes. Cigarettes and toothbrushes—with its tiny tube of paste—are now distributed in that fashion. Uncle Sam has been experimenting with automatic stamp-selling robots.

With a million and a half retail establishments in the nation, or about one for every fifty Americans, it hardly seemed that they needed to be supplemented by vending machines.[2]

On the other hand, diversification also seemed to be a fact of life in American business by the late 1920s. *Literary Digest* wrote late in the decade: "Perhaps the average housewife might think it strange that 'a widely used salad-dressing is made by one of the largest varnish and painting companies in the world,'' which, through a subsidiary, also made "meat sauces, pickles, spices, and condiments, in addition to margarine and other eatables based upon oil basis." The diversification trend had been "gathering great momentum of late, until they are talking about it in Wall Street much as crop diversification was being discust in farm circles a few years ago as a solution of the problems of agriculture." Colt Firearms was now into adding machines, dishwashers, molded specialty products of various kinds, compacts, and similar products. RCA now manufactured radio sets, talking machines, and talking motion-picture equipment, produced talking motion pictures, and owned a vaudeville circuit. Remington was manufacturing cutlery, business machines, vending machines, and cash registers.[3]

"Our whole distributing system is being made over," *Literary Digest* said, noting that in Providence, Rhode Island "eleven cigar sores are selling paint and varnish, eleven sell dry-good and notions, and forty-six carry groceries." Thirty-one butcher shops were selling tobacco in addition to meat. Now Montgomery Ward was opening chain stores, following the lead of Sears, Roebuck, the other major mail-order retailer, which planned to be represented in all 1,500 towns of 5,000 or more population. What would happen to independent retailers? Would they be forced to band together to get discounts.[4] It was, John Flynn wrote, the machines that were driving America into the arms of the chain stores.[5] While the chain stores were not established everywhere, in those areas they had penetrated their progress had been "amazing." Chain groceries and drug stores had largely driven independents out of business in the major eastern cities, Woolworth was driving neighborhood notion stores to the wall, and J.C. Penney's 1,000 department stores were doing the same to other department stores.[6] It seemed that only the chains were capable of the level of distribution required by machine mass production.

The 1920s also saw an explosion in installment buying, of which the *Literary Digest* wrote in early 1925:

> Not so many years ago selling on the installment plan was confined almost entirely to furniture. Now one can buy on this basis all kinds of labor-saving equipment, home appliances, heating-plants, clothing, musical instruments, radio receiving-sets, cash-registers, trucks, taxicabs, garages, and Diesel engines, locomotives, newspapers presses, rugs, and electrical appliances. And the financing of these sales has become such a gigantic problem that a new type of financial institution has sprung into existence to solve it. It is said that of the 4,000,000 automobiles sold in 1923 at a wholesale price of about $2,000,000,000 only 1,000,000 were sold for cash, the others being bought on the installment plan. And last year . . . there were 635 companies specializing in the financing of automobiles bought by installments.

Supporters of the practice argued that neither the automobile nor radio industries could have achieved their levels of success in the 1920s without it. And now department stores, too, were offering to sell on easy payments.[7]

Installment buying was a major fact of life in Middletown. The Lynds found the people living on a credit economy, with "the dollar-down-and-so-much-per plan" available to nearly every family and for virtually everything. "Living," they found, "in all its aspects leans upon money more than ever before."[8]

Specialization had even extended to the construction trades, Stuart Chase found, with house parts "being increasingly made in factories and then simply assembled by workers at the building site, using a host of new machines—pneumatic riveters, welders, nailing machines, etc."[9]

MANUFACTURING

One characteristic of business in the 1920s was the dispersal of manufacturing, partly under the impact of the growing use of automobiles and trucks, but also, as the Chicago *Journal of Commerce* pointed out, as a result of the spread of electricity. As the *Literary Digest* wrote:

> Of all the forces at work to halt the rush of population cityward, and turn people back again to the small towns, the most effective, it is generally agreed, is the network of electric-transmission wires that covers the country. More than 50,000 miles of these power-distributing lines have been built in the last eight years, at an expense of more than $1,000,000,000. So wide-spread has the power network become, says the Chicago *Journal of Commerce*, that much of the industrial activity formerly confined to the large cities may now be accomplished in the small town, and "some of the largest corporations have thus decentralized many of their operations."

Workers benefited from the lower cost of living in smaller towns. The Middle West Utilities Company of Chicago found that "industrial leadership of the country is being transferred to the less-populous centers." A government study showed that "the only present gain in number of industrial wage-earners is taking place in towns of less than 10,000 population," especially in "the new industrial areas of the South."[10] This would presumably arrest the migration from rural and small-town America to the cities, which was estimated in the late 1920s to have totaled about 800,000 since 1920.[11] By 1927 it was reported that over the past eighteen years the "center of industry" in America had shifted westward seventy-five miles to a point "about fifty miles southeast of Chicago."[12]

But manufacturing was also moving outside the United States. In 1929 the Metal Trades Department of the American Federation of Labor said that the American wage earner was being menaced by the "enormous scale on which American manufacturers are opening up branch factories in foreign countries, or even moving their whole enterprises to Canada, Europe, Argentina, or India, where they can employ the cheap labor which our immigration laws bar out at home." The trend was alarming for American workers, who faced the prospect of their jobs being exported along with the capital, and that national unemployment would increase as a result. The AFL called it "the greatest era of industrial migration ever known" with an estimated $3.5 billion invested in 2,000 branch or independent factories located abroad, led by some 150 of America's largest and most important companies. As the *Literary Digest* observed:

> The other day a jute-consuming plant was moved from Ludlow, Maine to a town in India ... leaving a group of high-standard white men out of jobs in Maine and placing a lot of thirty-cents-a-day brown men in jobs in India.... It is estimated that there are 2,000 branch or independent American factories under other flags ... and scarcely a day goes by without chronicling at least one more. Never before has there been such a migration of industry.

As one writer put it: "From a labor employment point of view the 'pauper labor' of Europe might as well be allowed to migrate to the United States as to permit American factories to migrate to Europe and employ it there to make goods that displace the products of domestic plants and labor."[13] Henry Ford moved the manufacture of his tractors to Ireland where he could use cheaper labor and still export the tractors to the United States duty-free.[14]

In part, however, the movement overseas was clearly in response to the rising cost of labor in the United States, caused by the expansion of the eight-hour working day and, later in the decade, by the five-day workweek.[15] Another form of response to higher labor costs was to mechanize. Stuart Chase reported that the number of factory workers had been declining since the beginning of the decade. "Mass production and the automatic function are relentlessly substituting machines for machine tenders. Between 1923 and 1928, total factory employees declined by 1,250,000." Had the "furious manifestation of mass production begun to eliminate workers faster than new tasks can be found for them, however long they wait?" The United States, he found, had "about the worst unemployment statistics of any civilized country. In the spring of 1928 the newspapers and magazines were filled for months with a vast debate as to whether there was, or was not, an unemployment crisis. Estimates of men out of work ranged from a few hundred thousand to six million—and nobody really knew anything conclusive about it."[16]

Chase wrote that the wave of prosperity had "brought mass production and the automatic process to heights undreamed of," but the suspicion was growing that it had reached the saturation point and that a growing number of unemployed was likely. "Accelerating unemployment is before us," he predicted, "and unless something is done, and that quickly, a very heavy bill, cast in terms of wretchedness and despair, will shortly be submitted."[17]

In 1929, however, the *Literary Digest* reported that:

> Repeated attempts to arouse Europeans in all stations of life to the growing menace of America's gigantic industrial invasion seem to be met with so little concern that some European editors begin to despair. They are especially pessimistic, they confess, when a great American encroachment in the European field takes place almost unnoticed, and the particular enterprise they have in mind is the purchase by the General Motors Company of the great German factories in which Opel automobiles are made. American control of the greatest German manufacturing organization of automobiles ... is a sensational

indication to the Paris progress civique that Europe is on the way to become "vassalized" by American industry.[18]

The overproduction that was resulting from machine production meant a battle for consumers that was waged through advertising and promotion. The expense of finding buyers began to eat up the savings that resulted from the lower costs of machine manufacturing. Still, business appeared prosperous at the end of the decade. Reporting on business in 1929, the *Literary Digest* found almost all lines of business had done better. "Competition was keen and profit margins were narrow," it said, "but the volume of business done assured higher profits than in the previous year." And consumer spending was up despite higher prices. It went on:

> It was a year when machinery, power, and individual efficiency came into their own. A year ago the country owed its prosperity largely to the agriculturist. To-day the country owes its prosperity to the industrialist. Scores of industries are venturing into new fields, and the trend toward the self-sufficient unit providing its own raw materials, its own manufacturing plants, its own distributive system, and its own retail outlets, is marked.

It found "conditions are favorable for a six-month period which will make the 1929 calendar year the greatest ever known from an industrial viewpoint. The danger lies in low prices for farm products and the uncertainty as to the future of the farmer." But others warned of a possible recession, a "breathing spell to allow consumption to catch up more closely to production."[19]

Stuart Chase found "all competent economists" agreed "that purchasing power has not kept step with invention. Purchasing power is the final arbiter of all jobs under the prevailing financial system. Unless prices fall as fast as labour-saving devices increase, the saved labourer must whistle for employment. With a static price level, he will have to keep on whistling. Prices have not been declining rapidly in recent years." He furnished the following table to illustrate the decline of productive workers based on U.S. Department of Commerce figures:

	1919	1925	Decline
Agriculture	11,300,000	10,700,000	600,000
Mfg and mech.	10,670,000	9,770,000	900,000
RR	2,035,000	1,860,000	175,000
		Total:	1,675,000

"For a hundred years," Chase wrote, "every census tabulated an increasing number of persons employed in factories; now suddenly since the War, with an increasing population, there are fewer persons in factories. Something cardinal has happened; some mighty corner has been rounded." While factory production was rising, the number of factory employees was declining. In the five years between 1923 and 1928, more than 1.25 million factory workers had been permanently laid off.[20] The same had been the result of mechanization of railroads and other industries. Some worried that the higher level of unemployment in the spring of 1928 was only a harbinger of more to come in the form of a higher permanent unemployment level, since a growing number of industries were equipped to produce more than consumers had money to buy, besides replacing workers with machines. Shoe factories, for example, were said to be capable of producing 730,000,000 pairs of shoes annually, but less than half that number could be absorbed by the market, and it was held to be "typical of many industries." Stuart Chase was "seriously afraid that accelerating unemployment is here; that the park bench is destined to grow longer. The advertisers may be able to stimulate new wants that will take care of some of the displaced men, but who is to stimulate the purchasing power that will absorb the commodities new and old?"[21] Similarly the quantity of manufactured goods was increasing far more rapidly than the population.[22]

THE STOCK MARKET

The 1920s began and ended in a frenzy of speculation, and the result in each case was a stock market crash. Of the one that ushered in the decade, the New York *Journal of Commerce* reported a year after the Armistice that the speculative mania had not been confined only to stocks, but had extended to commodities and real estate. The Federal Reserve Board had acted to check the speculative mania on Wall Street, but it was still rampant elsewhere in the economy. A writer in *The Financial World* reported:

> In this country speculation has been rampant for quite nine out of the twelve months ... since Armistice Day, 1918. Up to Armistice Day anniversary, November 11, 1919, the New York Stock Exchange has records showing sales of stocks ... totaling 295,000,000 shares, against 140,000,000 shares in the previous 12 months, and sales of bonds ... double the previous year.

In response, the New York Federal Reserve Bank had raised its interest rate on November 1 to insure "an orderly return to normal credit conditions" and had also warned the banks against abetting speculation.

The result, one writer observed, was that "the professional speculators saw that the game was up; they sold; the support to the artificial prices crumbled away, and the outside speculators had to sell whether they wished to do so or not." Although the Federal Reserve might have acted earlier and less drastically, its action was generally praised. One likely result was a drop in the inflation that had caused a serious rise in the cost of living since the Armistice. Money freed from gambling in stocks could now be used to increase production.[23]

Once turned downward, however, stocks continued their decline. The *Wall Street Journal* reported in early 1921:

Stocks started to decline in November, 1919, and on top of this decline comes the sharp break of the last several weeks. The fortunes of many multimillionaires have shrunk 50 per cent. In some cases the shrinkage has been even greater. Hundreds of individuals who made fortunes running from a quarter of a million to a million dollars over the last five or six years are back to where they started, and the market continues to go down.

Nevertheless, it found the impact on general business conditions to be minimal.[24]

There followed soon after a boom in the market that continued virtually unabated through the 1920s, drawing many first-time investors who sensed the opportunity to make an easy profit. Everyone else seemed to be doing it, and failure to be in, and talking about, "the market" stamped one as a sluggard. Conservative financial writers and editors warned that stocks were overpriced and predicted a "day of reckoning," but the bull market continued.[25] Looking at the "forces behind the fever," the financial editor of the *New York Evening Post* concluded in December 1928 that the boom psychology had exploded after Hoover's election the previous month, when the market had "swung forward at a dizzy pace." "The fever," he wrote, "is in the air," and he added:

The stock tables are crowding everything else off the financial pages of our newspapers. ... Roughly 4,000 miles of tape are consumed in a typical six-million-share day to tick off the stock trades on the Exchange. Over 2,100 telephones connect the outside world with the floors of the Stock Exchange and over these wires flow 1,500,000 calls in a five-hour session.[26]

Two books published in the mid-1920s were credited with providing a major stimulus to stock purchases—*Investing in Purchasing Power*, by Kenneth S. van Strum, and *Common Stocks as Long-Term Investments*, by Edgar Lawrence Smith. It was the theme of these two authors that common stock was a preferred investment to bonds, since only stocks were likely to keep pace with inflation. The result, one writer observed, was to set off "the wildest confusion between investment and speculation in the mind of the moneyed American public, and it gave everyone with an itch for speculation and some surplus cash exactly the excuse needed." And the common stock craze spread "into the management of trust funds, of life insurance companies and of savings banks" in the form of a liberalization of the standards applied to investments, and modifications in the laws that had hitherto confined their portfolios to "real investment securities."[27]

It was also, one writer observed, "one of the outstanding social phenomena" of the bull market of the 1920s "that in its course women for the first time in this country on a large scale financially became people." She explained:

They have been swept along by some of the same urges that have carried shopkeepers and day laborers, clerks and farm hands, from every nook and corner of the country suddenly into a market which has been 80 to 90 per cent, speculative. But many brokers insist that a special cause—namely, the radio—has been largely responsible for advertising stock trading to the home woman and the farm woman who never before thought of Wall

Street. The review of the market for the day and Wall Street closing prices come over the loud speaker in the leisure hours of her afternoon, after the dinner dishes are washed and before she has . . . to get supper. She listens in just as she does to the health and the travel talks.

One brokerage house advertised that "one out of five of its many thousands of clients was a woman." "In the past year," another firm announced, "the growth of the woman investor and the woman speculator has been amazing, and it is getting larger almost weekly." In a few instances women now owned the majority of stock in large corporations. And there were even brokers who believed that women had contributed as much as men to the speculative stock market of 1927–29. In 1928 some 95,000 women as heads of families had made income tax returns on $400 million, and others had paid taxes on $1.5 billion. One woman stockbroker who handled 300 accounts reported having mainly business women as clients—buyers for department stores, small-shop owners, advertising writers, and others. Some of them were earning only $15,000 per year, but living on half and investing the rest. And there was also a growing number of women with inherited wealth—widows and daughters. Many women's magazines were offering investment information and advice. Women were making more money in the 1920s than ever before, providing them with more to invest, and wives were being given greater discretion in dealing with the family income during this prosperous decade.[28]

It was the purchase of wartime Liberty Bonds that exposed many Americans for the first time to the experience of investing their money in pieces of paper and led them on after the war into the riskier business of investing in stocks and bonds. As one such investor recalled:

I began my brief financial career in all innocence. The war left me a small legacy of Liberty Bonds of a species highly desirable to people overshadowed by income taxes. They were worth more than I paid for them. On excellent advice I sold them, and my financial adviser picked up another bond for me and gave me the change. In a month or so he reported that he had sold the bond and here were two hundred dollars, come out of the nowhere into the here, as profit on the transaction.

The next step was stock, a sound stock earning its own keep and liable to grow nicely without watering. I learned to watch its doings from day to day and to make interminable calculations on the backs of envelopes. My eye began to roam hungrily over the stock reports, and in no time at all I thought I knew my way about. I learned to talk the language. And so at last I secretly dismissed my financial adviser and took to my bosom a broker of my own, who taught me that stocks were made to buy and sell, subject to brokers' discounts.

After making a considerable paper profit in this way, however, the writer's confidence overcame his judgment.

I set my teeth firmly into a stock on which I had an inside tip promising fabulous profits. I was moderate enough; believing firmly the stuff would go to 75 or maybe a full century, I was ready to get out at 40 with no more than a 23 point gain. It went up all right.

It went up to 39 and stuck. And then it slipped. I refused to believe it, but it kept on slipping. I renewed my faith in it with more margin, but it responded neither to my trust nor my prayers. It just died on me. It went miserably, ignominiously, and with the feeble fluttering of a dying duck, all the way down to the cellar, where they hung it on a hook at 11 and let it go at that. Somewhere on the way I dropped out with a dull sickening thud, and woke up broke.

"A lot of people," he wrote, "are using the stock market as savings bank, as investment, and as a focus for their sense of property, all of which they once preferred to find elsewhere."[29] In the aggregate, they numbered millions whose economic future depended largely on a continued bull market. But if it collapsed?

One writer estimated that only a half million Americans were trading in stocks before World War I, whereas some 15 million were "in the market" in some fashion by early 1929. "This is the result," he wrote, "of many causes."

The Liberty Loan campaign opened the eyes of millions to the fact that there were securities called bonds and that money could be kept in other places besides the savings bank or under the mattress. Later the Allied Governments distributed large volumes of their securities throughout the country.

To this he added nearly a decade of prosperity that had "left the country with a larger surplus for investment than ever before." Moreover, a number of companies had made their stocks available to employees and customers, and "New York Stock Exchange ticker quotations are available at reasonable cost throughout the country," making it almost as easy to invest and follow the market in Iowa or California as on Wall Street. But whether the result added up to "fever or foresight" was a debatable question.[30] To these causes should perhaps be added the reduced taxes of the 1920s, when increased exemptions reduced the number of taxpayers from more than 4 million in 1924 to less than 2.5 million in 1927.[31]

Installment buying of stocks was effecting a revolution in securities buying, making it possible even for laborers to buy.[32] "One of the most profound changes since the war is the beginning of the new era of 'democratic finance,'" one observed opined. Instead of a small investing class of "capitalists," there had come into being a great investing public, including people of all kinds of occupations and incomes. At the same time there had, as a result, been created a new "nationwide interest in financial news" and the selling of stocks and bonds through local or nationwide campaigns of advertising in magazines and newspapers. Financial advertising was a new feature of American life. The World War had caused European holders of American securities to dump their holdings on the American market increasing the number of railroad stockholders in America from 660,645 to 989,949 and—

In the entire field of finance, including all utilities, packers, oil, iron and steel, manufacturing and distributive industries, this story was paralleled. Three things had happened. The impact of the war had broken the levees of narrowly centralized control; the Government Thrift Stamp and Liberty Bond campaigns had given millions their first lesson in investing; America's huge gold reserve, with the collapse of foreign buying power, had turned inward a flood of productive capital incessantly seeking a wider investment market.

Capital immediately saw the possibilities of furthering and using this wide dispersal of securities in stabilizing industry and in building good-will. Employees were urged to purchase stock, intensive customer-ownership campaigns were carried on. In the above period of seven years, gas, electric light and power companies gained 815,955 customer stockholders, 75,000 employee stockholders, and 470,324 stockholders from the general public.

A study by the National Industrial Conference Board of the purchasers of fifty or more shares of a new stock issued by a large public utility corporation revealed fifty-seven occupations or trades, which included:

Accountants—166
Artists—81
Bakers—153
Barbers—155
Beauty culturists—52
Bricklayers—65
Butchers—115
Carpenters—483
Chauffeurs—601
Clerks—2,987
Domestics—623
Draftsmen—149
Dressmakers—372
Electricians—582
Engineers—558
Factory workers—1,058
Foremen—518
Housekeepers—4,029
Janitors—119
Laborers—499
Laundry workers—65
Machinists—499
Metal workers—157
Mail carriers—115
Mechanics—530
Messengers—91
Nurses—274

Painters—182
Plasterers—60
Plumbers—257
Policemen—347
Printers—335
Railroad men—312
Seamen—51
Secretaries—314
Bankers and brokers—65
Dentists—63
Doctors—146
Lawyers—77
Managers—496
Manufacturers—153
Merchants—926

As only purchasers of fifty shares were included, each of the above subscriptions represented an investment of at least $5,000.

Two electric companies also analyzed their sale of stock to 13,856 purchasers. Here are the occupations of the nine largest groups who purchased:

Housewives—3,347
Miners—1,054
Clerks—949
Salesmen—401
Schoolteachers—336
Laborers—326
Stenographers—256
Farmers—237
Grocers and butchers—178

One of the smallest groups in the above was listed as "capitalists." The housewives outnumbered them one hundred to one.[33]

Clearly, America had suddenly become a nation of savers and investors. In 1925 savings per capita were double the figure in 1912. The American Bankers Association reported that total savings deposits had increased during that period from approximately $8.5 billion to nearly $21 billion, while per capita savings had increased from $89 to $186, and the number of depositors tripled. While the ABA may have exaggerated the increase, it is clear that savings in commercial banks, savings banks, and savings-and-loan companies at least doubled in total between 1921 and 1925, as did investments in common stocks. Ironically in 1925 consumer credit had also quadrupled the total the previous year. Instead of diverting savings to consumption, Americans seemed to be resorting to installment buying. In 1925 installment credit for automobiles, alone, surged about 40 percent past 1924 to over $900 million, as auto sales jumped by about 20 percent to over 3.7 million vehicles.[34]

The New York *Journal of Commerce* pointed out that banks needed to find investments for these burgeoning deposits, but noted that the opportunities for sound investments were limited, and it worried that the unused savings were tempting banks to make unwise investments. Even school students were involved, with over 3 million of them enrolled in "school savings banks" with deposits of $20.5 million in 1924.[35] While all savings entered the stream of investment, they were separate from the money invested directly by individuals, many of whom were, as noted earlier, using the stock market as their savings bank.

In 1928 the State of New York, under Governor Franklin D. Roosevelt, liberalized its investment laws to allow savings banks and insurance companies to invest in classes of securities heretofore barred to them. Clearly the feeling was growing that the field of safe investment was widening. Financial authorities estimated that somewhere between $2,000,000,000 and $3,000,000,000 worth of electric, gas, and telephone bonds would now be eligible for investment by New York savings institutions.

One banker argued that the increase in savings bank deposits in New York State had made it necessary to expand the list of investments. "While deposits have doubled in the last ten years, and in the year just ended have increased over $300,000,000, the available legal bond investments have remained about stationary." But now investors could buy new classes of municipal bonds, railroad bonds, gas and electric company bonds, and telephone company bonds.[36]

In 1928 Federal Reserve Banks raised rediscount rates from 4 to 4½ percent "following an increase in Wall Street brokers' loans to a total of over $4,000,000,000 and a spurt of the time money rate up to 6 per cent." This was expected to dampen speculation, since easy money had been "one of the fundamental supports of the present market." The FRB had reported brokers loans totaled $4,129,001,000 on April 18, 1928, and these "enormous sums are being devoted to speculation instead of business."[37]

In early February 1929, the Federal Reserve Board tried again to put a psychological damper on the frenzied stock market by warning that for the past year the "excessive amount of the country's credit absorbed in speculative security loans" was having "detrimental effects on business and may impair its future." The effect was to increase the cost of credit for "legitimate" business use. But the "Fed" was loath to do much more than scold. Raising the interest rate to curb borrowing for stock speculation would likewise make credit more expensive for business and would also attract a flow of gold from England in search of the higher rates. Since 1927 the Fed had followed a policy designed to stimulate gold exports rather than imports. However, the British raised their interest rate early in February, which now made it possible for the FRB to do the same. The combination of the FRB's "scolding" and the British interest rate increase caused a sharp dip in stock prices.[38]

The New Republic pointed out that many speculators were buying stocks on the margin—paying a small amount of cash and borrowing the rest. It added:

> Brokers belonging to the Stock Exchange had by the end of January [1929] borrowed $6,735,000,000 to lend to their customers just for this purpose. That amounts to about one-fourteenth of the entire national income for a year. How much more the purchasers borrowed from other sources than these brokers it is impossible to say.

The speculative fever had made investors impervious to the high interest rates being charged on broker loans, but the effect had been to make credit too expensive for business borrowing.

> It has, for example, tightened building credit. This is beginning to restrict construction—one of the mainstays of prosperity. The high rates which call loans command have also attracted large sums from business concerns.... This money is, while it is loaned to speculators, not being used for current production of goods or new construction. The credit resources of the country, while large, are not inexhaustible. The more they are attracted to loans to speculators, the less they can be employed for the actual production and exchange of goods which make the profits anticipated by the speculators.

And the higher stock prices rose, the greater the demand for broker loans by speculators. Absent a brake on such loans, the country seemed headed for a smashup.[39]

Some, however, wondered how much impact the Federal Reserve could have, since, as the *Washington Star* pointed out, "most of the money used in speculation is coming not from member banks of the Federal Reserve System, but from individuals and corporations over whom the banks exercise no direct control."[40]

Noting that brokers' loans had increased from $3 billion in February 1927 to nearly $7 billion just two years later, Charles Merz wrote:

> There are still men left in the spring of 1929 who do not thumb their way straight to the stock news when they have had one fleeting glance at the first-page headlines in their evening papers, but the number of such men is smaller than in the spring of 1928; and the account-books of every brokerage firm in a broad nation show the names of schoolteachers, seamstresses, barbers, machinists, necktie salesmen, gas-fitters, motormen, family cooks, and lexicographers who have taken their first dip in the market in the last two years. The ticker tape runs on. And to a greater extent than ever before in its history the whole country has been buying stocks, selling stocks, trading stocks, assessing profits, covering close margins with fresh capital, and following with increasing interest the broad line in the market graphs....

The impact on American life, Merz concluded, had been profound. For one, there had been a "breaking down ... of certain ethical values and many household mottoes which were recently in their prime." Speculation was no longer regarded as a form of gambling, and few still believed that "a penny saved is a penny earned." "The spectacular profits reaped by nit-wits at some points in this astonishing bull market," Merz explained, "have come among these maxims with the disruptive force among the fables of the Bible." For another, the stockbroker had achieved new prestige: "Like the Advice-to-the Lovelorn columns and the modern psychologist, he is that combination confessor-advisor which the stress of strenuous times demands. . . . " The branch offices of brokerage firms had become the 1920s equivalent of the preprohibition saloon, with "the same swinging doors, the same half-darkened windows, the same community of interest once the threshold has been crossed." Speculation had become the "new national sport" that had replaced all other fads of the 1920s in popularity. Finally, it had "profoundly altered the attitudes of a great many Americans toward 'Big Business.'" Merz explained:

> A fabulously rich and prosperous corporation may be an octopus when it is selling gasoline at twenty-two cents a gallon instead of seventeen, but it is no octopus when some of its stock, even on margin, is in the hands of the customer who has recently been groaning. In this case it becomes either a benevolent philanthropic institution whose purposes have been greatly misunderstood and whose services to humanity are ridiculously undervalued, or a jolly partner in an admitted hold-up which must not be complained of too vociferously lest Congress come along with an investigation.

This change in attitude toward business had "contributed vastly to the political conservatism which has been characteristic of this country in recent years," a marked break from the prewar political currents "when the American people were deeply suspicious of huge alliances of capital and stubbornly determined to break them into manageable units." The nation, in short, had wrapped its political insurgency, at least temporarily, in ticker tape from the stock exchanges.[41]

A prominent psychologist had his own explanation for the speculation phenomenon. Dr. John B. Watson opined: "Even sex has become so free and abundant in recent years that it no longer provides the thrill that it once did, and gambling in Wall Street is about the only real excitement that we have left."[42]

By April of 1929, however, there was increasing attention being given to the "war" on speculation by the Federal Reserve Board. While most agreed that the frenzy needed to be tamed, for a variety of reasons already touched upon, the issue was how to do so without creating a panic in the market. The whole base on which this grotesque house of cards now rested, including the $7 billion worth of broker loans, was the expectation that stock prices would continue to rise. Withdraw that likelihood and the market must inexorably collapse, wiping out millions of investors and in the process making much of that $7 billion unrecoverable. Yet it appeared that the speculators who were driving up stock prices and the volume of brokers' loans could not be dissuaded by anything short of a full-blown panic. The Federal Reserve Board clearly should have acted before the boom psychology of 1928–29 had taken the situation beyond control.[43] But even in mid-1929 the speculators were fighting "like tigers against restraining action," *The New Republic* observed a week later, "And why shouldn't they? The stakes are immense, speculation being now a major industry." Speculation in 1928 had been twice as great as in 1925. It was an "exceedingly prosperous" industry, yielding greater profits than any other. *The New Republic* explained:

> While the net income of all corporations declined slightly in 1927 over 1923, the net income of financial institutions (other than insurance) increased 93 per cent.... The profits of 1,042 industrial and commercial corporations in 1928 increased 17 per cent over 1927, against 70 percent for financial institutions.
>
> Speculative profits reported by income-taxpayers in 1925–1927 increased 250 percent over 1918–1920—from $2,311,091,000 to $8,122,268,000, while corporate dividends increased only 85 percent.
>
> The earnings of brokers on the New York Stock Exchange in 1928 amounted to more than $400,000,000, an average of $367,000 for each of the 1,100 members, exclusive of speculative profits.

"But," it added, "while speculation flourishes, mass prosperity is comparatively stagnant," the frenzy of speculation since 1925 roughly coinciding "with a relative decline of prosperity measured in terms of the production and mass consumption of goods."[44] Even in 1926 there were 11,000 millionaires in the United States—one out of every 10,450 Americans.[45] A New York investment banker analyzed 1928 income tax returns and concluded that 41 percent of the nation's wealth was controlled by women.[46]

The Federal Reserve's "jawboning" of speculation in early February had only a brief impact on the market. By May *World's Work* was editorializing about "Another New High," writing:

> The entire world is possessed of an up-and-up frenzy at the present moment. Everything is going higher, nothing can go lower. So buy, buy, buy! There is a bull market in stocks, a bull market in real estate, a bull market in antiques, in works of art, in books. Millionaires are multiplying so rapidly that the income-tax collectors can hardly keep track of them. It is difficult to meet anyone anywhere who will not tell you about his or her latest gambling profit. Up and up! Up and up! No wonder this extraordinary phrase is the latest thing in slang. No one anywhere wants anything to come down.[47]

Wall Street, one writer recalled, had within the lifetimes of many around in 1929 been regarded as the

> festering place of our national ailments, breeding place of dastardly, but legal skullduggery. There dwelt the Morgans, the Goulds, the Carnegies, huge bloated figures with dollar signs on their waistcoats and widows' scalps on their belts.... Wall Street stood for a good part of what was detestable upon the American financial scene; and the men who moved there were carnivores of the more loathesome sort. But that was yesterday.... Today Wall Street is the nation and Wall Street is more Wall Street than Wall Street ever was—or probably ever will be. Wall Street is a state of mind; 20,000,000 men and women—investors and speculators—are its corporeal being; and the chattering tape that runs under the glass domes of 12,000 tickers, up hill and down dale, are its hypersensitive nervous system.... Prosperity is the match-maker that inspired this mating which,

twenty years ago, would have been damned as miscegenation.... Go anywhere in the country, look east or west, and you will observe, wherever there is a city of respectable proportions, there is at least one brokerage house.... Pennsylvania has 599 New York Stock Exchange bond and stock tickers, Illinois has 428, Virginia has 46, Ohio has 155, Oklahoma has 15, Texas has 38, California has 155, and Michigan, with 110, has only 59 less than Massachusetts.... Thousands of direct wires link these brokerage houses to the floor of the Exchange in New York.[48]

From time to time, as the bull market kept on soaring to new record heights, it was realized that money must have been going out of the savings banks into speculative Wall Street accounts. But until recently, as a writer notes on the investment page of the *New York Evening Post,* figures have failed to show any actual decline in savings deposits, "altho the shrinkage has been gaining momentum." Now, however, comes the definite statement that after twenty years of annual increase, the savings accounts of the country show a decline. According to the American Bankers' Association report, savings accounts for the year ending June 29 last showed a total drop of $195,305,000 below that of the previous year. This is attributed to "the lure of profits to be made in stocks." Also a decline in the number of savings depositors of over 50,000. Some suspected there had been an even larger drop for the second half of 1929.[49]

In mid-1929 the federal government launched a campaign against "stock swindlers, 'racketeers,' operators of 'financial speak-easies,' and all kinds of shady brokerage houses and bucket-shop keepers" that was attracting considered media attention as "being the first instance in which the Government has made a determined and sweeping attack on nationally operated stock swindles" using the federal government's authority over the mails. The campaign was "aimed at four targets—those selling stocks in worthless companies, those who sold stocks and then left without delivering the goods, those who run bucket-shops, and those operating through fraudulent tipster sheets," and it had already "started several on the road to Atlanta [prison], and ... caused a legion of financial racketeers to fold their tents and silently steal away."[50]

And then came the crash, with the vindication of all those who had voiced warnings of its inevitability. The explanations for the crash, in hindsight, were for the most part the same as those given for its inevitability. Predictably, most blame was placed with the Federal Reserve Board. *The Nation* wrote:

The trouble began in the summer of 1927, when the Federal Reserve gambled on the chance of precipitating a speculative orgy in this country by reducing its discount rate with the object of aiding the financial rehabilitation of Europe. In the succeeding fall and winter it released some $500,000,000 to $600,000,000 of credit available for speculative purposes by its purchases of government bonds. As the speculative fever rose the Board, instead of gradually curtailing credit, helped it to expand, putting out increasing quantities of Reserve notes and actually maintaining for some time a discount rate lower than the market rate for prime commercial paper. Leading financiers and the editors of financial journals pointed out again and again the danger of the policy which was being pursued, but with as little apparent effect as if they had spoken to the wind. When, at last, the situation began clearly to spell disaster and far-seeing investors prepared to get out of the market, the Board bludgeoned the market with veiled threats; when finally it acted, its action was drastic and too late.... The responsibility of the Federal Reserve, weighty as it is, must be shared by the Coolidge and Hoover administrations. For two years and more, while calamity was preparing, the country was again and again assured from Washington that everything was all right—industry prosperous, business good, savings increasing, the outlook fine. No warning has come from the Potomac to give the country pause—nothing but smug official complacence in a situation rotten to the core. One wonders, now that the mischief is done, whether the people who have been misled will forget, or whether they will remember.[51]

New York's Guarantee Trust Company voiced a slightly different perspective, both on the causes of the runaway bull market and the reasons for its collapse, laying the blame largely on the millions of inexperienced investors who had entered the market and on the "mob psychology" that influenced their actions. The company wrote that the perfectly normal bull market of the 1920s had been

immensely exaggerated by the changed character of the investing public ... partly as a result of the wide buying of government securities during the war and partly by reason of the diffusion of income in the last decade which has enabled vast numbers of people to enter the investment field on their own account for the first time. Security dealers were quick to take advantage of this change by establishing offices in cities and towns throughout the country. These offices, in turn, attracted thousands of inexperienced persons into the ranks of stock-market speculators, where neither their financial knowledge nor their financial strength entitled them to be.

Thus, the public that has, to a considerable extent, determined the course of the stock market in the last few years is a public uninformed as to intelligent procedure in buying and selling securities. It was easily subjected to psychological reactions of an exaggerated sort, buying and selling en masse without any clear understanding of the reasons for doing so. Altho [sic] there has always been an element of mob psychology in the actions of the investing public, this element has been increased manyfold by the changes of recent years.... When the realization finally came that prices of many securities were out of all proportion to present and prospective earning power, the reaction was similarly exaggerated. Not only did the fear of loss impel a rush of liquidation, but the disorder was increased by the fact that innumerable small speculators, unable to supplement their impaired margins, were precipitated into the market against their own will. Just as the efforts of the public to make the most of the rising prices results in a buying wave that pushes values too high, so the fear of loss forces a reaction that inevitably depresses the prices of stocks below their true worth.

Echoing the Guaranty Survey, another investment authority suggested that one salutary outcome of the crash was likely to be a search for sound financial advice by investors in the future, rather than a reliance on "the butcher, the baker, and the candlestick maker." The "new economics" of the 1920s was also discredited, an economic doctrine that had held:

(1) That common stocks are good or better investments than bonds—that with diversification they are just as safe and hold more chance of profit. (2) That stock prices, partly

because of public belief in the above theory, were permanently on a higher plane. (3) That the investment trust has stabilized the market. (4) That the public has maintained such heavy margins that no break is possible. (5) That because of these facts stock speculation had in fact become safe for the average man, and that almost any one could make money at it. (6) That the day of severe Stock Exchange breaks was over.[52]

6
Eugenics and Intelligence Testing

EUGENICS

The image of an ebullient and optimistic America in the 1920s is only part of the story, as we have seen. The decade was also one of a profound pessimism that expressed itself in some of the more negative movements and ideas of the 1920s, including eugenics, intelligence testing, immigration restriction, the Ku Klux Klan, fundamentalism, and birth control. The intent of all these movements was to try to preserve the control over America of the "best" classes in the country, at a time when that control seemed threatened by their declining numbers in the face of the rising numbers of the "less desirable" classes, and to turn back the clock and calendar to simpler times.

Horace Kallen, reviewing Seth Humphries' *Mankind: Racial Values and the Racial Prospect*, touched critically on these concerns, but conceded much to the eugenicists, when he wrote:

> The pity of his utterance lies in the perversion it operates on certain eugenic considerations of great importance, and altogether independent of the mythology with which it is applied. That the superior are for a variety of reasons infertile, that the multiplication of the inferior is excessive, that the war has produced an inevitable disproportion of females to males, in which the breeding of the superior is placed at a still greater disadvantage, are all matters deserving the greatest attention of the classes concerned with the conservation of the race, in whatever nation. That the principle which must govern the use of any chosen remedy in this situation must involve an enhanced reproduction of the eugenically fit and a greatly diminished reproduction of the eugenically unfit cannot be too much stressed. And it is true also that such a principle must needs generate very definite changes in the conventions of sex.

What Kallen deplored was the injection of race into such considerations, which served only to "blur and depreciate important conceptions of this sort."[1]

An article by Professor Leon J. Cole for *Scientific Monthly* traced the racial aspect of the eugenicist argument to Darwinism as interpreted by the Germans. Quoting from a collection of essays by Professor Vernon Kellogg, late of the Belgian Relief Commission and the American Relief Administration, Cole cited the creed of German biologists and natural philosophers "of a natural selection based on violent and competitive struggle." According to the Germans:

> The struggle not only must go on, for that is the natural law, but it should go on, so that this natural law may work out in its cruel inevitable way the salvation of the human species. By its salvation is meant desirable natural evolution. That human group which is in the most advanced evolutionary stage as regards internal organization and form of social relationship is best, and should, for the sake of the species, be preserved at the expense of the less advanced, the less effective.

Thus the whole racial thrust of the eugenics movement was based on an attempt to twist Darwinism to justify the dominance of some races over others in the name of an evolution that would benefit the human race in general.[2]

In a review of a work by Dr. Robert H. Lowie, *Current Opinion* wrote:

> The processes of natural selection are painfully slow, explains Doctor Lowie, but a conscious controller who should prevent the propagation of inferior strains and promote the early and prolific multiplication of superior individuals might greatly accelerate development along the predestined path. Mankind would then rapidly gain a higher evolutionary stage, at which the average representative of the species might well equal today's exceptional genius.[3]

In an address to the Eugenics Association in 1920, its president, Dr. Stewart Paton, of Princeton, called attention to the pivotal moment in world history that existed after the war and wondered if democracy would be equal to the opportunities and challenges of the postwar years. He questioned whether there could be "any more important service ... rendered to a government than is expressed in the purpose of this society to study man in order to find out first, what the forces are in his personality that would both quicken the development of his reasoning power and second assisting in the gradual elimination from the human race of those traits that make it easy for man to-day to wish intemperately while limiting his capacity to reason connectedly."

The Eugenics Society, he said, could not "afford to be even indirectly associated with any propaganda or uplift that is purely emotionally directed." He then told the society:

> The science of eugenics, as we all know, is still in its infancy, and its development should be directed along rational lines. A false step, the result of an enthusiasm often born of the best intentions, but not held strictly in check by reason, may have unfortunate results and give some justification to the the reproach that this movement ... is a fad. The possible good that may eventually be accomplished by the selective breeding of

human beings is a subject making such a striking appeal to the active imagination that the preliminary preparation necessary for the patient search for the essential facts may be forgotten or completely ignored.

The groundwork needed to be prepared by a study of the human personality at least as rigorous as those of "dogs or horses used for breeding purposes," together with studies of human anatomy, physiology, and psychology. This meant that an enormous amount of work must "be accomplished in laying the foundations of the science of eugenics before positive direct recommendations for improving the racial prospects are made to the public; except urging the use of selective methods in breeding to eliminate the unfit."[4]

When Professor Irving Fisher of Yale University was elected president of the Eugenics Research Association in 1921, his inaugural address told eugenicists:

> There is now a golden opportunity for eugenicists to "gear in," so to speak, with the great world of events. It was the dream of [Sir Francis] Galton that eugenics should not forever remain academic, but that, being the vital concern of us all, it should become a sort of religion. Hitherto eugenics has been largely studied "microscopically," that is, by special technical laboratory investigations. The next step is to study it more "telescopically," that is by observations of the general facts of human history.

The loss of 7 million of the best-fitted men in the World War was one that could not easily be made up without progress in eugenics. Fisher wrote:

> If nothing of the sort happens and there should be lacking the brains and energy to accomplish at least some of these things, then surely the dark ages lie ahead of us. The Nordic race will, as Madison Grant says, vanish or lose its dominance if, in fact, the whole human race does not sink so low as to become the prey, as H.G. Wells imagines, of some less degenerate animal!

Fisher opposed specialized care for the "biologically unfit, especially when such differential care is not accompanied by safeguarding against the marriage of the unfit." The population of the earth was growing so rapidly, and the empty spaces filling up, that the expansion in numbers must end within a generation or two.

> What will be the eugenic significance of this future limiting of population? This is one of the great questions for eugenic research. The answer will doubtless depend largely on which of the two checks will be put on population, whether it is to be the check from an increased death rate operating through lack of subsistence or the check from a decreased birth rate operating by volition of parents.
>
> The former check shown by Malthus led Darwin to conceive his theory of natural selection, which in turn led Galton to suggest eugenics.... To-day we have, in a way and to a degree of which Malthus probably never dreamed, the exercise of this prudential check under the title of neo-Malthusianism or birth-control.
>
> Until recently this subject was not discussed in the open, partly because the movement had not gained sufficient momentum, partly because of the conventional reticence on all matters of sex and partly because of the continual existence (in this country alone

among the nations of the earth) of laws passed at the instigation, chiefly of Anthony Comstock, forbidding the dissemination of information on birth-control.

But the subject is one especially deserving eugenic research; for, of all human inventions, those relating to birth-control probably have the most direct bearing on the birth rate and its selective possibilities.

Birth control was "largely a development of 'feminism' in the interests of women" that opened "up amazing possibilities of race extinction or, on the other hand, of race betterment." Fisher explained:

If the birth-control exercised by individual parents could itself be controlled by a eugenic committee it could undoubtedly become the surest and most supremely important means of improving the human race. We could breed out the unfit and breed in the fit. We could in a few generations and, to some extent even in the life time of us of to-day conquer degeneracy, dependency and delinquency, and develop a race far surpassing not only our own but the ancient Greeks.

Unfortunately, the educated class was bearing few children, leading Fisher to write:

At present, then, our educational system seems to be destroying the very material on which it works! Colleges seem to be engines for the mental suicide of the human race! Are the colleges of to-day sterilizing our scholars as did the monasteries and nunneries of the middle ages? Such race suicide of scientific and educated men and of the well-to-do classes means that their place will speedily be taken by the unintelligent, uneducated and inefficient.

To that point, then, birth control seemed to be working against the race, a situation that could only be rectified if birth control was extended to all classes instead of just the higher classes. Fisher then took up the issue of immigration, noting that "the character of the present immigration will make a great difference in the character of our future inhabitants." Moreover,

If we allow ourselves to be a dumping ground for relieving Europe of its burden of defectives, delinquents and dependents ... it would be quite contrary to the interests of humanity for the future. Not only should we be giving these undesirable citizens far greater opportunity to multiply than they had at home, but we would be taking away the checks on the multiplication of those left at home. It would be a step backward, a step towards populating the earth with defectives, delinquents and dependents. That the foreign born multiply faster than the native stock has been shown by the Immigration Commission and by East, Dublin, Baker and others. There is great danger, therefore, not only to this country, but to the whole world, of injuring the germ plasma of the human race by the indiscriminate immigration of recent times.... If it be granted that, from our standpoint, at least, indiscriminate immigration is dysgenic, a discriminating exclusion must be eugenic.

Fisher then took up another aspect of the movement, intelligence testing, writing:

> In our public schools should also be included educational and mental measurements. They are rapidly coming into use in our colleges and universities throughout the nation. They emphasize individual differences and will serve to correct the view that "men are created equal" in the biological sense while leaving them equal in opportunity before the law.

Fisher concluded:

> I believe in Galton's idea that eugenics must be a religion. It will prove a wonderful touchstone by which to distinguish between what is racially and radically right and what is racially and radically wrong.... It will throw its searchlight into every nook and cranny in the life of the individual and of society.
>
> Therefore it will help mould all human institutions. Especially will it help mould that fundamental institution, human marriage. While marriage is a most intensely individual and private matter, it has been regarded, from time immemorial, as of vital concern to society.... And just as law and religion discriminate and refuse their seal of approval to alliances which are found improper from their respective viewpoints, so must science discriminate. Dysgenic marriages must be discountenanced just as bigamous or incestuous marriages are discountenanced.[5]

Following the International Eugenics Conference held in New York in September, 1921, Edwin Slosson wrote in *The Independent*:

> The foundations of the science of eugenics have now been solidly laid in the vast amount of statistical and experimental work that has been done on heredity during the present century. Psychology has recently come to the aid of eugenics in devising tests of inborn intelligence, which are sufficiently and measurably accurate and are independent of education, wealth, race, and social position. Stock and strains bearing the determinants of the highest intellectual and moral qualities, as well as dangerous and incurable defects, can now be identified and traced with considerable certainly, But it does not yet appear how this new knowledge can be applied for the advance and salvation of the race.

The leaders of the movement, he wrote, were

> looking forward to the education of the people and the cultivation of "the eugenic conscience" in individuals, so that it will come to be regarded as a public disgrace and personal sin if those who have received a fine inheritance fail to pass it on to the coming generation, and if those who have a serious hereditary taint should perpetuate it in their posterity. To educate a whole people to such a sense of their duty to their race would seem an impossible prospect. Yet it is the best and perhaps the only way to accomplish this vital aim.[6]

A Harvard psychology professor described "Eugenia," his eugenic utopia, for *Scribner's*:

> Civilizations decay because they die off at the top; because, as they become increasingly complex, they cease to produce in sufficient numbers men and women of the moral and intellectual caliber needed for their support. So long as a nation produces in each generation a fair number of persons of first-rate caliber, it can carry an enormous tail, without fatal decline. But the number of such persons tends to become not only relatively but ab-

solutely fewer with each generation; because civilized societies breed from the bottom and die off at the top. . . . The supply of persons of first-rate caliber can only be maintained by the fruitful mating of persons of superior strains. At present, as in all highly civilized societies, such persons tend to be absolutely or relatively infertile. Eugenia is a scheme for bringing persons of such strains together in fertile unions which will give to the world an increasing number of persons of similar caliber.

This was not as selfish and elitist as it sounded, since:

Eugenia is not to be ruled by a selfish regard for itself. It will be animated by the spirit of world-service. Its children will be brought up with the noble ambition to serve the world. They will be aristocrats, but their tradition will be *noblesse oblige*. The community will be a closed one for the purposes of marriage and education only. Membership in the community will be attained in every case by formal admission, after fullest inquiry into the family history and intellectual and moral qualifications of each candidate.[7]

The president of a British eugenics society visiting the United States, told his audience:

Eugenics aims at increasing the rate of multiplication of stocks above the average in heritable qualities, and at decreasing that rate in the case of stocks below the average. But if the banner under which we are to fight should only have inscribed on it some such arid definition of policy as this, our defeat would be certain. We must prove that we are under the guidance of a noble ideal. We of this generation are responsible for the production of the next generation and, therefore, of all mankind in the future; and all in whom this sense of racial responsibility acts as a deep-seated sentiment . . . are in truth guided by the eugenic ideal. The belief that man has been slowly developed from some ape-like progenitor came toward the close of the last century to be nearly universally held by thoughtful persons; this belief gave rise to a new hope that this upward march of mankind might be continued in the future; and out of this new hope sprang the eugenic ideal.[8]

Present modes of breeding were dangerously unscientific, Albert Edward Wiggam wrote, and the only hope of civilization was to keep the unfit from breeding. "We are anti-Burbanking the human race at every point. Burbank selects his best species for parents. There is no mystery about it. Farmers have done this ever since Eden. But in the human family, when civilized, we select our worst." By setting up high rewards for ambition, civilization sterilized its strongest and ablest men and women, because few could have their selfish desires gratified and still have time or money left for children. "We can not select parents as the farmer selects his plants and animals," Wiggam wrote. "But we can absolutely prevent the criminalistic, pauperistic, feeble-minded, insane and epileptic stocks from reproducing their kind."[9]

In an article by Ellsworth Huntington in the *Yale Review*, he pointed out that in the past the upper classes had increased more rapidly than the lower, due to higher birth rates and lower mortality, but the opposite was now true. Various factors, including industrialization, urbanization, ease of divorce, improved public health, and birth control, had caused the upper classes to decline in numbers, while the lower classes were burgeoning. The progress of science, moreover, had made it possible for people "to increase and multiply as never before." The time had come, however, when this increase in population must stop." The abundant new freedoms available to people had given "nature an unexampled opportunity to preserve one kind of people rather than another." The group that was increasing most rapidly was that "useful only for manual labor, they are relatively stupid even at that, and their present freedom from disease, war, famine, and the other ills that reduced the number of their kind in the past makes it possible for them to increase enormously. They are the sort who make democracy a farce because millions of them can be led by the nose." Unfortunately, the birth rate fell as the scale of ability rose, so that it was not only the "excessive survival rate among the relatively stupid and incompetent" that was a problem, but also "the low survival rate close to the top among some millions of people—perhaps ten or twelve—who are endowed with high intelligence and high ability." If the trend continued, the valuable types would decline even more in relation to the numbers of the incompetent. Eventually, the "intelligent middle class, who form the very life of our civilization, will almost disappear," leaving a country populated with "a vast body of ignorant and rather stupid lower class people," dominated by a small number of upper-class aristocrats. "Is that we want?" Huntington asked. "Can such a condition be stable?" The only way to avoid it was to "cut off the great surplus of children among the less competent" and build the number among the upper middle class," thus producing "a population which is biologically sound, and which is able to maintain a civilization that constantly makes greater demands upon the human intellect and upon man's moral nature." But Huntington furnished no strategies for accomplishing that end.[10]

An anonymous author in *Harper's* gave a "biological forecast" of the national future. On interbreeding and amalgamation of races:

> All this will make for extreme variability in the future American race; and if only we had the means of eliminating all inferior combinations, as the breeder of animals and plants does, we might expect to produce a very superior race in future America. Unfortunately, we do not now have this power, and there is little probability that we shall ever be able to apply to our human stock the principles of good animal breeding.
>
> Under these circumstances it seems probable that our history will repeat that of many ancient civilizations. There are many parallels between our history and that of Greece and Rome at the height of their greatness. Now, as then, we see a general decadence of the family and of marriage, a great extension of voluntary birth-control and sterility among the better classes, and the consequent breeding of the race from the lower levels rather than from the top. Now, as then, we see the importation of vast numbers of alien and inferior stock and general race mixture. Now, as then, we see the gradual extinction of the most gifted lines as a result of the dry-rot of luxury, the subordination of social duties to personal freedom, the demand for pleasure at any price. Now, as then, we hear the counsel of despair, "Let us eat, drink and be merry, for tomorrow we die."[11]

Citing results of the army's IQ testing during World War I, Professor Carl Brigham, of Princeton, developed an argument in behalf of "Nordic" intellectual supremacy, only to be challenged by other scholars with having left out consideration of the effects of education and training. Professor William Bagley pointed out that the children of African Americans who had moved north, and had been educated in northern schools, often got better scores than southern whites. He also pointed out that states "in which the white population shows the highest proportion of Nordic blood have both the poorest schools and the lowest white 'intelligence,' as measured by Army [tests], by adult white literacy, by the distribution of public libraries, by the proportion of leaders produced, and by every other standard that has been suggested."[12]

By the late 1920s concern over such changes in the internal character of the nation's population were in part being superseded by concerns over the "decline and fall" of the white race, in relation to other races, as birth rates in Great Britain and its dominions, as well as in the United States, began to suggest a declining population in the Anglo-Saxon world.[13] But into the early 1930s the link between birth control and eugenics continued to be made, an English writer observing in 1932 that eugenicists advocated birth control for very different reasons than many of its supporters. The eugenicist would "not be primarily actuated by a desire to spare the working-class mother avoidable suffering, but rather by the consideration that on racial grounds the fertility of the 'lower orders' should be restricted." This was "negative" eugenics, "positive" eugenics being the encouragement of larger families on the part of the more desirable classes. But there was strong opposition to "negative" eugenics:

> While freely conceding that "heredity plays a part" in the breeding of race-horses and live-stock, and that it has been the dominant factor in the process of artificial selection by which we have acquired our domesticated plants, many people refuse to acknowledge that it has any significant bearing on human beings. The man who fervently believes that all men have equal rights, often further believes that they have equal endowments and attitudes.

Nevertheless, there were "two large groups of people who should be supplied with means for limiting or preventing the output of children." These were those "who exhibit or carry hereditary diseases or defects," and "those who are innately so ill-endowed in respect of the characteristics that make for useful citizenships that they prove themselves to be incorrigibly burdensome to the community."[14]

Late in the 1920s, George A. Dorsey essentially demolished the eugenicists and Nordic supremacists, calling them "heredity mongers," and writing that

> the amount of false biology, infantile logic, and bad faith that these heredity mongers bring to bear on our enormously complicated and complex racial and cultural problems is unbelievable. Wittingly or unwittingly, they juggle biologic, psychologic, and cultural factors to suit their convenience, and pour forth flimsy arguments based on dogmatic and unfounded assumptions as scientific facts to gratify their race phobia. They demand attention solely because of their prominence or academic standing, or because as 'best sellers' they attempt to mould American civilization in ways biologically unwarranted and socially false and misleading.

"The World War," he wrote, "produced a recrudescence of race phobia that has not yet run its course or possibly reached the height of its virulence." He traced the obsession with pure Aryan or Nordic races to a Scotsman, Houston Stewart Chamberlain, and its movement to America to Alfred P. Schultz, who wrote *Race or Mongrel* in 1908. Madison Grant's *The Passing of the Great Race* (1916) had then "let loose" on the public "the doctrine of a specific Nordic race." The book, he wrote, could not have attained the standing it did were it not for the endorsement of Professor Henry Fairchild Osborn, who wrote prefaces for two editions. Another spurious advocate of the doctrine was Professor William McDougall, who was professor of psychology at Harvard. There was also Albert Edward Wiggam, who, in his *The New Decalogue of Science* and *The Fruit of the Family Tree*, had, Dorsey wrote, "broadcasted more false views about race and civilization than any other one man. He is *the* spokesman of the Nordic faction, the silver-tongued champion of the eugenics cult, the popularizer of genetics *par excellence*." There was also Lothrop Stoddard, author of *The Rising Tide of Color*, introduced by Madison Grant, and Dr. Ellsworth Huntington, of Yale, a "confirmed Nordic propagandist," author of *The Pulse of Progress*, and Edwin M. East, professor at Harvard, author of *Mankind at the Crossroads* and *Heredity and Human Affairs*, another preacher of white supremacy. "The chief difference between these heredity mongers and the Ku Klux Klan," Dorsey wrote, "is the difference between kid gloves and a nightgown—they have the same ethics.... In fact between the religious prejudice of a Bryan's ignorance and the class prejudice of a McDouglas, Grant, East, or Osborn, there is little to choose and less to excuse."

Dorsey also debunked intelligence tests, saying that they "may furnish samples of knowledge, but there is no way whereby inborn capacity for intelligent behavior can be directly measured.... Whatever the tests showed, they did not measure capacity to learn, and they are therefore, so far as criteria of innate 'racial' capacity are concerned, worthless." He concluded: "The argument put forth by our racial purity propagandists falls to the ground. There is no evidence for pure races, no evidence that the extreme forms of any type represent the purest, nor any evidence for the assumption that inter-breeding of different types in any respect lowers their capacity for culture or civilization."[15]

INTELLIGENCE TESTING

As noted, the eugenicists seized on the use of intelligent tests when faced with the problem of deciding who was fit for their "Eugenia," and who was not. Intelligence tests seemed to offer a "scientific" method for such a determination, rather than to base it simply on class. Fortunately, such a "scientific" device seemed to have come to hand as a result of World War I in the form of intelligence testing.

Mental testing, as it was originally called, was tried in England and the United States in the late nineteenth century, with the first scholarly article on the subject published by an American, James McKeen Cattell, in the British journal *Mind* in 1890. By 1895 the American Psychological Association had become so interested in the concept that it appointed a committee "to consider the feasibility of cooperation among the various psychological laboratories in the collection of mental and physical statistics." The first tests created by this and subsequent committees had, however, disheartening results when their results were compared with the academic grades of the subjects, for they seemed to show no correlation at all.

Meanwhile, a French psychologist, Alfred Binet, was experimenting with quite a different approach to measuring intelligence. Beginning in 1905, he and a colleague, T. Simon, set out to measure the average intelligence of children at various ages, and then to test children in general to determine whether their intelligence matched that typical for their ages or was above or below it. The final revision in their test was made in 1911, but the concept had already spread to the United States where the Binet-Simon test began to be used and revised. By the time of the outbreak of World War I it has been estimated that over 300 monographs had been published in this country describing applications of the test and discussing the method. The most important revision was made in 1916 by Professor Lewis Terman at Stanford University, who not only revised the Binet-Simon tests radically, but also introduced the idea of dividing the subject's mental age by his/her chronological age in order to obtain an intelligence quotient.

One year after the Terman revision was published in the United States, this country entered World War I. The American Psychological Association quickly mobilized its members to aid in the war effort "by supplying reliable measures of intelligence." Psychologists then set to work trying to devise tests that could be applied to millions in the limited time available. Fortunately, it was discovered that a student at Stanford University, Arthur Simon Otis, had put together a series of tests that could be given simultaneously to great numbers of subjects. Psychologists now created two examinations: the Army Alpha, for literate personnel, and the Army Beta, for illiterates. Nearly 2 million recruits were tested, of whom 3 percent were found to be below the mental age of ten and about 20 percent of the mental age of twelve.

The potential for application of such testing to civilian life after the war was obvious—both for education and for industry.[16] As one writer observed in 1919:

> The uses made of intelligence tests in the army suggest that similar tests might be of considerable value to industry. The first use that at once suggests itself is in relation to hiring. Mental alertness is clearly an attribute that brings about success or failure at different kinds of work, and the employment manager who will inform himself of the amount of intelligence that various jobs require can assure himself that each applicant is at least intelligent enough so that he will suffer no handicap in becoming a satisfactory employee because of a slow or retarded mentality. The converse is also true, that applicants of superior intelligence need not be hired for positions in which high mental ability may be either unnecessary or misdirected.

The tests could also be useful in determining who should be laid off during slack periods and in locating present employees in positions that most corresponded with their intelligence level.[17] But a year later Ruml was sounding a more pessimistic note, writing that mental tests measured only in their particular direction, whereas intellect was of many dimensions. Absent an appreciation of this, the attempt to establish general mental laws on the basis of testing was flawed. He explained:

> The justification, that just as electricity is measured without too precise a knowledge of electricity, intelligence can also be measured without a final theoretical groundwork, has carried us too far.... It is not my intention to question the very real practical value of mental tests. But the usefulness of mental tests in concrete situations can not increase beyond a certain point unless, along with the activity in the field as an applied science, results of a speculative and interpretative value are secured. It is probable that many of the failures of mental tests can be traced to our present inadequate theoretical foundations.[18]

In education, between 1918 and 1923 more than thirty group tests for schoolchildren and college students appeared that were adaptations of the Army Alpha and Beta exams. The most common use was for identifying promising college students. A National Intelligence Test was on the market by 1921 and sold 575,000 copies during the first year it was available. However, a study in 1924 found no definite relation between scores on the intelligence tests and academic performance. A student's high-school grades turned out to be a more reliable indicator of college performance than the IQ tests. That discovery came at a time when the tests were under attack by skeptical laymen like the influential columnist Walter Lippmann. A 1929 article in *American Mercury* found psychologists, themselves, uncertain as to the value of the IQ tests, wondering whether they had ventured more into tests of personality and character.[19]

In that same year a school medical inspector questioned whether the mental tests might work to the detriment of students if not used slowly and with discretion. The tests did not measure character, he pointed out, which rendered their results incomplete. He wrote:

> Character is getting to be old-fashioned, with efficiency absorbing the attention of every one. The two combined stand for all that is best in the world. Efficiency by itself becomes a damnable thing because it ceases to be human. Our antagonist in the recent war is a striking example of this with an efficiency so perfect that a crime committed for the Fatherland became a virtue and received reward as such.

He warned:

> Let the children who test low get to know it and you might as well brand them as incompetents. If their school-work has been hard before, you will make it more so. "What's the use," they will say, and initiative will drop out of sight. "We are only capable of so much; why attempt to compete?" And when the time comes to go to work and make a living, efficiency will be slated for the job and character will be thrown into the discard.

The IQ tests were, he wrote, "a cold-blooded proposition with character excluded," which it must of necessity be since it could not be quantified. Yet it was those traits that comprised character that were the most valuable in making good citizens and good government.[20]

Already by early 1921 a New York University psychologist was writing in *Discovery* magazine that many, if not all, psychologists were skeptical about the value of the mental tests then in use. Those tests had made it possible to identify the feeble-minded, but had not shown their utility in determining abilities. Commenting on the article, *Current Opinion* wrote: "The new psychology can not tell us how able we are just yet, but in the meantime it can measure our imbecility, and that is something."[21]

A writer for *Harper's* noted that the Army intelligence exams had assigned grades ranging from A at the top to E at the bottom—the latter representing a mental age of 7–10 years. Of the D minds and below he wrote:

> They lack the mathematical vision to reckon consequences. They do not know enough to vote with discrimination, or to choose honest men for leaders, or to keep their promises. Stupidity will kill any organization, whether a hod-carriers' union or a trust company. It is the one dose fatal to democracy. Granted intelligence, and democracy is likely to worry through, one way or another, but where stupidity predominates the prospect is hopeless.

The writer advocated a universal test and grading system based on the Army tests. He wrote:

> Suppose every one were compelled either to submit to them or else to receive a rating too low to carry with it the privileges of citizenship. Then we could not cover our defects. Birth, family, education, would be powerless to save us.... This would be true democracy, for our souls would stand naked before the tests.

Opportunities in employment would be based on one's examination grade, and those of the lowest grades would be barred from the rights of citizenship.

In government it would eliminate the incompetent voters, and the demagogue would be the only one to suffer. The incompetent would be better off because they would live under better government. "Foolish ideas that are known to be vicious if realized would not be proposed as a lure for votes.... A great change might come over public opinion and public thought. We might seek the truth rather than seek what can be 'put over.'"[22]

An analysis of the results of the exams given to the Army showed that "the illiterate or those who are partially illiterate are largely the unintelligent, the ones having the least ability to learn." The results also indicated that

> in the classes of A and B intelligence are found the professional men, the leaders in engineering and the more successful business men.... In the C+ group are the bookkeepers and clerks.... The C intelligence is largely that of the skilled workman.... In the C− class [are] found the semiskilled and unskilled workman. The teamsters, miners, and laborers belong to this group.

The classes from C− and below consisted of the least intelligent and skilled among the population, fruitful targets for labor organizers and radical activists. They were also frequently foreign-born. The writer continued:

> at the present time we have many agencies that are working for the Americanization of foreigners; ... these various agencies are pointing out to the foreigner how he may become an American citizen; ... the necessary instruction is being given in evening classes by boards of education, and other educational agencies. It is true that in our large cities a good work is being done by teaching the uneducated foreigners. But most of this work assumes the character of teaching foreigners how to read and write, giving them the knowledge of our history, constitution, institutions and laws that will enable them to ... become American citizens. But it was only the more intelligent among the foreigners who were in the classes. What of the D groups, who lacked the ability to learn this material? A special effort should be undertaken to Americanize this group, using primarily lectures and other direct methods, rather than the printed word.[23]

At the end of the decade a writer observed that when psychologists brought psychology out of the laboratory and began applying it to practical uses in daily living, they "began a new epoch in the history of man's control over his own nature." The difficulty was that not all psychologists and psychiatrists agreed "on fundamentals, and on general conclusions," making it difficult for "a newly arrived practitioner in the field of education, in the field of business, or in the field of social work, to make selection of the sound, substantial contributions as against those which are either unsound or have not as yet been stripped of their false accoutrements, with the truth revealed as it really is." One of the choices was Freud, of whom he wrote:

> Once ridiculed and reviled, we now find the major contributions of Sigmund Freud accepted as sound and substantial. As time goes on, many of the fancy and elaborate decorations accompanying the Freudian contributions will be left in the discard and those mechanisms which have proven themselves, by test, to be true will find their proper place in the ultimate encyclopedia of human nature.
>
> On the other hand, many Freudian followers accept too readily, or are inclined to exaggerate, the dire results likely to follow the thwarting of the love-life, the operations of the censor, and the effect of repressions upon the normal self-expression of the individual.

The profession, in general, he argued, had created dangers for itself that threatened "the healthy development of guidance and adjustment work." Two of these were what he described as a "Blind Faith in Tests" and a belief in "Human Standardization." The former failed to recognize that the results of testing were "merely a means to aid in the interpretation of a considerable mass of other evidence"; the latter did not allow "for difference and for deviation" from "personal notions of the ideal man or the ideal woman." Another danger was in "Opposition to Self-Control," because of its

> opposition to inhibitions, repressions, self-control, and the latent possibilities of conscience in the direction of human conduct. To inhibit a little bit is not dangerous, and to repress a little bit, and on occasions, will also not make mental breakdown inevitable.[24]

DRUGS

Drug abuse was an ever-present problem in 1920s America. The *New York Times* reported in 1924 that annual per capita use of opium and its derivatives in the United States roughly equaled that in India, France, England, and Germany combined. It was estimated that one-fourth of the inmates in federal prisons were victims of the drug habit. Most users were comparatively young, with some being boys and girls under the age of twenty. The United States was spending $750,000 per year to enforce antinarcotic laws, but was clearly having no more success than in enforcing prohibition. International conferences designed to halt production of opium were likewise without results.[25]

Of particular concern was heroin use, which had grown rapidly after its introduction before World War I. The American Medical Association estimated in 1924 that there were 1,000,000 heroin addicts in America, with an average age of about twenty-two years. The head of the International Narcotic Education Association wrote:

> Heroin appeared in America only ten years ago. Its spread to the present proportions in so short a time is appalling and indicates new factors in the problem of addiction.... Every heroin addict, because of the drug's action on his brain, has a mania to spread his addiction to others; the drug is four times as powerful as morphin [sic] and comes in the convenient deceptive form of a white powder, called "snow," which is generally "whiffed" into the nostrils.

Although heroin use was illegal except by prescription, it was estimated that of 76,000 ounces of heroin consumed each year in New York City, only 58 ounces had been prescribed.[26]

Whether drug-induced or no, juvenile crime was a major concern in the 1920s. The precocity of crime, one magazine noted, was "a distinguishing feature of the great age of jazz." The jails and prisons were "recruiting as victims those who should still be playing marbles and dressing dolls." *Literary Digest* solicited the views of prominent prosecuting attorneys on the subject in early 1925. The general consensus was that a principal cause of the problem was a lack of respect for the law on the part of their parents, which set a bad example for the children. Another reason cited was the absence of working mothers from the home and the relegation of the home to a place simply for eating, sleeping, and changing clothes.[27]

7
The Ku Klux Klan and Fundamentalism

KU KLUX KLAN

A revivified Ku Klux Klan, bearing some resemblance to the notorious Southern organization of the nineteenth century, began to spread to the North in the winter of 1920–21, prompting a number of writers to examine the new group. One wondered what "crisis" or "menace" to American ideals had suddenly led to the resurgence of the Klan after a lapse of fifty years. Unless one existed, or was believed to exist, the Klan "must inevitably fall to pieces of its own weight." And if the Klan were to spread all over the country, as its promoters clearly intended that it should, that felt need must be a national one.

The Klan, he found, was quite obviously directed against those groups who were "the storm-centres of present-day racial antagonisms in the United States," which included the Jews, against whom anti-Semitic propaganda was "more open and active in America than at any time in recent history"; the Irish, who were the most obvious of Catholics in America in the twenties; the Japanese, who were widely regarded as undesirable landholders in California and as a potential enemy in war; and the resurgence of "the Negro question" as a result of World War I, which had brought many Afro-Americans north and raised them "for a time to unheard-of pinnacles of affluence," which had collapsed in the postwar years, but had left them determined "to assert their rights as citizens in a manner offensive to the dominant white race." The new KKK insisted that it was a law-abiding organization, intent on cooperating with the authorities, and that no law-abiding person of any race, creed, or color had anything to fear from them, but they did assert their intention to maintain Caucasian control of the United States.[1]

Another writer found little difference between the KKK's statement of purpose and the German "Me-und-Gott pronunciamentos with which the world was deluged about August, 1914." It was an organization that consisted of a

> secret body of hooded and masked men who seek to substitute for the regularly constituted bodies of law and order, an extra-legal "posse comitatus" method of vengeance. Into the tangled and muddled race relations of today, with the memory of disastrous riots between the races in Chicago, Omaha, Washington and other cities yet fresh, this organization is being revived, masking its purposes behind oratorical phrases of a half a century ago, and shouting its "Americanism" aloud from the house-tops.

It had been revived largely through the activities of William Joseph Simmons, who claimed a membership of 100,000 for the Klan and proclaimed an intention to spend $1,000,000 per year to spread its propaganda.[2]

The New Republic credited much of the success of the new KKK to Edward Young Clarke, "a professional publicity man and 'drive' promoter." It wrote:

> Here again, we have the note of a savage caricature. It has long been supposed, and it was pretty well demonstrated through the war, that almost anything can be "sold" to some section of the public if the right "technique" is employed. Mr. Clarke has gone beyond most drive promoters in being able to sell religious bigotry and race hatred at the cost of $10 per bonehead. By flattering the native-born Protestant gentile white American, by depicting the United States as secretly endangered by Jews, Roman Catholics, Negroes and foreign-born American citizens, a fair proportion of simple jungle-minded folk, all over the country, have been induced to take oaths of red-blooded Americanism.

It was, TNR opined, "plainly an outcropping in final idiocy of the many tyrannical manifestations with which this country has been afflicted since Woodrow Wilson as President yielded completely to illiberalism and gave Burleson and Palmer carte blanche." It was an outgrowth of the extremism of the National Security League, the American Legion, and other such organizations in their attacks on civil liberties during and immediately after the war.[3]

Literary Digest reported in September 1921 that some twenty newspapers, headed by the *New York World*, plus half a dozen weeklies, had printed exposures of the Klan. The *World*'s stories had included the revelations that the KKK had

> grown from a nucleus of 34 charter members to a membership of more than 500,000 within five years. Its "domains" and "realms" and "klans" have been extended until they embrace every State in the Union but Montana, Utah and New Hampshire.... When it was organized it was directed against the negro. Now the negro has become a side issue. To-day it is primarily anti-Jew, anti-Catholic, anti-alien, and it is spreading more than twice as fast through the North and West as it is growing in the South.

Much of that growth, it opined, was the result of the salesmanship of paid organizers, or Kleagles, who kept $4 of each $10 membership "donation." A flood of editorials from newspapers throughout the country were condemning the existence, and the alleged activities, of the Klan.[4]

By October the *Literary Digest* found the KKK being attacked by "practically the entire religious press of the country—Protestant, Catholic and Jewish" as "the most serious menace now threatening the national unity and religious harmony for which all the moral forces of the country are striving."[5]

Arthur Corning White found a deeper significance in the KKK than was evident from its pronouncements, writing in *The Forum* that the movement was, in fact, an American "Fascismo," although no other writer had yet seen beneath the surface appearances to the real significance of the movement.

The typical middle-class member, he wrote, was in the KKK "because he hopes to make more money being one." He explained:

> He hopes that in some way, as yet only dimly glimpsed, perhaps scarcely realized, the Klan will bring back the dear old days when income taxes were unknown, when you could ride a hundred miles on a good railroad for a dollar and a half, when coal was five dollars a ton, when you could hire an excellent gardener for twenty cents an hour, and when the cook in the kitchen knew her place and kept it. Oh, the Nineteenth Century was the real Golden Age!

Magazines were full of articles on the improvements "Fascismo" had made in Italy, particularly for the middle class.

> I do not for a moment believe that the Klan has its origin in Fascismo, but I am sure that the movements are essentially alike in purpose and that the apparent success of Fascismo in realizing its purpose will set the Klan to thinking about ways and means for an American application of the Italian method.

Already, he noted, the Klan had entered politics and seemed to control the state of Oklahoma.[6]

Judge Ben Lindsey wrote later in that same year that the "Ku Klux Klan has swept Denver like a prairie fire.... It was like the stampede of the herd in full tilt and it seemed almost as useful to try to stem its mad head-on rush." In none of his previous campaigns, he wrote, had he "ever seen such stark madness, such bitterness, such hatred" as he received for his anti-Klan position.[7]

The same magazine, however, observed a month later that if writers for "newspapers and periodicals would let their sense of humor aid their reason in contemplating the works of this order, warnings of the menace it presents might be less current." An Oklahoman, the writer dismissed the claims of KKK power and intimidation in that state. He wrote that all crimes committed by masked men had been conveniently "laid at the door of the Klan," even when there was no evidence of its guilt other than its reputation. Instead, the crimes had often been committed by others, who sought anonymity by adopting the supposed tactics of the Klan.[8]

Another writer, however, took the Klan much more seriously. William Robinson Pattangall, who had run unsuccessfully for governor of Maine against the KKK, told an interviewer:

The Klan is not dying; it is becoming more powerful, even if less noisy. And the real danger from it is not only to aliens and Catholics, although that is serious enough. The Klan's greatest threat is against American liberalism, which is and always has been the true Americanism; and the danger menaces all American liberals. So far we have had only a preliminary skirmish, and the Catholics and aliens have borne the brunt because they happen to be good fuel for prejudice. But already it has been made clear that, if the Klan wins power, it will substitute the deadly conservatism of ignorance and prejudice for the free spirit that has made America.

Moreover:

The Klan is more than an organization; it is a state of mind. The organization may not be so strong today, but the state of mind is stronger. The Klan's propaganda has caused a tremendous development of anti-Catholic, anti-Jewish, and anti-alien sentiment all through the country. It is now the rallying point for all the religious and race prejudice in the nation. Thousands who would not think of joining the organization support it and follow it politically.

The danger from the Klan was not overt political control, Pattangall told his interviewer. The problem was that

The Klan seeks a secret hold on legislators, judges, and other officials. It uses that hold to enforce its own demands, abandoning completely the American principle of rule by and for all. It maintains expensive lobbies, it acts secretly in both parties, it tries constantly for control—*secret control*—of elections, legislature, and government.

This was a far more serious threat than the occasional whipping or lynching that was publicized. Its greatest threat was to the Democratic Party, into which it had injected the religious issue. "The Klan is death to the Democratic Party," he said. "No one can subscribe at the same time to the creed of the Klan and the doctrine of Jefferson. A Klan-controlled liberal party is a contradiction in terms." And the Klan would destroy the party by driving away from it the northern industrial states.[9]

For his part, Hiram Wesley Evans, Imperial Wizard of the KKK, submitted to an interview by *The Forum* that was printed three months later. Evans defined the position of the Klan:

We believe that the pioneers who built America bequeathed to their own children a priority right to it, the control of it and of its future, and that no one on earth can claim any part of this inheritance except through our generosity. We believe, too, that the mission of America under Almighty God is to perpetuate and develop just the kind of nation and just the kind of civilization which our forefathers created. This is said without offense to other civilizations, but we do believe that ours, through all possible growth and expansion, should remain the *same kind* that was "brought forth upon this continent." Also, we believe that races of men are as distinct as breeds of animals; that any mixture between races of any great divergence is evil; that the American stock, which was bred under highly selective surroundings, has proved its value and should not be mongrelized; that it has automatically and instinctively developed the kind of civilization

> which is best suited to its own healthy life and growth; and that this cannot safely be changed except by ourselves and along the lines of our own character. Finally, we believe that all foreigners were admitted with the idea, and on the basis of at least an implied understanding, that they would become a part of us, adopt our ideas and ideals, and help in fulfilling our destiny along those lines, but never that they should be permitted to force us to change into anything else.

The traditional American spirit had "been bound up from the first with the spirit of Protestantism," and it was "a vital part of all Americanism, of all successful democracy."

He continued:

> We find as a fact that both the spirit and development of Americanism are threatened and have already been greatly weakened. After a century, we know that the melting pot has failed—the very phrase was coined by an alien! Except in small degree, the people we have recently allowed to come in not only do not become American, but they do not desire or attempt it.... When diverse groups live together, one must rule. Unless some one group does have control, the nation becomes to disunited that development is checked.... We are already seeing in America the workings of this law of disunity through alienism. Our counsels are divided, our progress is checked, our spirit weakened, our purpose as a nation confused and fumbling. We are drifting away from national unity; in fact, we are being carefully and deliberately driven away from it by alien ideas and excessive liberalism toward them. The Klan, knowing this, believes the whole tendency must be stopped....

Liberals, he argued, were to blame for much of the problem. "They have extended their liberality till they are willing to help the aliens tear at the foundations of the nation. They have become one of the chief menaces of the country, instead of the sane intellectual leaders they should be." Absent the leadership of the "best" people, it had fallen upon the common people to act.

Referring to the writings of the eugenicists, he observed:

> It is rather curious that science recently has been finding good grounds for supporting these very intolerances of ours. It has found, for example, that racial mixtures are unstable, and that the mongrel offspring of such mixtures is below the standard of either parent. It has shown, in addition, the great fundamental differences between races, and that the resistance to change in those fundamentals is very strong. It has emphasized the importance of heredity and inborn characteristics as against education. All this disproves the old hope that education could be depended upon to make Americans overnight of the most diverse people. It proves that the alien's ideas, which are so contradictory to ours, are a part of him and will remain a persistent danger to us. It justifies our racial exclusiveness.

The KKK's opposition to Catholicism lay not only in the political activities of the church, but also in the fact that most of its members in America were aliens whom the church was making no effort to help assimilate, but was instead working to "prevent this and keep the Catholics as a group apart." The Klan, he concluded was "the only leader in the effort to stop the perversion of our national character."[10]

A few months later, however, *The New Republic* thought it found the Klan losing out. It wrote that the evidence suggested the Klan was breaking up into splinter organizations and losing membership. The Klan had become a political party and in that role could not continue as a secret hooded society. Some within the Klan were attempting to preserve its old characteristics, "but theirs has been a losing battle. This has been true particularly because of the alliance between the Klan and Fundamentalism." It explained:

> Two interpretations of the present aggressiveness of the Fundamentalists are possible. One is that, seeing the country spiritually and emotionally exhausted by the War and its consequences, they have seized the opportunity to enforce their rule through legislation and through consolidating public opinion behind them. The other is that Fundamentalism is on the wane, and has just come to a panic realization of the fact.... Our own judgment is that the second explanation is more plausible than the first. In either case, it was inevitable that the Ku Klux Klan should become embroiled in the Fundamentalist struggle. The two types of mind not only resemble each other; they are one. At the same time, the agitation for Fundamentalist principles, even more than the other objectives of the Klan, is one which must be carried on in the open, and in itself insures the alteration we are discussing.... We may ... be sure that the Ku Klux Klan as we have known it in the past, with its secret membership, hooded parades, and solemn hocus pocus of burning crosses and open-air night meetings, is dead. Its spirit will go marching on, but the hooded figure on a horse must now give way to the perspiring orator and handbill distributor standing on the back seat of a Ford, using not the whip and tar-brush of yesterday, but the political argument and exhortation which are perennial.[11]

By late 1927, the TNR could herald "The Rise and Fall of the K.K.K." The Klan, it noted, had "undergone some serious setbacks in recent months."

> In Alabama, a state long completely dominated by the hooded order, thirty-six of its members have been indicted for a series of floggings of various men and women, white and black.... In Pennsylvania, court proceedings between two factions of the K.K.K. have resulted in some sordid revelations. Riots were artificially created, we learned, so as to herd new members into the organization—at ten dollars a head.... In Indiana, the statewide corruption and bribery by and for the Klan, which debauched the government of the commonwealth, has come to light as an aftermath of the case of D.C. Stephenson, former leader of the organization in that state, who is now serving a life sentence for the rape and murder of a young woman.
>
> In all these states, and in others, the enrollment of the Klan is diminishing. Thousands of sincere and honest men have quit the order in disgust after learning of the avariciousness and debauchery of their leaders.

The Klan was losing ground everywhere, it seemed, but New England, where it had started late.

In seeking the reasons for the brief rise of the Klan during the decade, *The New Republic* found one being that many Americans were frightened after a war "which thousands of them, especially in the Middle and Far West, never really understood or believed in." This caused them to cling to their neighbors and to seek some way to preserve the old institutions that seemed threatened. It continued:

> Another historical accident helped the Klan: the fact that prohibition began when the famous "wildness of youth" was at its peak. With prohibition came the bootlegger, and many anxious parents, seeing their sons and daughters going in for "petting parties," all-night automobile escapades and bad gin, sincerely thought the foundations of society were being undermined.... Another minor cause of the Klan's success was the general disbelief in the honesty of the press.... The anti-foreign aspect of the Klan was helped by yet another historical accident. The experience of the War had made the country acutely conscious of the large mass of undigested foreigners in its midst; the old idea of the successful melting pot was beginning to be subjected to a sharp scrutiny.... Never before had so many arguments existed in favor of restricting immigration; and the Klan organizers made good use of the threat that we should be "inundated" by "the undesirables of all Europe."

The Klan, it concluded, was an organization intent mainly "on preserving a status quo which seemed in danger of disappearing."[12] And those were concerns and goals with which many Americans could empathize in the bewildering 1920s.

The Lynds found that the Klan had come "upon Middletown like a tornado," turning "latent differences among the population into a frenzy of activity," emphasizing "potential factors of disintegration." It had been brought to Middletown originally by a few of the city's leading businessmen to act as a sort of vigilante group "to hold an invisible whip over the corrupt Democratic political administration and generally 'to clean up the town,'" but its ranks quickly burgeoned under the influence of a professional organizer, "and by 1923 some 3,500 of the local citizens are said to have joined. As the organization developed, the business men withdrew, and the Klan became largely a working class movement," whereupon it abandoned the original issue and adopted the issues of the national organization, with the city divided into hostile groups as the KKK's "Tales against the Catholics ran like wildfire through the city.... Klan feeling was fanned to white heat by constant insistence in season and out that 'every method known to man has been used and is being used by the alien-minded and foreign influence to halt our growth.'" The Klan, the Lynds concluded, had blown "off the cylinder head of the humdrum. It afforded an outlet for many of the constant frustrations of life." It had provided "a wealth of scape-goats against whom wrath might be vented for all of the economic tensions and social insecurity." But, they wrote: "The high tide of bitterness was reached in 1923, and by 1925 the energy was mainly spent," after which the Klan had largely disappeared, "leaving in its wake wide areas of local bitterness."[13]

FUNDAMENTALISM

It is ironic that even as more and more people drifted away from religion in the 1920s, many of those who remained within it became even more dogmatic and intolerant. As earlier noted, the goals of the KKK and of the fundamentalists were strikingly similar. The fundamentalists, however, attracted major attention for their opposition to the teaching of the Darwinian theory of evolution in the schools in the 1920s and their efforts to bring about state laws that would make it illegal. Their most publicized success was in the state of Tennessee, site of the famous Scopes "monkey trial" in 1925. The issue was typically defined more broadly, however, as one between science and religion, between "modernity" and "fundamentalism," and included a widely held belief that the two were mutually exclusive and irreconcilable.

The liberal *New Republic* took notice of the stirrings of the antievolutionists in early 1923, and wrote:

> Perhaps it is not a bad thing that Mr. [William Jennings] Bryan and the Fundamentalists are stirring up matters about evolution, and hence stirring up the evolutionists to interrupt for a moment their evolutionary research in order to take stock of their present knowledge, and to tell the public, in more or less intelligible language, just where evolution stands now. What has been learned about evolution since Darwin? What are the special things that still need to be learned?

Thomas Henry Huxley, however, had presented "enough evidence to convince any fairminded person," and "the silver tongue of Bryan cannot overcome the gold of ascertained fact," although it could "hypnotize many people for a longer or shorter time by its tinkling."[14]

The next month the Presbyterian General Assembly voted down an antievolution proposal of Bryan and adopted, instead, a substitute that was "said to have fallen far short of the wishes of the 'fundamentalists.'" The resolution written by Bryan provided that none of the church's educational funds should "be paid to any school, college, university or theological seminary that teaches or permits to be taught as a proven fact, either Darwinism or any other evolutionary hypothesis that links men in blood relationship with any other form of life." The resolution adopted was fairly close to Bryan's in instructing the synods and presbyteries of the church to "withhold their official approval from such academies, colleges and training schools where any teaching or instruction is given which seems to establish a materialistic evolutionary philosophy of life which disregards or attempts to discredit the Christian faith."[15]

In September of that year, *Literary Digest* found liberals mobilizing to fight the fundamentalists and adopt "a militant Liberal program." Harry Hibschman wrote in the Unitarian *Christian Register*:

> Denying the right of any man, even who acquired his scientific knowledge by self-communion on the windy plains of Nebraska [an obvious allusion to Bryan], to put my reason or that of my neighbor in a straitjacket, I refuse to stand complacently aside and let the hosts of intolerance, ignorance and bigotry sweep the field unopposed.

His call, and others like it, aroused immediate support.[16]

Early in 1924, Charles William Eliot wrote an article for *Atlantic* on "The Great Religious Revival." "The mass of the American people," he observed, "have always been Protestants," but divided into a variety of sects that produced "discord and divisions, not peace and unity." Then had come the tides of immigration of Jews and Catholics, which had further divided the religious scene.

> This heterogeneous and divided American people, which lives in many different climates and on many different soils, now finds itself divided in quite a new way into three parties or sections in regard to religion, the number of persons in each party being unknown, but variously estimated or guessed at with the most assurance by different guessers.

There were, first of all, the fundamentalists, who took their Bible literally, and who constituted "a strong effort to revive and spread the kind of religion which inspires and governs its devotees; and in this effort the movement has been strikingly successful.... It is a quickening revival and also a propaganda." The modernists, by contrast, respected "modern Biblical Criticism, and accepted its conclusions concerning both the Old and New Testaments." "These Modernists," Eliot wrote, "are inevitably bringing about a revival of interest of both sympathizers and opponents." The third group consists of the "tens of millions of men and women of scanty education who are not connected with any church and, apparently, take no interest in any religious doctrine or practice." Eliot wrote:

> In all probability a free people will always be divisible into three sorts, recognizable by their different faces, attitudes, and mental habits, all equally sincere, and all living side by side in peace and good will—those who prefer to live under a sacerdotal authority; those who prefer to take their opinions and beliefs from other minds, stronger, clearer, and more authoritative than their own; and those who habitually think for themselves, select their leaders on grounds of sympathy and intellectual fellowship, "look out and not in," welcome new thoughts and prospects, and live in the present and future rather than in the past.[17]

For *The Nation*, the fundamentalists were an appropriate study for psychoanalysts, writing: "What repressed desires, what envy and bitterness, find outlet in the zeal with which these Christian soldiers ... sentence to hell all poor sinners who happen to doubt, or not to care, whether Jesus of Nazareth was born of a virgin!" But it concluded that in the 1920s there was "nothing strange in intolerance."[18]

A professor at the Union Theological Seminar defined a fundamentalist as one "who accepts on authority certain doctrines or statements of fact regarding religion, science, and history, that were decided upon after much acrimonious discussion by men long dead," and who, "living ages ago, in the pre-scientific state of human experience, knew little concerning the nature of man, his origin, or the laws and constitution of this world; and this little was most of it incorrect." But the fundamentalist refused to reexamine or reevaluate those doctrines on the basis of modern knowledge and demanded a "similar surrender to authority on the part of others before he consents to associate with them as fellow-believers." While they took the Bible literally, they ignored the fact of the variety of translations and their differences.

On the insecure foundation of these imperfect translations of imperfect original texts, the fundamentalist bases his belief in the Scriptures as being inerrant, and so he accepts as true all the ideas of the Jews and the early Christians therein contained; all the Biblical myths, legends, tales, parables, and histories, whether as to the origin of the heavens and the earth, the creation of man, the conduct of the first pair, the universal flood, Joshua's command to the sun, Jonah and the great fish, the floating axehead, the revivifying effect of Elisha's bones, the immunity of the three young men in the fiery furnaces, etc., etc.

Whenever the accredited results of modern knowledge are found by him to differ from the notions of primitive science as contained in the Bible, the fundamentalist feels himself constrained to reject the former.

In opposition, a professor at the Princeton Theological Seminar argued that "Christianity, if it be true Christianity, must place itself squarely in opposition to the soul-killing collectivism which is threatening to dominate our social life; it must provide the individual soul with a secret place of refuge from the tyranny of psychological experts; it must fight the great battle for the liberty of the children of God." The churches, being voluntary organizations had every right to prescribe terms of admission and elements of the creed, which was not a violation of liberty.

One of the essential elements in civil and religious liberty is the right of voluntary association—the right of individuals to associate themselves closely for the propagation of anything that they may desire, no matter how foolish it may seem to others to be. This right is being maintained by "Fundamentalists," and it is being combated subtly but none the less dangerously by some of their opponents.

In an age of accelerating decadence, fundamentalism was "the only means of checking the spiritual decadence of our age."[19]

The dean of the Cathedral of St. John the Divine questioned the definitions of both fundamentalism and modernism. The fundamentalists, he found, placed their faith in the "divines" of the sixteenth-century Protestant Reformation and adopted their presuppositions. The fundamentalist

insists that the Bible be accepted after the manner in which Mohammedanism accepts the Koran, as a book written in heaven and free from any trace of human imperfection. He carries the cosmogony of the opening chapters of Genesis into the twentieth century, and flings defiance at the whole vast and noble structure of modern scientific knowledge. ... Like his sixteenth century predecessors the modern fundamentalist is a stout-hearted hater of heretics. He publishes from his pulpit lists of infidels ... and consigns them to the lower regions; he petitions State Legislatures to eliminate from schools and colleges text books containing the theory of evolution; he organizes a *posse comitatus* to hunt for heresy in theological seminaries and on mission boards.

What was not easy to forgive of fundamentalism was its

profound and perfect obscurantism, its hardening of heart against new revelations of truth through the noble medium of science.... It will not even tolerate the possession by

> others of a vision of God to which its own eyes are blind.... [It] does not believe that in the revelations of science, and in the results of scholarly study of the Bible, the Spirit of God is guiding men into new truth.

The modernists, on the other hand, practiced "pragmatism with a vengeance," denuding the "Christian tradition of the greater part of its historic significance while at the same time gallantly maintaining its ideal verity." It thus played "straight into the hands of scepticism on the one side and of superstition on the other."

Both fundamentalism and modernism were, then, misnomers. The fundamentalists did "not get down to the fundamentals of religion," and the modernists had not kept up with the march of science, but were more "characteristic of a bygone and materialistic age of science, not of a newer and more reverent age which already accepts many of the miracles of healing and is cautious and open-minded in its examination of the rest."[20]

The New Republic found it noteworthy that the conflict between fundamentalism and modernism had attracted such popular attention and interest—"conceive religion on the first page!"[21] A writer for the magazine wrote, somewhat tongue-in-cheek, that he was

> often impatient with the fundamentalists for throwing overboard so many planks for which they once battled even through blood. I don't think they had a right to do that. They assert that the basis of their religion is divine revelation, and they quite properly, under the circumstances, deny the theory of evolution, yet I catch them permitting religion to evolute. They ought not to do that. It is nothing less than backsliding. The Bible is crystal clear on the flatness and squareness of the earth, just as an example, yet very few Christians now defend these assertions.

And this was only one example of biblical statements that even fundamentalists no longer took as literal truth. Moreover, he found fundamentalists teaching comparative anatomy in their medical colleges, which was "at least a half-brother" to evolution. In the interest of a literal belief in the Bible they ought not to be doing so, nor should they be teaching modern surgery or any other kind of medicine, because "they have fought virtually every step of its advance, sometimes with the rack and bonfire." After all, the "Bible furnishes plenty of information on how to cure disease," as the Christian Scientists were quick to point out. As for prohibition, which was such a holy cause for fundamentalists, he found the Bible "not very explicit. Some authorities approved of wine, some didn't. All, however, seemed to drink it." Personally, the author hoped for a great increase in the number of agnostics, because: "When we don't know where we came from and haven't the slightest notion beyond a hope where we are going there is very little joy in killing each other."[22]

The New Republic also welcomed the activities of Bryan and the antievolutionists in the South, since it had focused public attention on what had been underway quietly in the Southern states—the teaching "of anti-evolutionism in the comparative obscurity of their classrooms in the theological seminaries," where they had "perpetuated indefinitely the kind of Christian education that kept clergymen from participating intelligently in modern life." It wrote:

> By his behavior Mr. Bryan has not done any harm to science or the teaching of science. He has himself begun the work of making the position of the anti-evolutionists impossible, and he has exposed to ridicule and contempt his own attitude and that of the people who agree with him.

It continued:

> At the root of the present explosion of "fundamentalism" are the intellectual standards of hundreds of seminaries which, with the approval of the leaders of the denominational churches, are educating Christian ministers who do not understand and owe no allegiance to scientific method and achievement.... These graduates are then turned loose on American society as the spiritual leaders of their generation, [but] the salient features of modern life are the direct and indirect results of scientific naturalism. The people who do not understand it and owe no allegiance to its methods and standards are as unfitted for religious as they are for secular leadership.[23]

In 1926, Mississippi joined Tennessee in enacting an antievolution bill that forbade the teaching in the public schools of any theory that "man is descended from a lower order of animals." The Ohio State *Journal* saw the movement as motivated by a desire for "a union of Church and State.... Not only is the anti-evolution movement in conflict with free educational progress, but in spirit, at least, it is an assault upon a great and essential principle of liberty laid down in the American Constitution." But the *Detroit Free Press* considered the fundamentalists as

> essentially a backwash from the stream of progress and enlightenment.... But in the course of time their areas will be caught in the current, or if they are not, will remain small isolated points. That, at least, is a justifiably optimistic view of the matter. Any other concedes an early recession of the country generally into the dusk and mud of medievalism, and that is scarcely thinkable.[24]

The Nation wrote, in the year following the Scopes trial:

> When at the close of the Scopes trial, God removed his faithful servant, William Jennings Bryan, various men and newspapers announced that now the fundamentalist menace to freedom in education was over; now the path was once more open to the general teaching of modern evolutionary science. Events have crowded upon one another's heels to disprove the assertion. Not only is the fundamentalist opposition to the theory of evolution more and more dangerous than ever, but other fields of thought are also being invaded.

Forty states would be in legislative session in 1927, "as against eight in 1926, and a flood of anti-evolution bills is threatened." Mississippi had already joined Tennessee in outlawing evolution in the schools; the school board of Atlanta,

Georgia had ruled against evolution; and the University of Louisiana had "refused a petition of students for a course on evolution." In Texas the antievolutionists "saved themselves the trouble of passing a law on the subject by working directly on the State Textbook Commission, which demanded of the publishers that they cut bodily out of all biology textbooks used in the State schools the pages referring to evolution." Antievolution bills were being pushed in Arkansas, Washington, Oregon, and California. There was the prospect of consideration by Congress of a national antievolution amendment drawn up by William Jennings Bryan.

Of the future of the fundamentalists, *The Nation* wrote:

> Who is to be Bryan's successor still remains undecided. His son has neither the personal influence nor the prestige to be very dangerous. The chief contestants for the honor seem to be the Rev. John Roach Straton of New York, who says "Better wipe out all schools than undermine belief in the Bible by permitting the teaching of evolution," and Rev. William B. Riley of Minneapolis and Los Angeles, executive secretary of the World Christian Fundamental Association, who predicts the organization of every State against evolution within twelve months. A Southern aspirant is Rev. T.T. Martin, of Tennessee and Mississippi, who ornamented Dayton with his "Hell in the High Schools" banner. Billy Sunday, is, of course, a perennial, but his power seems to be waning.

The Nation regarded the organization of new national antievolution societies as an ominous sign, writing that "the avowed purpose" of these groups, was "to establish a fundamentalist theocracy in America." Clearly the fight against them had only begun.[25]

A year later, however, *The New Republic* found the fundamentalists in retreat, despite evidence of their activities in trying to push legislation like the Tennessee law through the legislatures of twenty-two states. It wrote that there were still "plenty of persons who would like to see an anti-evolution law on the statute books of every state," and doubtless they would try to bring this about, but it was "safe to say that the period of most serious danger from activities of this sort is now past."

The churches that had been in the forefront of the movement, and many of their leaders, had begun to realize that the effort was a mistake, and the efforts of the antievolutionists had "been checked by, among other influences, the laughter of the world. They are not insensitive to the fact that nearly all intelligent people looked upon them and their activities as the hugest, albeit the most dismal, joke of the decade." *The New Republic* continued:

> In that drive, the personality of William Jennings Bryan was the most important factor. To his great oratorical gifts and his political shrewdness he added an unbelievable intellectual naivete—which is always a dangerous assortment of qualities. A few years before his death, Bryan decided that the country must be saved from the "rising tide of atheism," and set out single-handed to save it—the fact that the crusade was very profitable to himself, financially and politically, being at least no disadvantage in his eyes. He prepared an eye-popping set speech about the terrible perils by which "this Christian na-

tion" was confronted, and went about in the darkest parts of the South delivering this to joint sessions of the upper and lower houses of the state legislatures. His prestige with these loyal Democrats, who were often as ignorant, credulous and pious as himself, was, of course, enormous. The real wonder is that we did not get ten anti-evolution statues instead of two. His death took away the main driving force of the movement. No one has yet arisen capable of filling his shoes, nor is there any sign that anyone will.

It added that another cause for the wave of fundamentalism was the war, and explained:

The Allied propaganda in America had as one of its most effective arguments the charge that Germans were all Nietzscheans. The doctrine of the ruthless superman easily and quickly became interchangeable with that phase of "Darwinism" dealing with the survival of the fittest. The biologist in the popular view, was practically indistinguishable from the Hun. Moreover, the scientific attitude of mind was itself repudiated during and immediately after the War. From the anguish of the battlefield, missions turned to a mysticism which repudiated intellect because its fruits were so bitter on the tongue. The movement was accelerated by the contemporaneous work of the physicists who abandoned the mechanist doctrine of the last century and began to talk about the ultimate unknowable reality of the universe. Today, the wild swings of the post-war philosophic pendulum are moderating, and the results are certainly not favorable to the cause of the Fundamentalists.[26]

Literary Digest, too, found the "Anti-Evolution Agitation Waning," in June 1927, writing that antievolution bills had recently been "defeated in six states—Oklahoma, West Virginia, Arkansas, Missouri, New Hampshire, and Minnesota—and there is at least a lull in the battle." It continued:

These defeats, remarks the New York *Christian Advocate* (Methodist), indicated that the agitation has about exhausted itself. The only States that actually have the statute on their books are Tennessee and Mississippi, and "they are allowing it to become a dead letter and are expected to repeal it within a year or two."[27]

A year later the state of Arkansas, however, enacted an antievolution bill. The *Literary Digest* explained:

The Arkansas bill banning the teaching of the theory of evolution in State-supported schools was passed in a popular referendum at the general election, two years after it had been passed by the State House of Representatives and killed in the Senate by a small majority. Critics, however, pointed to the rise in sales of scientific books in Tennessee and Mississippi as a portent of what was likely to happen in Arkansas. It seems that banning evolution from the schools was only making it more popular as an illicit study![28]

Dr. Albert C. Dieffenbach, Unitarian, editor of *The Christian Register*, arch foe of Fundamentalism, and a leader of "Modernism's apparently dwindling forces," was pessimistic, however, writing in his book *Religious Liberty: The Great American Illusion* that the Reformation had exchanged an infallible pope for an infallible book, replacing one master with another. Now America was in danger of getting a state church. He explained:

> The dogmas which have been the bane of Protestantism these four hundred years are again triumphant, and the organized religions of Jesus, whose charter is liberty and whose service is perfect freedom, passes into a period of intolerance not equaled since the Chaos. Protestantism enters a new dark age.
>
> Dogmatism is in control of more than 90 per cent of the people in the denominations. ... Today Protestantism is creed-bound with new fetters of triple brass. Instead of the marvelous promise of spiritual rebirth that one sensed on every side, at the opening of the present decade, we have witnessed the disastrous defeat of freedom. The opportunity for liberation came, but our prophets were found wanting.
>
> In one church after another—Baptists, Episcopalian, Presbyterian, Methodist, and all the others—the holy warfare has ceased. The Fundamentalists have overwhelmed their liberty-loving brethren. The strife is over and peace prevails. The churches have denied to their ministers by one form of declaration or another the freedom of individual conscience, and their laity have meekly acquiesced.... [29]

Dieffenbach's point was well taken. Fundamentalism's strength or weakness in America could not be judged simply by its success or failure in the fight against evolution. By the same token, the ebbing membership of the KKK did not necessarily signal a decline in the mentality that had inspired its growth. Both represented a state of mind that had been revealed all too clearly in the 1920s.

8
Pastimes

PLAY

Stuart Chase estimated the annual cost of play in America as:

Pleasure motoring: $5 billion
Vacations and travel: $2 billion
Movies: $1.5 billion
Newspapers, tabloid, light fiction (in part): $1 billion
Radio: $750 million
Phonographs, etc.: $250 million
Telephone for pleasure: $100 million
Flying, bicycling, etc. for pleasure: $25 million

The popularity of second-hand amusements, he estimated at:

Newspapers and tabloids: 35 million readers a day
Radio: 30 million listeners a night
Record players: 15 million listeners a night
Movies: 50 million admissions a week
Theaters, concerts, lectures, etc. 5 million admissions a week
Popular magazines: 15 million readers a month
Baseball: 40 million admissions a year
Football: 10 million admissions a year
Etc.[1]

Of the type of play that Americans were indulging in during the 1920s, Chase wrote that "with the coming of the machine, and particularly in the United States of America, the age-long biological balance is threatened by monotonies and muscular repressions in work which give play an unprecedented significance. Increasingly it becomes the flywheel of modern life."[2] Play had, he wrote, "grown year by year with the industrial revolution. It has matured with steam turbines, turret lathes, and giant power. Inevitably like every other factor of human life in the Western World, it has been profoundly influenced by these instruments." For one, it had given Americans "more playthings; more physical and mechanical apparatus with which to amuse ourselves," and also the "machine age has given us more leisure in which to play." It had also given families more income "with which to buy the increase in the output of playthings," but had made the cities more congested so that opportunities "for free play are normally at a minimum."

> Finally, the machine age has given us mass production in amusement, run according to up-to-date business methods. We have been "sold" on play precisely as we have been sold on tooth powder, bathtubs, snappy suits and electrical refrigerators. Motors, bicycles, baseball, moving pictures, Broadway, night clubs, college football, prize fights, Coney Islands, radios, victrolas, lecture bureaus, tabloids, confession magazines, best sellers, horse-racing, travel bureaus, plus fours, revival meetings, Boy Scouts, cigarettes, antique furniture—all have gone into quantity production, following accepted formulae of advertising, salesmanship, the limit of price the traffic will bear and all have proved soundly profitable, with wide margins of credit from the banks, and as often as not a listing on the stock exchange.[3]

But what the Machine Age had given in increased leisure time, it had also taken away "by degrading the opportunities which that time affords; by standardizing our recreations on a quantity production basis, by making us watchers rather than doers, by exploiting our leisure for profit, by surfeiting us with endless mechanical things to monkey with . . . , by forcing the pace of competition in play until it turns into work, and above all by brutalizing in recreation millions of human beings who are already brutalized by the psychological imperatives of their daily labor."[4]

The Machine Age, Silas Bent opined, had produced impatient people who were "chary of attending affairs where there's nothing doing." They fed on "swift superficial excitement," like movies, tabloid picture newspapers, and fast automobiles.[5]

The Lynds found that in Middletown leisure-time activities tended to be "largely passive., i.e., looking at or listening to something or talking or playing cards or riding in an auto," with most of them related "to the coming of inventions, the automobile, the movies, the radio, that have swept through the community." Virtually all women, and most men over thirty, tended to spend most of their leisure time sitting down.[6] A considerable part of it was spent reading what the Lynds called "a ceaseless torrent of printed material," in the form of magazines and newspapers, that exposed them to the "new tools and habits of thought" of the Machine Age.

A writer for the *Magazine of Wall Street* estimated that one-quarter of the national income—over $21 billion—was being spent every year on luxuries and amusements like movies, phonographs, radio, candy, chewing gum, tobacco, and ginger ale. He wrote:

> The trend of America's expenditures for amusements and luxury items is very clearly upward, reflecting the steadily growing national income and rising standard of living. Net incomes of many companies catering to our love of entertainment and pleasure are gaining rapidly and the securities issued by some of these concerns have achieved recognition as genuine investments.

Radio and movie industries, in particular, seemed good investments offering great growth potential.[7]

SPORTS

As leisure time grew, sports became more and more popular. As a consequence the 1920s saw the development of the newspaper sports section. By the end of the decade from one-eight to one-quarter of the typical newspaper was being devoted to athletics. The headliners of the sports pages tended to be one star who dominated each sport, Red Grange in football, Babe Ruth in baseball, Bobby Jones in golf, Bill Tilden and Helen Wills in tennis. This popularization of sports heroes was only a part of the larger phenomenon of hero worship in America that was a product of the Machine Age. As Bruce Bliven explained it:

> What we have witnessed in recent years is the creation of a vast new machinery resting in the first place on mechanical invention, a machinery for acquainting every one with any new person or idea. Of this machinery the movies and the radio . . . are but a part, although an important one. Let any one emerge over the horizon who has said or done anything interesting, and within a week every one in America has heard his voice on the radio, seen his photograph and read his interviews in the newspapers (of which 40,000,000 copies are circulated daily), seen and heard him in the talking movies.

And to all this must be added the contribution of a new figure in American life, the publicist, or public relations man:[8]

One characteristic of the 1920s was the growing popularity of golf, as it was transformed from its earlier perception as an activity of the well-to-do to a pastime of a broader cross section of Americans. Some, indeed, began to wonder if golf would replace baseball as the leading sport in America as the whole country seemed to be in the grip of golf fever, while baseball appeared to have reached its saturation point.[9]

Baseball, meanwhile, was going through a period when hitting was dominating pitching, leading some to suspect that the ball, itself, had been changed to become more "lively." *Literary Digest* in 1924 lamented "the scarcity of good pitching material," quoting a writer in *Baseball* magazine: "A few years ago, young pitchers were a drag on the market, The slingers had everything their own way, and had the batters so buffaloed that the magnates hated the sight of any additional hurdlers. Pitchers who could fool the hitters were thicker than bees on a honey tree.... All is changed today, thanks to the lively ball. The sluggers dominate and the scouts are seeking pitchers in all directions. Pitchers who can keep the ball inside the limits of the park are in furious demand. Old pitchers who dropt out of major service three or four years ago are coming back, just because they seem to have developed some new stuff during their exile.... It's the batters' era, but it's also the day of great opportunity for the pitchers. Thinking of present conditions and the men of long ago, the writer can not help wondering how certain stars of the past would have held up under the present conditions. The lively ball would have utterly ruined some of the fanciest pitchers of the olden time, while sundry others would have been as great as ever." One problem was that new pitchers had not bothered to master the curve ball. Part of the problem, the writer concluded, was "the abolition of all freak deliveries except the spit-ball." Since pitchers had heretofore been able to use "foreign" substances on the ball, few had felt it necessary to develop a substance-free curve ball.[10]

Late in the decade critics were still charging that home runs were ruining baseball. Pie Traynor, third baseman of the Pittsburgh Pirates, predicted that continued use of the lively ball would bring about the demise of the game. *Literary Digest* opined that "few would deny that the ball was livelier than the one a few years ago," and reprinted a diagram from the *Philadelphia Public Ledger* showing the difference in construction. The new ball had more cork, livelier rubber, and less yarn. But the manufacturer of the balls conceded nothing, insisting that the balls had not changed.[11] But home runs added to the excitement of the game, attracted fans to the games, and helped to make major league baseball into a big business in the 1920s, with 20 million paid admissions per year and a payroll of over $2 million annually. It was estimated that the appearance of legendary home-run hitter Babe Ruth in games was worth at least $1 million in additional ticket sales every year.[12]

But baseball was only one sport that became big business in the 1920s. Boxing promoter Tex Rickard transformed that sport in the 1920s, with his Madison Square Garden voting trust certificates listed on the New York Stock Exchange. Rickard had profited $437,000 on the first Jack Dempsey–Gene Tunney fight, taking boxing "into the category of big business, financed by the banks, issuing securities, and licensed by the state—like banking and insurance."[13]

Football, however, was only making its first stirrings in the direction of big business in the 1920s, since it still faced competition from the popularity of college football. These first stirrings took the form of recruiting the most popular college player, Red Grange, to the professional ranks and thus giving status to the professional game. One writer observed of the event:

On the day Red Grange left the amateur ranks, he cleared $375,000, with the promise of making a million before the winter was over. At the same time the use of his name was sold to a sweater manufacturer for $12,000, a shoe manufacturer for $5,000, a cap maker for $2,500, and to a cigarette company for $1,000—the latter bargain figure doubtless due to the fact that Red never smokes. A candy company sold six million "Red Grange Chocolate Bars" in thirty days, for a consideration not disclosed.[14]

Meanwhile, it was generally conceded in the 1920s that college football, though "amateur in name is professional in spirit," with a good college football team serving not only as a boon to its school, but also a source of considerable profit—sometimes as high as $500,000 per year.[15] The Carnegie Foundation for the Advancement of Teaching made public in 1929 a report on college sports that had been 3½ years in the making. After visiting 130 college and universities over that period of time, the Carnegie report described the subsidization of athletes as "the darkest blot upon American college sport" and charged that one out of every seven engaged in intercollegiate competition was subsidized to a point "bordering upon professionalism."[16] The commercialization of one outdoor sport in the 1920s lifted it to near-vaudeville status. Starting out as a competition in horsemanship between cowboys in the west, its profit potential was quickly recognized by entrepreneurs who added a number of attractions like bulldogging and a few cowgirls and brought the show east. Like the Wild West show of Buffalo Bill at the turn of the century, the rodeos circuited the large cities east of the Mississippi performing before crowds of 10,000 spectators.[17]

THE AUTOMOBILE

Stuart Chase claimed for the automobile "the lion's share" of the time and money spent on play in the 1920s, writing:

> In the aggregate, it is the most powerful prime mover we possess; it is the outstanding exhibit in mass production; it is the rock upon which the whole structure of American "prosperity" is founded; it is the chief creator of the new labour burden; the mightiest reason for the congestion of cities and the desolation of the countrysides; and the leading national plaything.[18]

Silas Bent added that the automobile had "quite altered the economic and industrial reflexes of the country, as well as its social life.

> It has made the suburb possible for city dwellers, changed country life, and brought about the construction of hard roads throughout the United States. It has given birth to a million roadhouses. It has evoked a new vocabulary, in the forefront of which is "joyrider"; and it has meekly taken the blame for a lot of the faults attributed to the Younger Generation. It has given us the ubiquitous taxicab, and all but driven the beloved horse from our streets. It has been estimated that New York City's taxi bill was one hundred and sixty million dollars in 1928, a sum greater than the revenue of all the subways, elevated lines, and surface systems there.

And it had created time-consuming and costly urban traffic congestion.[19] A study by the University of Nebraska College of Business Administration showed that the impact of the automobile on that state had been the decline of villages having populations under 1,000, with those over 1,000 showing healthy growth, and especially those over 5,000. General stores in smaller villages were declining, with only grocery stores still viable. The viability of small villages and more general products had depended on the horse-and-buggy level of mobility. Now, with cars, people could travel farther for other than staples.[20]

In addition to the obvious effects of increasing the mobility of workers and consumers, and facilitating the movement of materials via trucks in and between cities, the use of motor vehicles also began to modify the spatial pattern of the cities. In the late nineteenth and early twentieth centuries cities had spread out along the lines of the trolleys and interurban railroads, radiating outward from the city itself like fingers, or blood vessels, or tentacles, with very little development between these tentacles beyond walking distance of them, because there was no other way to get back and forth to the city. But now the automobile made possible new suburbs, and the pattern that began to prevail in suburban growth was the one made possible by the automobile, not the older tentacle pattern. The great expansion of road building that began with the Federal Highway Act of 1916 led to the interstices between the tentacles being filled in. For the older cities, with already developed central business districts, the effect was that the new highways funneled traffic to the urban center, worsening congestion there. For newer cities, like Los Angeles, business tended to become decentralized along the highways.

It was during the 1920s that engineers perfected, and governments gradually adopted, various devices to speed up traffic, including grade separations of highways from city streets, traffic circles, divided dual highways, and synchronized stoplights. These, plus other innovations like the Holland Tunnel under the Hudson River, made possible easier movement of automobiles into and through the cities. Once there, parking became a problem, but New York City took a step forward in resolving that dilemma with a twenty-four-story wholly automated parking garage that guaranteed delivery of the vehicle in three minutes.[21]

The expanded economic opportunities and movement that were provided by the automobile stimulated an urban land boom that radically inflated property values in American cities, especially where automobile routes followed essentially the same corridors already established by the older forms of urban transportation. The expansion that followed in central business districts encouraged optimism that more would follow and triggered the kind of speculative boom that was so characteristic of the 1920s. Property values soared.

Higher land values forced developers to devise new ways to jam more people into the urban space that was becoming increasingly expensive. The inflation of land values, combined with the prosperity of the 1920s, stimulated the great era of skyscraper building in America. By 1929 American cities contained 377 skyscrapers of more than 20 stories in height, most of them built with no concern for the effects they would have on traffic and the surrounding urban areas. Many of them were begun in 1928 and 1929, not to be completed until after the Great Depression had begun. The Empire State Building, the tallest and most famous of them of all, was not completed until 1930 and went begging for tenants. Some blamed skyscrapers for much of the urban traffic congestion and suggested rationing so many of them to a city block. Building more subways, they said, was not the answer since they could not keep pace with skyscraper building.

At the same time, the growth of suburbia naturally led to an expansion of business away from downtown, making shopping more convenient for suburbanites. Where previously such suburban business ventures had followed the earlier corridors, they now developed along the new streets and highways. Moreover, the availability of trucks for the transport of goods freed some businesses from their dependence on trains for that purpose and made it possible for some industries to move away from the large cities. The move was also a response to the growing use of the assembly line in manufacturing in the 1920s, which required greater horizontal space at cheaper cost than could be obtained in the cities.

By the mid-1920s railroads were already suffering from the competition presented by trucks for cargo and by buses for passengers. Some railroads were abandoning lines made unprofitable by the competition, others had gone into the motor bus business themselves. A writer in *Nation's Business* reported that during 1924 1,500 bus lines had been established with over 5,000 buses. More and more tourists were also using their automobiles for travel rather than relying, as in the past, on railroads.[22]

Three billion bus passengers paid $350 million for travel in 1928 on 92,000 buses. The *St. Paul Pioneer Press* reported that the rate of increase of bus transportation exceeded even that of air transportation, or of motor trucks. "The number of buses," it reported, "has increased from 15,000 in 1920 to about 90,000 in 1928, and the mileage of their routes now comprises a transportation system of 270,000 miles, which is greater than the extent of railroad lines in the United States. This growth has come partly at the expense of the railroads, whose annual passenger revenue has declined $300,000,000 since 1920." Automobiles were taking most of railroad passengers away, though.[23] The *Electric Railway Journal* found trolleys still carrying 80 percent of city traffic and was optimistic that this would continue. Commuters were avoiding congestion and parking problems and expense and wear and tear on a car of exposing it to elements all day, so were using cars mainly for pleasure.[24]

Florida was the mecca of real estate speculation in the 1920s, induced by the flow of winter tourists who could now flee the cold and snow in their automobiles. But Florida went all out to lure these winter visitors to become year-round residents. In 1924, Florida courted the rich by adopting a constitutional amendment forever prohibiting inheritance or income taxes. The people voted 6–1 in favor of the amendment. One Florida newspaper predicted that the result would be a doubling of the population of the state within a decade.[25] An added attraction was the opening of the first railroad connection between east and west Florida, which was expected to open up for development "hundreds of thousands of new acres."[26]

A reporter told the *Literary Digest* that "half of Florida has gone wild over real estate," with small and large fortunes being made every day by people of all classes. He wrote:

> The little trader is making his along with the big trader. Take the case of Samuel Untermyer, the New York lawyer. Seven years ago he bought an ocean front tract at Palm Beach for $75,000. He sold it the other day for $700,000. Back in the lake section, touched by the new cross-state railroad, one small lot was sold four times between sunrise and sunset. The first sale was made for $400. The fourth sale—all in a day—was made for $1,800.[27]

Such tales could be multiplied almost endlessly.

Literary Digest wrote:

> Payments are small and easy. That catches the little fellow. He may know a man in the real estate business, so he takes the man's word, and he doesn't bother his brain with location. He seems to think it is a case of throwing a hook anywhere in the water and bringing up a fish.

Florida was getting an enormous amount of advertising, but the most effective was by word of mouth, and particularly about the fortunes that were being made.

Then came the hurricane. The bubble burst among shoddily constructed homes destroyed and lots under water. The hangover from the Florida boom was a precursor of the greater hangover that would begin late in 1929 when the stock market collapsed. Stuart Chase wrote of these "ill-advised real estate booms":

> Take Florida, which I have recently visited. Throughout the state today one may view the ruins of a grandeur which never materialized. Here are hundreds of miles of paved subdivision roads in which the grass is sprouting; abandoned public utility systems; thousands of sagging monolithic entrance gates; enormous dredging, leveling, and sand pumping enterprises so remotely placed as never to be practicable. The best engineering talent in America was called to Florida in 1925, taking with it a vast labour force. They planned and dug and hoisted and leveled and built. The jungle is now reclaiming the bulk of what they did, and a rusting steam dredge, one crazy arm aloft, stands as the tombstone of their labour.[28]

The Florida land boom even inspired a musical comedy, *The Cocoanuts*, with music by Irving Berlin, starring the Marx Brothers.[29]

Reference has already been made in previous chapters to many of the influences exerted by the automobile in the 1920s—its impact on dating, for example. In 1929 Charles Merz published a book on Henry Ford and the automobile, *And Then Came Ford*. In vivid language, Merz traced the rise of the motor car and its impact on America. Merz wrote that there had been a million and a half cars manufactured in 1921, then:

Two million and a half in 1922. Three million and a half in 1923 and 1924. Four million in 1925 and 1926. By 1926 there were twenty-two motor cars in the United States to every twenty-three families.... Fifteen hundred towns and cities established automobile camping parks along the open road. Two billion dollars' worth of gasoline and oil was sold by filling stations and repair shops to the swarm of motor cars that swept across the countryside like locusts.... the motor tour had become as casual as a walk to the street corner, a mere incident in an average day's routine.... Year by year since the annual production of automobiles in the United States first mounted above a hundred thousand cars in 1909 a remorseless urban civilization had been marching on to new frontiers. Year by year the cities pushed their smokestacks farther into the countryside as the conveniences of motor travel widened the orbit of suburban life. Year by year new interests and enthusiasms were carted up and down the country.

This was an America in which no traveler from East or West could lose his own home town, however far he rambled. For the rubber wheels of the Motor Age had ironed out the traits that once distinguished one community from another. Titusville was only a lap behind Broadway.[30]

The 1920s saw the original open cars abandoned in favor of closed models, the adoption of automatic starting in place of hand cranking, and the growing use of balloon tires over cord ones, and, of course, the addition of radios. Automobile manufacturers also took the lead in initiating the frequent style changes that characterized most industries in the 1920s, hoping thereby to create sales to consumers who were afraid to be seen with a product that was out of style. Yet, as Merz pointed out, the used car market was a sizable one by the mid-1920s, with some "four million cars in various stage of preservation ... on the auction block in 1926."[31]

Ford's promise that his customers could have their Model T in any color they wanted as long as it was black is well known, but by the mid-1920s black was being abandoned for virtually every color in the rainbow, largely due to the invention of pyroxylin finishes. The *New York Times* reported that by 1926 the trend toward color had become a "stampede." Fifty new colors debuted at the 1926 automobile show, from Florentine cream to Versailles violet. The *New York Times* reported: "One car at the new show is expressive of the Georgian era, painted Wedgwood green with white striping. Similarly, the Chinese influence is carried out in a four-passenger coupe, the Egyptian in a two-window berlin, the Roman in a convertible club roadster finished in red with gold striping and the Gothic in a seven-passenger limousine."[32]

Many automobiles were bought on the installment plan, and it was, in fact, the automobile that pioneered this practice. There were estimates of $3 billion in auto paper for 1925.[33] A writer in that year wrote that he believed people were now relying more on their cars than their houses as indicators of social position, because "the house stands still; only a chosen few can see the inside. But the car goes about; everybody sees it, and many observers know what it cost." He added:

Given the choice of a fine home without a car and a modest one with a car, the latter will win. Real-estate men testify that the first question asked by the prospective buyer is

> about the garage. The house without a garage is a slow seller. While the country makes an appeal of its own, it has an added lure if it can be enjoyed through the medium of the car, and many a man has moved from city to country in order to get away from the high cost of maintaining an automobile in the city. The whole scheme of domestic life centers about the motor-car.
>
> I do not believe the middle classes are getting ahead as they once were. What formerly went into the bank now goes into the motor-car. The thought in the minds of many workers is not how much they can save, but how long it will be before they can have a motor.
>
> The avalanche of automobile-owners is not a good omen. It signifies that the people are living either up to their means or beyond them; that the old margin of safety no longer obtains.... The ease with which a car can be purchased on the time-payment plan is all too easy a road to ruin. The habit of thrift can never be acquired through so wasteful a medium as an automobile.[34]

In Middletown the Lynds found that families sometimes mortgaged their homes to buy cars. They wrote: "The automobile has apparently unsettled the habit of careful saving for some families.... Men in the clothing industry are convinced that automobiles are bought at the expense of clothing, and the statements of a number of working class wives bear this out." But many families, they found, justified automobile ownership as "an agency for holding the family group together." Above all, they found, the automobile had "revolutionized" the leisure of Middletown's residents, even more than the movies. It was "making leisure-time enjoyment a regularly expected part of every day and week rather than an occasional event." Whereas in the past holidays like Fourth of July had been community events, now the city tended to empty out as people took to their cars. Most workers did not have paid vacations, but could take off without pay for up to two weeks.[35]

Besides the plethora of filling stations, automobile tourists spawned the growth of tourist camps and roadside eating stands. An examination of 170 tourist camps in the state of New Hampshire found that at an estimated total of 6,393 people could be housed in one night. Practically all had double beds, most did their own laundry, the larger ones had regular laundry rooms with washers and mangle irons. A few had running water in each cabin and at least two had flush toilets in each cabin. Most, though, had community toilets. The study reported that tourists were "using the camps more and more, preferring the quiet airiness and natural location. And with increased use the public has raised its demands to a higher level, until the 'camping' element of stopping overnight has largely disappeared." The camps all charged $1 per person, with the manager, his wife and assistant doing all of the work. The largest class of patrons was the family on tour.[36]

The *Ohio Health News*, published by the State Department of Health, reported that the wayside eating stand continued to be a problem for automobile tourists, and in many instances a menace. In both numbers and types they had experienced an enormous growth during the last years of the decade. The Ohio State Department of Health concluded that conditions would only improve if travelers, themselves, demanded better conditions in them.[37]

Meanwhile, filling stations had begun to displace the old country stores by carrying sundries, sandwiches, coffee, hot dogs, pie, candy, tobacco, canned goods, lipstick, cold cream, soap, pots and pans, swimsuits, and other sundries. Unlike the mom-and-pop stories, the filling-station stores were always open.[38]

Charles Merz wrote:

The rise of the filling station is coincident with the standardization of America. The same successful methods of efficiency and comfort have swept across the country and the filling stations stand as symbols of their progress. Not by so much as three dents in the counter of its battered water-can does one station differ from another. Each is the produce of a national art, perfected and unchanging.... Here is a scene which can be reproduced in any corner of the country: people doing the same thing in the same way in vast numbers for the same purpose.[39]

Stuart Chase observed that until recently machines had largely been confined to industry. He continued:

The bicycle started the stampede over the line, followed by the telephone and the phonograph, and now it would appear ... that probably the bulk of the outlay for new consumer goods goes for machines, primarily the automobile. Over half the articles listed in the catalogues of the great mail order houses are machines and their accessories and parts.

Which brings us to a brief philosophical interlude. How far is the whole phenomenon of prosperity, progress and mass production, since 1920 in America, but the shadow of the automobile? Without it, should we have had the phenomenon at all? It was the motor car which brought installment selling to perfection, and so created some six billions of temporary purchasing power out of nothing at all. Then the technique welcomed radios, phonographs, player pianos, electric refrigerators and the rest, into the fold. If we should cease to buy automobiles at the present rate, what would happen to "prosperity"; would it go down like a house of cards?[40]

Throughout 1927 America was agog over the imminent appearance of Ford's successor to the venerable Model T. The unveiling of the new Model A was representative of much of the change that had taken place in American life in the 1920s. First, the unveiling itself, and the advertising that went with it. The *Springfield Union* wrote:

With the simultaneous "unveiling" in all cities in the United States, as well as in many foreign cities, of the new Ford models, Mr. Henry Ford takes his place as the master showman of all times. The mystery with which the new car has been surrounded, the tremendous interest aroused in this and other countries, and the huge volume of newspaper publicity which has attended the change of the Ford designs constitute an advertising feat which never has been equaled. Best of all, it has been legitimate advertising, a wholly proper as well as amazing use of publicity for the promotion of business.

The *New York Evening Post* added:

The old Ford dript oil into our upturned faces as we lay under it on country roads at midnight. The new Ford is shown off like a modiste's mannikin to a generation which has lost the joy of getting its hands dirty. The old Ford ruined ten million pairs of overalls. The new Ford is unveiled in hotel ballrooms by salesmen in dinner jackets.

The new Ford is new; but it isn't a Ford. It has theft-proof coincidental locks, pressure grease-gun lubrication, and five steel-spoke wheels; it is as silky as a debutante and as neat as a watch; it will go sixty-five miles an hour and thirty miles on a gallon; it has a gas-tank behind the engine and a switch for all lights on the steering post, ... and it wipes its own windshield.

It is a remarkable piece of machinery, but it isn't a Ford, because the Ford was an educational institution as well as a machine. The old Ford, the old, black, rusty, cantankerous, obstinate, sputtering Ford, brought wisdom to many fools and made many wise men go raving, tearing mad. This new lily-of-the-valley isn't going to teach us anything. It looks as if it would run indefinitely without complaint, which is all wrong. It is made for serenity and comfort, which is also all wrong. Where is the gas-tank? Out in front where it can be reached. Where is the timer? Up on top where it can no longer bark your knuckles. Where are the brake-bands? In a ridiculously exposed position where their value as trainers of character and refined language is completely lost.

We are degenerating. We are entering a period of Roman luxury. The new Ford is a garage car. Back to the pioneer days when we threw sand under the fan belt and tightened the horn with a dime.[41]

READING

A common charge against Americans, uttered by both domestic and foreign critics, was that they did not read. Americans, they pointed out, bought few books and read even fewer. A technological people had become captive to its machines, reading standardized newspapers, watching motion pictures, and listening to the radio. Clifton Fadiman estimated the number of book readers in America at only a half million people, most of them "idle middle-class women, school-children, shop-girls, and a sprinkling of the laboring class." But Fadiman pointed to the widespread newspaper and magazine readership, with over 44 million newspapers circulated daily, and numerous popular weekly and monthly magazines. The five-cent weeklies, including the *Saturday Evening Post, Liberty*, and *Collier's*, were read, he said, "by the great middle class, the buying power of America." He explained:

> Even more clearly than their contents, their advertisements give as a good a picture of the American psyche as one would wish to find. Their influence is profound. In these columns the American middle-class philosophy finds itself completely expressed. Read indiscriminately by men, women and children, they publish nothing unsuited to the intelligence of a fourteen-year-old.

In addition, there were the many monthly magazines whose circulation was also in the millions, and the "pulp" magazines that catered to special groups. Americans, in short, were readers who did not want to waste their time, but who wanted in succinct form that reading material that confirmed their prejudices and met their desires. As Fadiman put it, "In the most direct and honest fashion, the magazines satisfy our life urges. They say little but when they talk it is the voice of America speaking."[42] But the 1920s also witnessed the launching of *The New Yorker*, which quickly established itself as required reading among America's cultured citizens.

Newspapers, Robert Benchley charged, were "machine-made" and "stereotyped," but "efficient and . . . entirely trustworthy," relying on features like personal columns, comic strips, and sports pages to build circulation. To the extent that the newspaper exerted any influence on its readers, that influence probably was the result of its political cartoons, for few Americans went to the trouble of reading editorials. Being on the whole colorless and uninspired, newspapers had inspired competitors in the form of tabloids, which attracted "readers" by exploiting photographs, sex, and lurid stories. As Robert Benchley wrote, they did not "attempt to cover any news which cannot be sensationalized or adapted to the camera's uses." They were a striking bit of evidence as to the level of the typical American mind in the 1920s.[43]

For the estimated half-million serious readers in America in the 1920s, the dominant literary influence was undoubtedly Henry Louis Mencken, the famed "Sage of Baltimore." This largely self-educated reporter for the *Baltimore Evening Sun* became, in the words of columnist Walter Lippmann, "the most powerful personal influence on this whole generation of educated people" in the 1920s.[44]

Most literate Americans in the 1920s considered the periodicals that he edited—*Smart Set* in the early years of the decade, then *American Mercury* into the early 1930s—as their bibles where literature and political/social criticism were concerned. For others, Mencken and the periodicals he edited epitomized all that was wrong with America during the decade. A Seattle Doctor of Divinity, for example, was quoted as saying: "Christian public school educators today are crying to the churches for help in combating the menace of Menckenism," while another complained of the *American Mercury*, which Mencken edited: "Mercurianity is the name of a new religion, the Bible of which is a green-covered monthly magazine."[45]

Mencken was simultaneously a champion of the new literature of the 1920s, a leading foe of censorship, and a critic of virtually everything that the American masses (the "booboisie") held dear. No political figure or area of the country was spared his relentless criticism, although his sharpest attacks were on Woodrow Wilson ("the perfect model of a Christian cad") and the South ("The Sahara of the Bozart"). He was unsparing in his attacks on fundamentalism and the Ku Klux Klan, although he regarded them as quintessentially American and unfailingly amusing.[46] Mencken traveled to Dayton, Tennessee to cover the Scopes trial and to study the backward culture that was so virulent in its opposition to science. His newspaper stories were reprinted in Tennessee newspapers, making him very unwelcome in Dayton. When William Jennings Bryan died a few days after the trial ended, Mencken penned some of his best prose in writing an epitaph for the fallen leader of the fundamentalist attack on science.

> Thus he fought his last fight, thirsting savagely for blood. All sense departed from him. He bit right and left, like a dog with rabies. He descended to demagogy so dreadful that his very associates at the trial table blushed. His one yearning was to keep his yokels heated up—to lead his forlorn mob of imbeciles against the foe. That foe, alas, refused to be alarmed. It insisted upon seeing the whole battle as a comedy. Even [Clarence] Darrow, who knew better, occasionally yielded to the prevailing spirit. One day he lured poor Bryan into the folly I have mentioned: his astounding argument against the notion that man is a mammal.... There stood the man who had been thrice a candidate for the Presidency of the Republic—there he stood in the glare of the world, uttering stuff that a boy of eight would laugh at. The artful Darrow led him on: he repeated it, ranted for it, bellowed it in his cracked voice. So he was prepared for the final slaughter. He came into life a hero, a Galahad, in bright and shining armor. He was passing out a poor mountebank.[47]

Through the 1920s Mencken was also publishing books, particularly his series of "Prejudices" volumes, which contain his best essays from the decade. In 1925 Mencken also struggled with the first work that he described privately as a "treatise." It was the book published in 1926 as *Notes on Democracy*, but Mencken was not satisfied with it. The writing had been interrupted by the death of his mother in 1925 and then by censorship battles in 1926.[48]

The principal problem with the book, however, was that its pages laid bare all of Mencken's rage over the events of the decade just passed—events that confirmed him in his contempt for the "American booboisie," its political leaders, and its religion. From the ease with which it swallowed "Dr. Wilson's" arguments for entering World War I and the eagerness with which it joined in the repression of civil rights during the war years and in the "Red Scare" that followed, to its support of prohibition and censorship, the picture was not one that saddened Mencken, but one that sickened, disgusted, and enraged him. Those emotions made *Notes on Democracy* the bitterest book that he wrote, eclipsing any of the Prejudices series in that respect. His later attempts to write scholarly treatises would turn out better, with *Treatise on the Gods* (1930) and *Treatise on Right and Wrong* (1934). In the meantime, Mencken had also published a work on the origins and nature of *The American Language* (1919), which, much to his surprise, quickly snowballed into a multivolume reference work that established him as the leading authority on the subject. A man who had little but disdain for pedants, now found himself included in their ranks.

By the end of the 1920s the passage of time had cooled much of Mencken's rage over the events of the World War I years and those that had followed that war, and many of the targets of his rage had disappeared from the scene. His advancing age, and changes in his personal life, also combined to alter his temperament and interests. The result was that the dominance of Mencken during the 1920s would not continue into the decade of the Great Depression.

One of the storms that raged through the literary world in the 1920s surrounded Sinclair Lewis' debunking of American sacred cows in his novels. Typical was the storm of protest that erupted over his portrayal of a Protestant minister in *Elmer Gantry*, from Billy Sunday and other defenders of the faith.

Literary Digest noted, though, that "H.L. Mencken, arch apostle of advanced and advancing thought, to whom Mr. Lewis plays the beloved disciple in his dedication, greets the book with becoming praise, and finds *Elmer Gantry* a typical, made-in-America man of God, and the book a lever which will begin moving Methodists, Baptists, etc., from the path of progress up which Mr. Mencken and others of the vanguard of civilization are so painfully toiling." Mencken, himself, wrote of the book:

> Elmer Gantry is American from the first low cackle of the prolog to the last gigantic obscenity—as American as goose-stepping or the mean admiration of mean things. And out of it leaps the most vivid and loving, the most gaudy and glorious, the most dreadful and perfect portrait of a man of God that has got between covers since Rabelais painted Friar John.... I am no prophet, but it seems to be quite possible that this simple (but far from idle!) tale may accomplish at one stroke what ten billion kilowatt hours of argument and invective have failed to accomplish. It may awaken the Americano to the dangers of the Methodist tyranny, as "Babbitt" awakened him to the imbecility of the Rotary-Kiwanis blather. In six months every Wesleyan spouter in the land may be jeered at as a *Gantry*, as every gabby tradesman is now sneered at as a *Babbitt*. The book may turn out to be a bugle-blast to topple over the evangelical wall, now so high and frowning. It may be the bomb foreordained to blow up the citadel.[49]

Joseph Wood Krutch, reviewing it for *The Nation*, wrote: "In a manner that seems to be merely the almost too literal truth but which manages nevertheless to contains its own criticism, Mr. Lewis has" in his trilogy *Main Street*, *Babbitt*, and *Elmer Gantry*, recorded a reign of grotesque vulgarity which but for him would have left no record of it because no one else could have adequately recorded it."[50]

Looking at the impact of the Machine Age on literature, Carl Van Doren wrote that it had produced "as in other forms of activity, such a division of labor and such a specialization that something very like a system of castes has arisen." Literature, journalism, oratory, history, drama, and the movies had begun each to inhabit its separate sphere, with even the bulk of verse and prose fiction considered somewhat inferior. Van Doren wrote: "The term literature, in a world in which nearly everybody is literate, is as a rule held to apply, not to whatever is written to be read, but only to what is written in certain ways for the benefit of those who will read it in certain ways." However, the leisure of the Machine Age had also stimulated such a demand that it had resulted in a flood of inferior writing, which could not really be considered literature at all. Moreover, the demands produced by the machine age had created, Van Doren wrote, "a demand, beyond the strength of publishers or writers to resist, for written matter which would serve various purposes not served by the classicals. Easy instruction, entertainment, news—these have been the demands most frequently insisted upon." But the Machine Age had also impacted the writers of genius, by giving them "impulse to productivity.... Somewhere in almost everything now written there is a sense of the audience. But that sense of an audience shows itself in more ways than has ordinarily been noted. It may lead to simplicity of language, to the avoidance of controverted themes, to the repetition of literary devices so often tried that they can be certain of effect, to a concession to vulgar prejudices."

Including movies as a form of literature, Van Doren wrote that it was the form of literature "most completely characteristic of the machine age, and it is the form which is, on the whole, most dependent upon machines. In it may be seen the full extent to which machines can liberate an art and the full extent to which they narrow it ... the moving picture, aiming always at the eyes of so many millions, notoriously prefers being below the few to being above the many. As a rule its plots are conventional, its characters stereotyped, its sentiments banal. Machines can photograph better than they can think."[51]

But literature in the 1920s was also infected by the disillusionment that came out of American participation in World War I, a disillusionment that led many to abandon the United States altogether during at least part of the decade, and to make Paris for a time the center of American letters. Included in their ranks were such noted names as Ernest Hemingway, John Dos Passos, Thomas Wolfe, and William Faulkner. It was also the decade of Theodore Dreiser and his celebrated battles with censorship, as well as humorists like Robert Benchley and Ring Lardner.

SMUT

One form of "literature" was relatively new to the United States, at least in the volume that appeared in the 1920s. This was smut. A writer in the *Saturday Review of Literature* wrote in 1926:

> Sins have their ups and downs, like the cost of living. Each generation has its pet aversion and saves for that the word immorality.... To get rid of the inhibitions of the Victorian period where the writer was not allowed so much as to mention things that everyone knew, is a great gain for honest readers and an immeasurable relief for honest authors. But this by no means tells the whole story. In poetry, in the novel, on the stage most of all, the suggestive situation, the risque line, cynical laughter at restraint, leering praise of the grosser instincts, have an astonishing place in popular favor. They get the laugh, they sell books, plays built upon them succeed, novels compounded of them are sure of discussion....
>
> Every newstand is dripping with magazines the entire purpose of which is to suggest, to arouse, to gratify eroticism under the thinnest veil of a language from which certain words are excluded (by legal advice) and by plots which always turn aside before the obvious conclusion. The joint circulation of such magazines is sufficient to put a copy into the hands of one out of every five or ten readers in the United States.... The age by comparison with earlier generations is sex mad (without being necessarily more licentious in deed); a fact at least as worthy of consideration as alcohol percentages or a belief or disbelief in evolution.

It was difficult, the writer admitted, to tell the difference between "a study of human nature, or a play upon human frailities," but "the vulgar dirt that floods the magazine market must be condemned."[52]

Midway through the decade, *Literary Digest* found the United States bidding to take the "lead in lewd literature away from France." It wrote: "Some scores of short-story magazines, it is said, are exploiting strictly sex emotions with a libidinous appeal that constitutes a grave social problem." One writer had estimated that "there are in all human probability 222,240,000 readings of sex-thrill magazines in the United States each year." The reaction against them had forced some out of business, but the only permanent solution would be through federal legislation and the use of the powers of the Postal Department. Frank Kent, columnist for the *Baltimore Sun*, wrote:

> In one small city in Ohio, of approximately 25,000 inhabitants, out of 110 weekly and monthly periodicals on sale, sixty-eight were either out-and-out devoted to "sex stuff," or were so close to the border-line as to be almost over it.... Then there are a whole flock—fifteen or twenty—monthlies of the "Hot Dog," "Red Pepper," "Whiz Bang" types, which add to the suggestiveness of the French a coarseness and vulgarity that are entirely American. All these periodicals are openly and frankly pornographic ... and are shipped to the dealers by express, so as to avoid going through the mails. They are of the type that have to be read by stealth and hidden in the desk.

So insatiable was the demand that new sex magazines were being launched every month, and Kent estimated that within a year there would a hundred of them. He went on:

> The rapid and remarkable rise of these publications—it has all occurred within the past eighteen months—is certainly the most sensational development in the publishing business ... in the last five years. Yet it has seemingly attracted little attention either from the daily newspapers or from the decent magazines.[53]

But *The New Republic* did take up the subject of what it called "Gutter Literature" the next year, writing:

> Within the last year or two a whole new type of periodical literature has sprung up in this country—most of it new in substance, all of it new in that it is now displayed openly where anyone, of any age, who possesses the requisite ten or twenty cents, may walk up and buy. The simplest, most accurate phrase by which to describe it is "gutter literature." Taken in the mass, it represents a social phenomenon of decided importance, which merits far more attention than it is getting.

The "newest and one of the most popular" of the magazines relying on sex for their appeal was the "Art magazine," of which there had been "a deluge in the past year." Despite their pretense of purveying art, they had "one idea and one alone: the portrayal of nudity." It went on:

> Some of my readers may be surprised to know that a majority of all the publications I have been discussing are planned by their publishers for women readers. Rightly or wrongly, the editors believe that the ladies are more voluminous printer-consumers than the men, even when it comes to stuff of this sort. While there are some of these periodicals which seek to interest men—and boys—there are three times as many which do not.

Most of these journals, of course, and particularly the very popular confessional type, base their appeal on the fact that for the average man, and even more, for the average woman, leading the common existence in this country, only partially literate, with limited financial resources, real life is a drab, dull and sordid affair. For such individuals the keenest pleasure, and almost the only pleasure, comes with temporary escape into a world of illusion and fantasy. . . . For this reason, the literature of escape which these magazines offer in such direct and simple form makes a powerful appeal, and one which it would be very difficult to break down. It is perhaps also for this reason that moral reformers, so busy with other aspects of our national life, have almost entirely ignored the growth of these new periodicals.[54]

Reformers took up the battle against smut. Hendrik Willem van Loon challenged a New York newspaper editor to accompany him to a newstand where he promised would be found at low cost "the foulest collection of smut, dirt, and plain pornography ever offered to an unsuspecting public in the guise of literature." In a magazine article he charged that America was "being overrun with . . . a putrid stream of the most despicable, the most iniquitous, and on the whole the most dangerous form of a degraded form of literature."[55]

Liberal reformer Oswald Garrison Villard took up the topic, too, in a May 1926 *Atlantic* article, writing that any American who had checked out the newsstands or village drugstores could not but be aware of:

a great new American literature, "throbbing with personality," "baring the human soul in all its elemental passions," letting in the light upon all mysteries of sex, and serving its country by brushing aside the last of our mid-Victorian reserves, reticences, and retirements. . . . Overnight a dozen readers grow where but one grew before. No low-descending sun but beholds the rise of a lodestar of the new monthly journalism. The reception of each one leaves no doubt that the little red schoolhouse is at last coming into its own; its graduates are proving in large numbers that they are ready for the high school of the sex magazines.

Villard pointed out that the American smut publishers faced competition from European magazines, like *La Vie Parisienne,* which American servicemen had grown familiar with during World War I.[56]

In early 1927 a campaign in New York City succeeded in driving the smut magazines from its newsstands, as a result of a campaign launched by the *New York World.* Thus, *Literary Digest* reported,

what Henrik van Loon two years ago described as the "foulest collection of smut, dirt, and plain pornography ever offered to the public in the name of literature" is sent to the garbage pile in the city where most of it is said to have originated.

And similar campaigns were underway in other cities, including the nation's capital, Atlanta, St. Louis, Boston, Baltimore, and Syracuse.[57]

Conclusion

The leitmotiv throughout the 1920s was the impact of science, particularly the machine, on the daily lives of the American people. The application of the machine to mass production for seemingly limitless profits was credited by many astute observers with being the driving force behind virtually every aspect of the decade, from the collapse of moral standards and the frenetic form of play to art and architecture. There seems little doubt that it injected a large element of uncertainty and insecurity into the lives of many Americans, causing them worry about their ultimate place in the new machine economy and fear about their prospects after they reached their forties or fifties. This was an age without the emphasis on retirement plans, Individual Retirement Accounts, and all of the other devices by which people can now provide for their old age, not to mention the absence until the 1930s of the federal social security system. That fear doubtless drove many into the stock market speculation of the 1920s.

The effects of World War I on the 1920s would doubtless have been profound in a variety of ways even without the inexorable force of the machine, but almost certainly not as profound as they were. Perhaps the greatest impact of the war, in fact, was the impetus it gave to the American economy and to the exploitation of machine production on a scale unheard of before then. Time-tested values and standards were blown by the wayside. The machine brought to most Americans devices unheard of before the war or limited to a very wealthy few. The advantages of those devices were many and have been much described, but as the Lynds' study of Middletown showed, they promoted changes that might have been better adapted to had they occurred separately and over a period of time. But all intruded into the lives of Americans simultaneously—the automobile, motion pictures, radio, home appliances, thus challenging traditional family life, dating patterns, even long-ingrained habits of thrift as the necessity for them was pounded into the people daily by the variety of advertising media and by peer pressures.

Some lashed out blindly at the influences they saw around them, attacking symptoms rather than the cause. Ministers castigated the loose morals of the 1920s, blaming them on everything from Freudianism to jazz and the dances. Fundamentalists retreated into a dogmatic shell and battled the influence of modern science. Others joined the Ku Klux Klan in seeking to bring a return to a more stable past, one free of the influences of those groups they blamed for the deterioration of America. Eugenicists sought to restore to influence the racially pure Nordic group they credited with America's progress by increasing its progeny and reducing the numbers of those of the "less desirable" groups. Guardians of the country's morals also tried to censor those books they condemned for their lewd content and themes. Prohibitionists never tired of seeking to eliminate the evil influences of alcohol all through the 1920s. These are all the actions of a society torn by insecurity about the present and future.

America has historically cleaved between its rural/small-town values and standards and those of the city, all the way back to Jefferson and Hamilton. There was also cleavage between North and South, with the latter regarded as more backward, what Mencken called the "Sahara of the Bozart." Both cleavages were present in the 1920s, the former accentuated by the depression in agriculture that continued through the 1920s in stark contrast with the prosperous image of the cities, and by the fact that prohibition tended to be identified by Northern city dwellers with the parochialism of the South and rural areas, where its strongest supporters did, in fact, exist. Yet, the reaction against the influences of the 1920s cut across those lines and revealed itself in North and South and in cities and rural areas alike. We have already seen the observation in Chapter 6 of Dr. Albert C. Dieffenbach, Unitarian, editor of *The Christian Register*, arch foe of fundamentalism, but hardly an alarmist, that the mind of fundamentalism cut across Christians in most states. The ebb and flow of fundamentalism in the 1920s tended then and since to be measured in terms of its successes and failures in the battle against the teaching of evolution, but such a yardstick did nothing to measure the hold its fundamental tenets continued to hold on people or where. The success, even if brief, of the Ku Klux Klan in a variety of Northern areas is also an indication of the depth to which the reaction cut across traditional lines of separation. The reaction also cut across class and intellectual lines, with the eugenics movement, for example, attracting a number of otherwise respectable scholars, while the Ku Klux Klan was attractive, at least initially, to many businessmen in much the same way that Fascism attracted many of them in Italy.

Some reacted to the uncertainties and apparent normlessness of the 1920s with hedonism, others with a dogmatic attempt to restore the certainties and predicability of the past. So widely separated in response and behavior, however, both groups were reacting to the same stimulus—the seemingly inexorable march of Mammon and the Machine and the disruptions being caused in their daily lives.

Notes

PREFACE

1. Charles Merz, *And Then Came Ford* (Garden City, NY, 1929), pp. 318–19.
2. *President's Research Committee on Social Trends*, 2 volumes (New York, 1933).

INTRODUCTION

1. See *Literary Digest*, 16 November 1929, p. 64.
2. In Fred J. Ringel, ed., *America: As Americans See It* (New York, 1932), p. 16.
3. Stuart Chase, *Men and Machines* (New York, 1929), pp. 12–13.
4. Sila Bent, "Advertising," in Ringel, pp. 280–87.
5. Silas Bent, *Machine Made Man* (New York, 1930), p. 11.
6. Clarence Britten, in Harold Stearns, ed., *Civilization in the United States* (New York, 1922), p. 111.
7. Chase, p. 162.
8. R. Austin Freeman, *Social Decay and Regeneration* (Boston and New York, 1921), p. 3.
9. John Dewey, in Charles A. Beard, ed., *Whither Mankind* (New York, 1928), pp. 322–24.
10. Freeman, p. 181.
11. Everett Dean Martin, in Beard, pp. 363–34.
12. Ibid., p. 365.
13. Lewis Mumford in Stearns, p. 13.
14. Martin, p. 373.
15. Eugene O'Neill, *Dynamo* (New York, 1929).
16. See *Literary Digest*, 26 May 1928, p. 25.
17. Quoted in ibid., October 1927, p. 28.

18. Bertrand Russell, in Beard, p. 72.
19. Robert S. and Helen Lynd, *Middletown* (New York, 1929), pp. 32–33.
20. Ibid., pp. 34–35, p. 493.
21. See *Literary Digest*, 19 May 1928, p. 23.

CHAPTER 1: THE REVOLUTION IN MORAL STANDARDS

1. Joseph Wood Krutch, *The Modern Temper* (New York, 1929), pp. 23–24.
2. Ibid., p. 94.
3. Ibid., p. 105.
4. Ibid., p. 114.
5. "Is Freudism Destined to Live?" *Current Opinion*, September 1920, pp. 355–57.
6. A.A. Roback, "Quacks," *Forum*, May 1929, pp. 263–69; "Excess of the Sex-Factor in Freud's Methods," *Current Opinion*, April 1921, pp. 523–24.
7. Karl Menninger, "Pseudoanalysis: Perils of Freudian Verbalisms," *Outlook*, 9 July 1930, pp. 363–65.
8. Alfred B. Kuttner, "Nerves," in Stearns, p. 434.
9. John Crowe Ransom, "Freud and Literature," *Saturday Review of Literature*, 4 October 1924, p. 161.
10. Viola Paradise, "The Sex Simplex," *Forum*, July 1925, p. 108.
11. George Sylvester Viereck, "Freud: Columbus Of the Subconscious," *Forum*, March 1925, pp. 302–12.
12. Cornelia Stratton Parker, "The Capital of Psychology," *Survey*, 15 August 1925, pp. 551–55.
13. Aldous Huxley, "Our Contemporary Hocus-Pocus," ibid., pp. 313–20.
14. Havelock Ellis, "A Tribute to Freud," *Forum*, July 1926, pp. 150–53.
15. A.A. Roback, "Quacks," *Forum*, May 1929, pp. 263–69.
16. Max Plowman, "Beauty and ... Freud," *Living Age*, December 1930, pp. 378–80.
17. Silas Bent, *Machine Made Man* (New York, 1930) p. xvi.
18. See *Catholic World*, November 1930, pp. 225–27.
19. See *New York Times*, 29 February 1920.
20. See *Literary Digest*, 9 February 1924, pp. 32–33.
21. See *New York Times*, 12 February 1927.
22. See *Literary Digest*, 31 December 1927, p. 51.
23. See *New York Times*, 19 April 1927.
24. Ibid., 4 November 1927.
25. Ibid., 28 April 1927.
26. Ibid., 5 May 1930.
27. Ibid., 16 April 1928.
28. Joseph Wood Krutch, "Love—Or the Life and Death of a Value," *Atlantic*, August 1928, pp. 199–210.
29. William Orton, "Reconstructing the Sex Ethic," *The New Republic*, 15 February 1928, pp. 339–42.
30. Gilbert Murray, "The Crisis in Morals" *Harper's*, January 1930, pp. 133–40.
31. Harvey O'Higgins, "The New Morality," *New Outlook*, 16 January 1929, pp. 83–85.
32. Ralph W. Sockman, "Morals in a Machine Age," *Harper's*, February 1931, pp. 365–74.

33. Emily Post, "What! No Chaperons?" *Collier's*, 7 September 1929, pp. 20, 66.
34. See *Literary Digest*, 21 February 1925.
35. Ibid., 26 April 1919, p. 47.
36. James F. Gillespie, with Wesley Stout, "Hot Music," *Saturday Evening Post*, 19 March 1929, pp. 10–11.
37. See *Literary Digest*, 12 March 1924, pp. 29–30.
38. Ibid., 5 January 1929, p. 23.
39. Ibid., 2 October 1926, p. 28.
40. Ibid., 30 October 1926, p. 29.
41. Silas Bent, pp. 297, 321.
42. See James Weldon Johnson, in Ringel, p. 163.
43. See *Literary Digest*, 13 November 1926, p. 32.
44. Ibid., 9 February 1929, p. 21.
45. Sydney Grew, "War and Music," *Contemporary Review*, December 1920, p. 850.
46. See *Literary Digest*, 14 May 1921, pp. 11–12.
47. Gilbert Seldes, "Shake Your Feet," *The New Republic*, 4 November 1925, pp. 283–84.
48. David Ewen, "Popular Music of the Decade," in Barbara A. Solomon, ed., *Ain't We Got Fun*, New York, 1980, p. 149.
49. See *Literary Digest*, 19 October 1929, pp. 46–48.
50. Ibid., 25 July 1931, p. 22.
51. Isaac Goldberg, "Jazz," *Forum*, April 1932, pp. 234–36.
52. See *Literary Digest*, 12 April 1930, p. 20.
53. Ibid., 5 January 1924.
54. Ibid., 5 November 1927, pp. 27–28.
55. Ralph W. Sockman, "The Vanishing Sinner," *Harper's*, November 1930, pp. 676–84.
56. Gilbert Murray, "The Crisis in Morals," *Harper's*, January 1930, pp. 133–40.

CHAPTER 2: MANNERS, MODES, AND FADS

1. See *New York Times*, 4 September 1921, p. 8.
2. Elizabeth Robins Pennell, "Our Democracy of Bad Manners," *Forum*, April 1925, pp. 504–12.
3. Mr. Grundy, "'Polite Society,'" *Atlantic*, May 1920, p. 608.
4. Willing Ratray, "Divorce as Manners and Customs," *The New Republic*, 9 December 1925, p. 81.
5. Reid Byron, "Death to Propriety," ibid., 26 December 1928, p. 161.
6. See *Literary Digest*, 2 February 1929, p. 26.
7. Robert S. and Helen Lynd, *Middletown*, (New York, 1929), pp. 154–55.
8. "The Family Goes On," *The New Republic*, 16 November 1927, p. 327.
9. Silas Bent, *Machine Made Man*, New York, 1930. pp. 48–50.
10. *Middletown*, pp. 94–95.
11. Ibid., pp. 98–99.
12. Ibid., p. 171.
13. Ibid., p. 172.
14. Ibid., p. 173.
15. Bent, pp. 5, 103.

16. See *Literary Digest*, 29 September 1928, p. 31.
17. *Middletown*, pp. 499–500.
18. See *Literary Digest*, 13 July 1929, p. 56.
19. Stuart Chase, *Men and Machines* (New York, 1929), pp. 279, 281–82.
20. Walter Pitkin, in Ringel, p. 203.
21. Ibid., p. 212.
22. "The Civilizing of Divorce," *Literary Digest*, 1 August 1928, p. 266.
23. Ibid., 11 April 1925, p. 32.
24. Bishop Frederick Burgess, quoted in Gustavus Myers, "The Rapid Increase of Divorce," *Current History*, 14 August 1921, p. 816.
25. In Ringel, p. 218.
26. Myers, p. 816.
27. See *Literary Digest*, 12 January 1929, p. 26, and 10 December 1927, p. 28.
28. Charles Platt, "Is Prohibition Worth While?" *Nation*, 14 January 1925, pp. 33–34.
29. Charles Merz, *The Dry Decade*, passim.
30. Ben Dixon MacNeill, "Report from North Carolina," *American Mercury*, January 1930, p. 98.
31. See *Literary Digest*, 12 April 1930, pp. 33–34.
32. Ibid., 21 July 1928, p. 46.
33. Charles Merz, *The Great American Bandwagon* (New York, 1928), pp. 53, 56, 58, 60–61, 67.
34. In Ringel, pp. 282–83.
35. See *Literary Digest*, 23 February 1923, p. 17.
36. Quoted in *Literary Digest*, 28 June 1919, p. 76.
37. Walter Pitkin, in Ringel, p. 203.
38. See *Literary Digest*, 22 November 1924, p. 28.
39. In ibid., 19 December 1925, pp. 31–32.
40. Allan L. Benson, "Smokes for Women," *Good Housekeeping*, August 1929, pp. 40, 194.
41. Philip Wagner, "Cigarettes vs. Candy," *The New Republic*, 13 February 1926, pp. 343–45.
42. See *Business Week*, 28 October 1931, p. 14.
43. Frances Warfield, "Lost Cause," *Outlook*, 12 February 1920, pp. 244–47.
44. Chase, *Men and Machines* p. 271.
45. See *Literary Digest*, 7 March 1925, pp. 21–22.
46. See *North American Review*, August 1920, pp. 252–53.
47. See *Literary Digest*, 6 December 1924, p. 29.
48. Ibid., 29 March 1924, pp. 54–55.
49. Merz, *Bandwagon*, p. 256.
50. Charles Merz, *And Then Came Ford*, Garden City, 1929, pp. 259–60.
51. Paul Poiret, "Will Skirts Disappear?" *Forum*, January 1927, pp. 32–33.
52. Chase, *Men and Machines*, p. 268.
53. S. N. Behrman, "The Advertising Man," *The New Republic*, 20 August 1919, pp. 84–85.
54. See *Atlantic*, October 1919, pp. 572–75.
55. "The Hand of the Designer in Advertising Art," *Arts & Decoration*, March 1921, pp. 384–85.
56. "Advertising for Health," *Literary Digest*, 29 November 1919.

57. "A Note on Advertising," *The New Republic*, 8 July 1925, p. 180.
58. Sinclair Lewis, "Publicity Gone Mad," *The Nation*, 6 March 1929, p. 278.
59. Silas Bent, pp. 385, 390.
60. Stuart Chase, "The Tragedy of Waste," *The New Republic*, 19 August 1925, pp. 342–45.
61. Stuart Chase, "Six Cylinder Ethics," *Forum*, January 1928, pp. 22–34.
62. Ibid.
63. In Ringel, p. 286.

CHAPTER 3: THE QUEST FOR BEAUTY

1. M.D.C. Crawford, "Weaving the Orient into American Industry," *Journal of the American Asiatic Association*, January 1920, pp. 58–64.
2. R. Austin Freeman, *Social Decay and Regeneration*, Boston and New York, 1921, pp. 183–86.
3. See *Literary Digest*, 19 April 1924, pp. 28–29.
4. Lewis Mumford, "Machinery and the Modern Style," *The New Republic*, 3 August 1921, pp. 263–65.
5. Walter Pach, in Stearns, p. 241.
6. Gilbert Seldes, "Industrial Design," *Saturday Evening Post*, 5-28-1932, p. 34.
7. Lewis Mumford, "Modernism for Sale," *American Mercury*, April 1929, pp. 453–55.
8. See *Literary Digest*, 2 June 1928, pp. 25–26.
9. Ibid., 1 September 1928, pp. 22–23.
10. See Charles Merz, *Ford*, p. 284.
11. Lewis Mumford, in Beard, pp. 296–97, 302.
12. Charles Merz, *Ford*, pp. 281–82.
13. C. Matlack Price, "The Trend in Architectural Thought in America," *Century*, September 1921, pp. 708–22.
14. Lewis Mumford, "The Architecture of Escape," *The New Republic*, 12 August 1925, pp. 321–22.
15. Harvey W. Corbett, "New Heights in American Architecture," *Yale Review*, July 1928, pp. 690–701.
16. Lewis Mumford, "The Brown Decades: Architecture," *Scribner's*, April 1931, pp. 385–95.
17. See *Literary Digest*, 21 May 1927, pp. 26–27.
18. In Charles Ringel, pp. 47–49.
19. See *Literary Digest*, 28 September 1929, p. 29.
20. Stuart Chase, *Men and Machines* (New York, 1929), pp. 246–47, 249.
21. Ibid., p. 251.
22. See *American Mercury*, January 1931, pp. 164–65.
23. Merz, *Bandwagon* (New York, 1928), pp. 120–21, 123.
24. Stuart Chase, *Men and Machines*, pp. 276–77.
25. *Literary Digest*, 29 March 1924, pp. 27–28; 23 November 1929, p. 19.
26. In Charles Ringel, pp. 254–59.
27. Robert Hughes, *American Visions* (New York, 1997), pp. 360–435.
28. Walter Pach, in Stearns, p. 229.

29. See *Literary Digest*, 30 November 1929, p. 21; See *Current Opinion*, October 1919, p. 243.
30. See *The New Republic*, 25 November 1931, pp. 40–43.
31. Dorothy Cocks, "What about Plastic Surgery?" *Good Housekeeping*, June 1930, pp. 109, 150–51.
32. Jeanette Eaton, "The Cosmetic Urge," *Harper's*, February 1931.
33. See *New York Times*, 13 April 1922.
34. In Ringel, pp. 96–97.
35. In Ringel, p. 203.
36. Jeanette Eaton, "The Cosmetic Urge," *Harper's*, February 1931.
37. Paul W. White, "Our Booming Beauty Business," *Outlook*, 22 January 1930, pp. 133–35.
38. "Is the Younger Generation in Peril?" *Literary Digest*, 14 May 1921, pp. 9–10.
39. "On Being in the Fashion," *Living Age*, 17 July 1920, p. 164.
40. Harvey Maitland Watts, "The American Age," *Forum*, March 1925, pp. 373–74.
41. See *Literary Digest*, 18 July 1925, pp. 65–66.
42. Bruce Bliven, "Flapper Jane," *The New Republic*, 9 September 1925, pp. 65–66.
43. Carrie Chapman Catt, "Short Skirts and French Dictators," *Forum*, 4 April 1927, pp. 578–85.
44. Fannie Hurst, "Let's Not Wear Them!" *The New Republic*, 30 October 1930, pp. 293–94.
45. Letter from Harry Collins to *New York Times*, 2 September 1922.
46. *Independent*, 12 February 1927, p. 181.
47. Marian Hertha Clarke, "The Sheep Decide," *North American Review*, August 1929, pp. 234–37.
48. Fannie Hurst, p. 294.
49. "The Battle of the Styles," *The New Republic*, 11 December 1929, p. 58.
50. "The Female Form Divine," *The Nation*, 13 November 1929, p. 540.
51. *New York Times*, 28 July 1929.

CHAPTER 4: THE IMPACT OF RADIO AND MOVIES

1. Stuart Chase, "Play," *Whither Mankind*, pp. 333–34.
2. Robert S. and Helen Lynd, *Middletown*, (New York, 1929), pp. 217, 269–70.
3. Creighton Peet, "Music as a Narcotic," *Forum*, August 1930, pp. 113–15.
4. George W. Gray, "Signing Off on the First Ten Years," *World's Work*, December 1930, p. 46.
5. Bent, p. 127.
6. See *Literary Digest*, 20 November 1926, p. 20.
7. Ibid., 2 October 1926, p. 13.
8. Marc A. Rose, "Radio or Newspaper—Can Both Survive?" *The Nation*, 24 December 1924, pp. 699–700.
9. See *Literary Digest*, 12 January 1924, p. 12.
10. John R. Tunis, "Sport and the Radio," *Outlook*, 16 October 1929, p. 276.
11. See *Literary Digest*, 24 January 1925, p. 29.
12. Leon Whipple, "The Red Radio," *Survey*, 1 July 1925, pp. 406–8.
13. Gilbert Seldes, "Listening In," *The New Republic*, 23 March 1927, pp. 14–15.

14. *Bandwagon*, pp. 46–47, 48, 50.
15. In Charles Ringel, pp. 275–76.
16. L.W. "No News on the Air," *Survey*, 1 October 1926, p. 53.
17. "You're on the Air," *Saturday Evening Post*, 1 May 1926, pp. 14–15.
18. See *Literary Digest*, 10 January 1925, pp. 63–65.
19. "The Voter and the Radio," *The New Republic*, 23 May 1928, pp. 6–7.
20. See *Literary Digest*, 7 May 1927, p. 46.
21. Ibid., 1 December 1928, p. 13.
22. Ibid., 3 January 1925, p. 232.
23. Ibid., 14 May 1925, pp. 23–24.
24. Ibid., 17 May 1924, p. 27.
25. Ibid., 30 July 1927, p. 30.
26. Harvey O'Higgins, "To What Green Altar," *The New Republic*, 15 February 1919, pp. 80–81.
27. *Middletown*, p. 263–64.
28. Walter P. Eaton, "Latest Menace of the Movies," *North American Review*, July 1920, pp. 80–87.
29. Elizabeth R. Pennell, "Movies as Dope," ibid., November 1921, pp. 619–27.
30. Bent, p. 308.
31. Deems Taylor, in Stearns, pp. 212–13.
32. Floyd Parsons, "Everybody's Business," *Saturday Evening Post*, 26 March 1921, pp. 26, 29.
33. "Photoplay Finance," *Literary Digest*, 4 June 1921, pp. 83–84.
34. Ralph Block, "The Movies versus Motion Pictures," *Century Magazine*, October 1921, pp. 889–91.
35. Gilbert Seldes, "Theory about 'Talkies,'" *The New Republic*, August 1928, pp. 305–6.
36. R.E. Sherwood, "Renaissance in Hollywood," *American Mercury*, April 1929, pp. 431–37.
37. See *Literary Digest*, 11 August 1928, pp. 8–9.
38. "A Year of Talkies," *The Nation*, 26 June 1929, p. 772.
39. "The 'Talkies,'" ibid., 20 February 1929, p. 236.
40. See *Literary Digest*, 12 October 1929, p. 21.
41. See *Bandwagon*, pp. 169–81.
42. "The Talkies' Future," *The Nation*, 15 January 1930, pp. 61–62.
43. M. Mermey, "Vanishing Fiddler," *North American Review*, March 1929, pp. 301–7.
44. Alexander Bakshy, "Color," *Nation*, 19 March 1930, p. 337.
45. Alexander Bakshy, "Vaudeville Must Be Saved," ibid., 24 July 1929, pp. 98–99.
46. Alexander Bakshy, "Vaudeville's Prestige," ibid, 4 September 1929, p. 258.
47. Nick Grinde, "Where's Vaudeville At?" *Saturday Evening Post*, 11 January 1930, p. 44.
48. A.B. Walkley, "The Theatre and the War," *Living Age*, 15 November 1919, pp. 407–13.
49. Oliver M. Sayler, "New Movement in the Theatre," *North American Review*, June 1921, pp. 761–71.
50. Montrose Moses, "New Trends in the Theatre," *Forum*, February 1925, pp. 231–37.
51. See *Literary Digest*, 26 October 1929, p. 32.
52. Earl Chapin May, "A Calamitous Stage Slump," *World's Work*, May 1929, pp. 58–61.

53. George Jean Nathan, "The Living Corpse," *American Mercury*, April 1929, pp. 500–5.

54. George Jean Nathan, "The Theatre" pp. 245–48 in Stearns.

55. Theresa Helburn, "What's Right with the Theater?" *The New Republic*, 10 April 1929, pp. 226–27.

56. T. McKnight, "Wall Street Marries Broadway," *Scribner's*, August 1929, pp. 164–68.

57. Otis Skinner, "What's Wrong with the Theater To-day?" *World's Work*, October 1929, pp. 93–96.

58. Jane Cowl, "The Collapse of the Drama," *Pictorial Review*, September 1929, p. 27.

59. "Hey Rube," *The Nation*, 6 November 1929, p. 513.

CHAPTER 5: BUSINESS AND LIFE

1. Robert S. and Helen Lynd, *Middletown*, (New York, 1929), pp. 44–45.
2. Silas Bent, pp. 192, 194.
3. See *Literary Digest*, 21 December 1929, p. 64.
4. Ibid., 4 April 1928, p. 87.
5. In Charles Ringel, p. 297.
6. In ibid., p. 299.
7. See *Literary Digest*, 28 February 1925, p. 78.
8. Robert S. and Helen Lynd, *Middletown*, (New York, 1929), pp. 46, 49.
9. Stuart Chase, *Men and Machines* (New York, 1929), p. 179.
10. See *Literary Digest*, 17 August 1929, p. 58.
11. See *Literary Digest*, 8 October 1927, p. 76.
12. Ibid., 7 September 1929, p. 11; 12 October 1929, p. 11.
13. *Men and Machines*, p. 137.
14. Silas Bent, p. 268.
15. Stuart Chase, pp. 208–9.
16. Ibid.
17. Ibid.
18. See *Literary Digest*, 29 November 1929, pp. 17–18.
19. Ibid., 26 February 1929, p. 64.
20. Stuart Chase, pp. 209–10.
21. Ibid., pp. 214–15.
22. Ibid., p. 210.
23. See *Literary Digest*, 29 November 1919, pp. 17–18.
24. Ibid., 26 February 1921, p. 64.
25. Thomas Gammack, "In Defense of the Bull Market," *Outlook*, 12 December 1928, p. 1330.
26. Quoted in P.W. Garrett, "Forces behind the Fever," *Outlook*, 26 December 28, p. 1391–92.
27. F.D. Bond, "Common Stock Racket," *North American Review*, April 1929, pp. 444–48.
28. Eunice Fuller Barnhard, "Ladies of the Ticker," ibid., April 1929, pp. 405–10.
29. "Bulls, Bears and Lambs," ibid., January 1929, pp. 28–29.
30. Paul Abbott, "Fever or Foresight?" *Outlook*, 23 January 1929, pp. 142–43.
31. See *Literary Digest*, 3 July 1926, p. 50.

32. Ibid., 11 June 1927, p. 72.
33. Bent, pp. 206–7.
34. Figures are from *Historical Statistics of the United States* (Washington, DC, 1975), pp. 264–66, 1009.
35. See *Literary Digest*, 3 January 1925, p. 68.
36. Ibid., 28 April 1928, p. 65.
37. Ibid., 12 May 1928, p. 76.
38. Thomas Gammack, "Scolding by the Federal Reserve," *Outlook*, 20 February 1929, p. 306.
39. "Four Wheel Brakes for Speculation," *The New Republic*, 20 February 1929, pp. 4–5.
40. See *Literary Digest*, 23 February 1929, pp. 78–82.
41. Charles Merz, "Bull Market," *Harper's*, April 1929, pp. 640–46.
42. "Behind the Credit Battle," *The New Republic*, 10 April 1929, pp. 212–13.
43. Lewis Corey, "Who Gains by Speculation," ibid., 17 April 1929, pp. 247–48.
44. See *Literary Digest*, 25 September 1926.
45. In Ringel, p. 310.
46. See *Literary Digest*, 13 April 1929, p. 56.
47. See *World's Work*, May 1929, p. 33.
48. C.J. Murphy, "Wall Street Branches Out," *Outlook*, 18 September 1929, pp. 85–89.
49. See *Literary Digest*, 30 November 1929, p. 56.
50. Ibid., 21 September 1929, p. 72.
51. "The Men Who Did It," *The Nation*, 13 November 1929, pp. 539–40.
52. See *Literary Digest*, 9 November 1929, pp. 72–75.

CHAPTER 6: EUGENICS AND INTELLIGENCE TESTING

1. Horace Kallen, "Eugenics—Made in Germany," *Dial*, 11 January 1919, pp. 28–29.
2. Leon Cole, "Biological Philosophy and the War," *Scientific Monthly*, March 1919, pp. 247–57.
3. "Risks Involved in the Effort to Breed Superior People," *Current Opinion*, October 1920, pp. 499–500.
4. Stewart Paton, "Democracy's Opportunity," *Scientific Monthly*, September 1920, pp. 254–62.
5. Irving Fisher, "Impending Problems of Eugenics," ibid., September 1921, pp. 214–31.
6. Edwin Slosson, "The Survival of the Unfittest," *The Independent*, 8 October 1921, pp. 24–25.
7. William McDougall, "The Island of Eugenia: The Phantasy of a Foolish Philosopher," *Scribner's*, October 1921, pp. 483–91.
8. Leonard Darwin, "The Aims and Methods of Eugenical Societies," *Science*, 7 October 1921, p. 322.
9. See *Literary Digest*, 12 January 1924, p. 25.
10. Ellsworth Huntington, "Our Biological Future," *Yale Review*, XVII (October 1927), 136–52.
11. See *Literary Digest*, 21 April 1928, p. 46.
12. Ibid., 14 June 1924, p. 23.
13. Ibid., 14 July 1928, p. 17.

14. C.P. Blacker, "Birth Control and Eugenics," *The Nineteenth Century*, April 1932, pp. 464–77.

15. George A. Dorsey, "Race and Civilization," in Charles A. Beard, ed., *Whither Mankind*, New York, 1928, pp. 229–63.

16. Grace Adams, "Measuring the American Mind," *American Mercury*, June 1929, pp. 194–98.

17. Beardsley Ruml, "The Extension of Selective Tests to Industry," *Annals of the American Academy*, LXXX (January 1919), 38–42.

18. See *Literary Digest*, 28 February 1920.

19. Grace Adams, "Measuring the American Mind," *American Mercury*, June 1929, pp. 194–98.

20. See *Literary Digest*, 24 July 1929, pp. 80–81.

21. "Ascertaining a Man's Ability by Scientific Tests," *Current Opinion*, February 1921, p. 236.

22. Ellwood Hendrick, "The Shadow Side," *Harper's*, August 1920, pp. 394–400.

23. See *School and Society*, 22 January 1921, pp. 97–102.

24. S.C. Kohs, "We've Gone Psychiatric," *Survey*, 15 May 1930, pp. 188–90.

25. See *Literary Digest*, 6 December 1924, pp. 8–9.

26. Ibid., 24 May 1924, pp. 32–33.

27. Ibid., 28 March 1925, p. 31.

CHAPTER 7: THE KU KLUX KLAN AND FUNDAMENTALISM

1. Frank Parker Stockbridge, "The Kuklux Klan Revival," *Current History Magazine of the New York Times*, April 1921, pp. 19–25.

2. Walter F. White, "Reviving the Ku Klux Klan," *The Forum*, April 1921, pp. 426–34.

3. "The K.K.K." *The New Republic*, 21 September 1921, pp. 88–89.

4. "For and against the Ku Klux Klan," *Literary Digest*, 24 September 1921, pp. 35–38.

5. See *Literary Digest*, 1 October 1921. pp. 30–31.

6. Arthur Corning White, "An American Fascismo," *The Forum*, November 1924, pp. 636–42.

7. Letter to *The New Republic*, 24 December 1924, p. 121.

8. Llewellyn Nelson, "The KKK for Boredom," ibid., 14 January 1925, pp. 196–97.

9. William Robinson Pattangall, "Is the Ku Klux Un-American?" *The Forum*, September 1925, pp. 321–32.

10. Hiram Wesley Evans, "The Klan: Defender of Americanism," ibid., December 1925, pp. 801–14.

11. "The Klan Sheds Its Hood," *The New Republic*, 12 February 1926, pp. 310–11.

12. See *The New Republic*, 30 November 1927, pp. 33–34.

13. Robert S. and Helen Lynd, *Middletown* (New York, 1929), pp. 481–84.

14. Vernon Kellogg, "Where Evolution Stands Today," *The New Republic*, 22 April 1923, pp. 179–81.

15. "The Presbyterian Church and the Teaching of Evolution," *School and Society*, 2 June 1923, pp. 606–7.

16. See *Literary Digest*, 15 September 1923, p. 34.

17. Charles William Eliot, "The Great Religious Revival," *Atlantic*, March 1924, pp. 379–85.

18. "The Case of the Fundamentalists," *The Nation*, 26 December 1923, p. 729.
19. "Does Fundamentalism Obstruct Social Progress?" *The Survey*, 1 July 1924, pp. 389–92.
20. Howard Chandler Robbins, "'Fundamentalism,' and 'Modernism,'" *The Forum*, May 1924, pp. 651–55.
21. See *The New Republic*, 6 February 1924, p. 275.
22. Chester T. Crowell, "I'm for the Fundamentalists," ibid., 18 March 1925, pp. 94–96.
23. "The Cure for Fundamentalism," ibid., 10 June 1923, pp. 58–60.
24. "Banishing Evolution in the South," *Literary Digest*, 3 April 1926, p. 30.
25. Miriam Allen DeFord, "After Dayton: A Fundamentalist Survey," *The Nation*, 2 June 1926, pp. 604–5.
26. "The Fundamentalists Retreat," *The New Republic*, 24 August 1927, pp. 8–9.
27. See *Literary Digest*, 11 June 1927, p. 33.
28. Ibid., 1 December 1928.
29. Ibid., 26 November 1927, pp. 26–27.

CHAPTER 8: PASTIMES

1. Stuart Chase, "Play," in Charles A. Beard, ed., *Whither Mankind*, (New York, 1928), pp. 336–39.
2. Ibid., p. 335.
3. Ibid., pp. 343, 347–48.
4. Ibid., p. 353.
5. Silas Bent, p. 10.
6. Robert S. and Helen Lynd, *Middletown* (New York, 1929), pp. 226, 232.
7. See *Literary Digest*, 29 March 1924, p. 50.
8. In Ringel, pp. 126–27.
9. See *Literary Digest*, 5 October 1929, pp. 78–79.
10. Ibid.
11. Chase, "Play," p. 349.
12. Ibid., p. 348.
13. Ibid., p. 349.
14. Ibid.
15. Bent, pp. 288–89.
16. Bent, p. 300.
17. Stuart Chase *Men and Machines* (New York, 1929), p. 257.
18. Bent, p. 175.
19. See *Literary Digest*, 8 October 1927, p. 76.
20. Bent, p. 177.
21. See *Literary Digest*, 14 August 1926, p. 23.
22. Ibid., 10 January 1925, p. 27.
23. Ibid., 21 March 1929, p. 13.
24. Ibid., 14 June 1924, pp. 70–71.
25. Ibid., 29 November 1924, p. 15.
26. Ibid., 7 March 1925, pp. 82–84.
27. Ibid., 24 March 1925; 2 October 1926, pp. 7–9; 9 October 1926, pp. 43–47.
28. *Men and Machines*, p. 191.

29. David Ewen, in Solomon, p. 158.
30. Charles Merz, *And Then Came Ford* (Garden City, NY, 1929), pp. 272–78.
31. Ibid., p. 271.
32. Merz, *Ford*, pp. 282–83.
33. See *Literary Digest*, 11 September 1926, p. 87.
34. William Ashdown, "Confessions of an Automobilist," *Atlantic*, June 1925, p. 786.
35. *Middletown*, pp. 255–57.
36. See *Literary Digest*, 26 October 1929, p. 31.
37. Ibid., 26 October 1929, p. 37.
38. Ibid., 21 August 1926, p. 68.
39. See *Band Wagon*, pp. 14–15.
40. *Men and Machines*, p. 227.
41. Ringel, pp. 75–77.
42. Ringel, pp. 338–39.
43. See *Literary Digest*, 17 December 1927, p. 10.
44. For example, Fred Hobson, *Mencken, a Life* (Baltimore, 1994), p. xi.
45. Both quoted in *Menckeniana: A Schimpflexicon* (New York, 1928), pp. 68, 85.
46. Two standard Mencken biographies are: William Manchester, *Disturber of the Peace* (New York, 1950); Edgar Kemler, *The Irreverent Mr. Mencken* (Boston, 1948).
47. Henry Louis Mencken, *A Mencken Chrestomathy* (New York, 1949), pp. 243–48.
48. Guy J. Forgue, *Letters of H.L. Mencken* (New York, 1961), p. 342.
49. In Ringel, p. 241.
50. See *Literary Digest*, 16 April 1927, pp. 28–29.
51. Carl Van Doren, "Literature," in *Whither Mankind*, pp. 390–91, 395–96.
52. "Dirt," *Saturday Review of Literature*, 6 March 1926, p. 608.
53. See *Literary Digest*, 19 September 1925, p. 33.
54. "Gutter Literature," *The New Republic*, 17 February 1926, pp. 350–52.
55. See *Literary Digest*, 21 February 1935, p. 31.
56. Oswald Garrison Villard, "Sex, Art, Truth, and Magazines," *Atlantic*, May 1926, pp. 388–98.
57. See *Literary Digest*, 12 February 1927, pp. 31–32.

Bibliography

BOOKS

Allen, Frederick Lewis. *Only Yesterday*. New York, 1931.
Beard, Charles A., ed. *Whither Mankind*. New York, 1928.
Bent, Silas. *Machine Made Man*. New York, 1930.
Chase, Stuart. *Men and Machines*. New York, 1929.
Forgue, Guy J., ed. *Letters of H.L. Mencken*. New York, 1961.
Freeman, R. Austin. *Social Decay and Regeneration*. Boston and New York, 1921.
Hobson, Fred. *Mencken, a Life*. Baltimore, 1994.
Hughes, Robert. *American Visions*. New York, 1997.
Kemler, Edgar. *The Irreverent Mr. Mencken*. Boston, 1948.
Krutch, Joseph Wood. *The Modern Temper*. New York, 1929.
Lynd, Robert S. and Helen. *Middletown* New York, 1929.
Manchester, William. *Disturber of the Peace* New York, 1950.
Mencken, Henry L. *A Mecken Chrestomathy* New York, 1949.
Menckeniana: A Schimpflexicon (New York, 1928).
Merz, Charles. *And Then Came Ford*. Garden City, NY, 1929.
———. *The Dry Decade*. New York, 1931.
———. *The Great American Bandwagon*. New York, 1928.
O'Neill, Eugene. *Dynamo*. New York, 1929.
Ringel, Fred J., ed. *America: As Americans See It*. New York, 1932.
Solomon, Barbara H., ed. *Ain't We Got Fun?* New York, 1980.
Stearns, Harold, ed. *Civilization in The United States* New York, 1922.

ARTICLES

Abbott, Paul. "Fever or Foresight?" *Outlook*. 23 January 1929.

Abels, Jules. "Personality Craze." In Barbara H. Solomon, ed. *Ain't We Got Fun?* New York, 1980.
Adams, Grace. "Measuring the American Mind." *American Mercury*. June 1929.
"Advertising for Health." *Literary Digest*. 29 November 1919.
"Ascertaining a Man's Ability by Scientific Tests." *Current Opinion*. February 1921.
Ashdown, William. "Confessions of an Automobilist." *Atlantic*. June 1925.
Bakshy, Alexander. "Color." *Nation*. 19 March 1930.
———. "Vaudeville Must Be Saved," *Nation*. 24 July 1929.
———. "Vaudeville's Prestige," *Nation*. 4 September 1929.
"Banishing Evolution in the South." *Literary Digest*. 3 April 1926.
Barnhard, Eunice Fuller. "Ladies of the Ticker," *North American Review*. April 1929.
"The Battle of the Styles." *The New Republic*. 11 December 1929.
"Behind the Credit Battle." *The New Republic*. 10 April 1929.
Behrman, S.N. "The Advertising Man." *The New Republic*. 20 August 1919.
Benson, Allan L. "Smokes for Women." *Good Housekeeping*. August 1929.
Blacker, C.P. "Birth Control and Eugenics." *The Nineteenth Century*. April 1932.
Bliven, Bruce. "Flapper Jane." *The New Republic*. 9 September 1925.
Bond, F.D. "Common Stock Racket." *North American Review*. April 1929.
"Bulls, Bears and Lambs," *North American Review*. January 1929.
Byron, Reid. "Death to Propriety." *The New Republic*. 26 December 1928.
"The Case of the Fundamentalists." *The Nation*. 26 December 1923.
Catt, Carrie Chapman. "Short Skirts and French Dictators." *Forum*. April 1927.
Chase, Stuart. "Play." In Charles A. Beard, ed. *Whither Mankind*. New York, 1928.
———. "Six Cylinder Ethics." *Forum*. January 1928.
———. "The Tragedy of Waste." *The New Republic*. 19 August 1925.
"The Civilizing of Divorce." *The New Republic*. 1 August 1928.
Clarke, Marian Hertha. "The Sheep Decide." *North American Review*. August 1929.
Cocks, Dorothy. "What about Plastic Surgery?" *Good Housekeeping*. June 1930.
Cole, Leon. "Biological Philosophy and the War." *Scientific Monthly*. March 1919.
Corbett, Harvey W. "New Heights in American Architecture." *Yale Review*. July 1928.
Corey, Lewis. "Who Gains by Speculation." *The New Republic*. 17 April 1929.
Cowl, Jane. "The Collapse of the Drama." *Pictorial Review*. September 1929.
Crawford, M.D.C. "Weaving the Orient into American Industry." *Journal of the American Asiatic Association* XX (January 1920).
Crowell, Chester T. "I'm for the Fundamentalists." *The New Republic*. 18 March 1925.
"The Cure for Fundamentalism." *The New Republic*. 10 June 1923.
Darwin, Leonard. "The Aims and Methods of Eugenical Societies." *Science*. 7 October 1921.
DeFord, Miriam Allen. "After Dayton: A Fundamentalist Survey." *The Nation*. 6-2-1926.
Dewey, John. "Philosophy." In Charles A. Beard, ed. *Whither Mankind*. New York, 1928.
"Dirt." *Saturday Review of Literature*. 6 March 1926.
"Does Fundamentalism Obstruct Social Progress?" *The Survey*. 1 July 1924.
Dorsey, George A. "Race and Civilization." In Charles A. Beard, ed. *Whither Mankind*. New York, 1928.
Eaton, Jeanette. "The Cosmetic Urge." *Harper's*. February 1931.
Eliot, Charles William. "The Great Religious Revival." *Atlantic*. March 1924.
Ellis, Havelock. "A Tribute to Freud." *Forum*. July 1926.
Evans, Hiram Wesley. "The Klan: Defender of Americanism." *Forum*. December 1925.

Ewen, David. "Popular Music of the Decade." In Barbara H. Solomon, ed. *Ain't We Got Fun?* New York, 1980.
"Excess of the Sex-Factor in Freud's Methods." *Current Opinion*. April 1921.
"The Family Goes On." *The New Republic*. 16 November 1927.
"The Female Form Divine." *Nation*. 13 November 1929.
Fisher, Irving. "Impending Problems of Eugenics." *Scientific Monthly*. September 1921.
"For and against the Ku Klux Klan." *Literary Digest*. 24 September 1921.
"Four Wheel Brakes for Speculation." *The New Republic*. 20 February 1929.
"The Fundamentalists Retreat." *The New Republic*. 24 August 1927.
Gammack, Thomas. "In Defense of the Bull Market." *Outlook*. 12 December 1928.
———. "Scolding by the Federal Reserve." *Outlook*. 20 February 1929.
Garrett, P.W. "Forces behind the Fever." *Outlook*. 26 December 28.
Gillespie, James F., with Wesley Stout. "Hot Music." *Saturday Evening Post*. 19 March 1929.
Goldberg, Isaac. "Jazz," *Forum*. April 1932.
Gray, George W. "Signing Off on the First Ten Years." *World's Work*. December 1930.
Grew, Sydney. "War and Music." *Contemporary Review*. December 1920.
Grinde, Nick. "Where's Vaudeville At?" *Saturday Evening Post*. 11 January 1930.
Grundy, Mr. "'Polite Society.'" *Atlantic*. May 1920.
"Gutter Literature." *The New Republic*. 17 February 1926.
"The Hand of the Designer in Advertising Art." *Art & Decoration*. March 1921.
Helburn, Theresa. "What's Right with the Theater?" *The New Republic*. 10 April 1929.
Hendrick, Ellwood. "The Shadow Side." *Harper's*. August 1920.
"Hey Rube." *The Nation*. 6 November 1929.
Huntington, Ellsworth. "Our Biological Future." *Yale Review*. XVII (October 1927).
Hurst, Fannie. "Let's Not Wear Them!" *The New Republic*. 30 October 1930.
Huxley, Aldous. "Our Contemporary Hocus-Pocus." *Survey*. 15 August 1925.
"Is Freudism Destined to Live?" *Current Opinion*. September 1920.
"Is the Younger Generation in Peril?" *Literary Digest*. 14 May 1921.
Kallen, Horace. "Eugenics—Made in Germany." *Dial*. 11 January 1919.
Kellogg, Vernon. "Where Evolution Stands Today." *The New Republic*. 22 April 1923.
"The K.K.K." *The New Republic*. 21 September 1921.
"The Klan Sheds Its Hood." *The New Republic*. 12 February 1926.
Kohs, S.C. "We've Gone Psychiatric." *Survey*. 15 May 1930.
Krutch, Joseph Wood. "Love—Or the Life and Death of a Value." *Atlantic*. August 1928.
Lewis, Sinclair. "Publicity Gone Mad." *The Nation*. 6 March 1929.
L.W. "No News on the Air." *Survey*. 1 October 1926.
MacNeill, Ben Dixon. "Report from North Carolina." *American Mercury*. January 1930.
Martin, Everett Dean. "Education." In Charles Beard, ed. *Whither Mankind*. New York, 1928.
May, Earl Chapin. "A Calamitous Stage Slump." *World's Work*. May 1929.
McDougall, William. "The Island of Eugenia; the Phantasy of a Foolish Philosopher." *Scribner's*. October 1921.
McKnight, T. "Wall Street Marries Broadway." *Scribner's*. August 1929.
"The Men Who Did It." *The Nation*. 13 November 1929.
Menninger, Karl. "Pseudoanalysis: Perils of Freudian Verbalisms." *Outlook*. 9 July 1930.
Mermey, M. "Vanishing Fiddler." *North American Review*. March 1929.
Merz, Charles. "Bull Market." *Harper's*. April 1929.

Moses, Montrose. "New Trends in the Theatre." *Forum*. February 1925.
Mumford, Lewis. "The Architecture of Escape." *The New Republic*. 12 August 1925.
———. "The Arts." In Charles A. Beard., ed. *Whither Mankind*. New York, 1928.
———. "The Brown Decades: Architecture." *Scribner's*. April 1931.
———. "Machinery and the Modern Style." *The New Republic*. 3 August 1921.
———. "Modernism for Sale." *American Mercury*. April 1929.
Murphy, C.J. "Wall Street Branches Out." *Outlook*. 18 September 1929.
Murray, Gilbert. "The Crisis in Morals." *Harper's*. January 1930.
Myers, Gustavus. "The Rapid Increase of Divorce." *Current History*. 14 August 1921.
Nathan, George Jean. "The Living Corpse." *American Mercury*. April 1929.
Nelson, Llewellyn. "The KKK for Boredom." *The New Republic*. 14 January 1925.
"A Note on Advertising." *The New Republic*. 8 July 1925.
O'Higgins, Harvey. "The New Morality." *New Outlook*. 16 January 1929.
"On Being in the Fashion." *Living Age*. 17 July 1920.
Orton, William. "Reconstructing the Sex Ethic." *The New Republic*. 15 February 1928.
Paradise, Viola. "The Sex Simplex." *Forum*. July 1925.
Parker, Cornelia Stratton. "The Capital of Psychology." *Survey*. 15 August 1925.
Paton, Stewart. "Democracy's Opportunity." *Scientific Monthly*. September 1920.
Pattangall, William Robinson. "Is the Ku Klux Un-American?" *The Forum*. September 1925.
Peet, Creighton. "Music as a Narcotic." *Forum*. August 1930.
Pennell, Elizabeth Robins. "Our Democracy of Bad Manners." *Forum*. April 1925.
Platt, Charles. "Is Prohibition Worth While?" *Nation*. 14 January 1925.
Plowman, Max. "Beauty and ... Freud." *Living Age*. December 1930.
Poiret, Paul. "Will Skirts Disappear?" *Forum*. January 1927.
Post, Emily. "What! No Chaperons?" *Collier's*. 7 September 1929.
"The Presbyterian Church and the Teaching of Evolution." *School and Society*. 2 June 1923.
Price, C. Matlack. "The Trend in Architectural Thought in America." *Century*. September 1921.
Ransom, John Crowe. "Freud and Literature." *Saturday Review of Literature*. 4 October 1924.
Ratray, Willing. "Divorce as Manners and Customs." *The New Republic*. 9 December 1925.
"Risks Involved in the Effort to Breed Superior People." *Current Opinion*. October 1920.
Roback, A.A. "Quacks." *Forum*. May 1929.
Robbins, Howard Chandler. "'Fundamentalism' and 'Modernism'." *The Forum*. May 1924.
Rose, Marc A. "Radio or Newspaper—Can Both Survive?" *The Nation*. 24 December 1924.
Ruml, Beardsley. "The Extension of Selective Tests to Industry." *Annals of the American Academy*, LXXX (January 1919).
Russell, Bertrand. "Science." In Charles A. Beard. ed. *Whither Mankind*. New York, 1928.
Sayler, Oliver M. "New Movement in the Theatre." *North American Review*. June 1921.
Seldes, Gilbert. "Industrial Design." *Saturday Evening Post*, 5-28-1932, p. 34.
———. "Listening In." *The New Republic*. 23 March 1927.
———. "Shake Your Feet." *The New Republic*. 4 November 1925.
Skinner, Otis. "What's Wrong with the Theater To-day?" *World's Work*. October 1929.

Slosson, Edwin. "The Survival of the Unfittest." *The Independent*. 8 October 1921.
Sockman, Ralph W. "Morals in a Machine Age." *Harper's*. February 1931.
———. "The Vanishing Sinner." *Harper's*. November 1930.
Stockbridge, Frank Parker. "The Kuklux Klan Revival." *Current History Magazine of the New York Times*. April 1921.
"The Talkies' Future." *The Nation*. 15 January 1930.
Tunis, John R. "Sport and the Radio." *Outlook*. 16 October 1929.
Van Doren, Carl. "Literature." In Charles A. Beard, ed. *Whither Mankind*. New York, 1928.
Viereck, George Sylvester. "Freud: Columbus of the Subconscious." *Forum*. March 1925.
Villard, Oswald Garrison. "Sex, Art, Truth, and Magazines." *Atlantic*. May 1926.
"The Voter and the Radio." *The New Republic*. 23 May 1928.
Wagner, Philip. "Cigarettes vs. Candy." *The New Republic*. 13 February 1926.
Walkley, A.B. "The Theatre and the War." *Living Age*. 15 November 1919.
Warfield, Frances. "Lost Cause." *Outlook*. 12 February 1920.
Watts, Harvey Maitland. "The American Age." *Forum*. March 1925.
Whipple, Leon. "The Red Radio." *Survey*. 1 July 1925.
White, Paul W. "Our Booming Beauty Business." *Outlook*. 22 January 1930.
White, Walter F. "An American Fascismo," *The Forum*. November 1924.
———. "Reviving the Ku Klux Klan." *The Forum*. April 1921.
"You're on the Air." *Saturday Evening Post*. 1 May 1926.

Index

About the Author

GARY DEAN BEST is Professor Emeritus of History at the University of Hawaii, Hilo. His previous books include *Pride, Prejudice, and Politics* (Praeger, 1990), *FDR and the Bonus Marchers* (Praeger, 1992), *The Nickel and Dime Decade* (Praeger, 1993), and *The Retreat from Liberalism* (Praeger, 2002).